Industrial Diversification and Innovation

NEW HORIZONS IN THE ECONOMICS OF INNOVATION

General Editor: Christopher Freeman, *Emeritus Professor of Science Policy, SPRU – Science and Technology Policy Research, University of Sussex, UK*

Technical innovation is vital to the competitive performance of firms and of nations and for the sustained growth of the world economy. The economics of innovation is an area that has expanded dramatically in recent years and this major series, edited by one of the most distinguished scholars in the field, contributes to the debate and advances in research in this most important area.

The main emphasis is on the development and application of new ideas. The series provides a forum for original research in technology, innovation systems and management, industrial organization, technological collaboration, knowledge and innovation, research and development, evolutionary theory and industrial strategy. International in its approach, the series includes some of the best theoretical and empirical work from both well-established researchers and the new generation of scholars.

Titles in the series include:

Industrial Diversification and Innovation

An International Study of the Aerospace Industry

François Texier
University of Linköping, Sweden

NEW HORIZONS IN THE ECONOMICS OF INNOVATION

Edward Elgar
Cheltenham, UK • Northampton, MA, USA

© François Texier, 2000

Published by
Edward Elgar Publishing Limited
Glensanda House
Montpellier Parade
Cheltenham
Glos GL50 1UA
UK

Edward Elgar Publishing, Inc.
136 West Street
Suite 202
Northampton
Massachusetts 01060
USA

A catalogue record for this book
is available from the British Library

Library of Congress Cataloguing in Publication Data

Texier, François, 1970–
    Industrial diversification and innovation : an international study of the
aerospace industry / François Texier.
    —(New horizons in the economics of innovation)
    Includes bibliographical references and index.
    1. Aerospace industries—Case studies. 2. Diversification in industry—Case
studies. 3. Aerospace industries—Technological innovations—Case studies.
I. Title. II. Series.

    HD9711.5.A2 T49 2000
    338.6–dc21
                                                                00–034830
ISBN 1 84064 452 4

Printed in the United Kingdom at the University Press, Cambridge

Contents

List of Tables

List of Abbreviations

ADD: Agency for Defence Development
CAA: Civil Aviation Administration or Civil Aviation Authority
CEV: Centre d'Essais en Vol – National Flight Test Centre
DTA: Direction du Transport Aérien – Directorate of Airborne
         Transportation
FAA: Federal Aviation Administration
FAR: Federal Aviation Regulations
FFRRT: First Flight Readiness Review Team
FMV: Försvarets Materielverket
FOA: Försvarets Forskningsanstalt
GAMD: Groupement des Avions Marcel Dassault
ITA: Institut des Transports Aériens – Airborne Transportation Institute
JAA: Joint Aviation Authorities
JAR: Joint Airworthiness Requirements
JVC: Joint Validation Committee
KARI: Korean Aerospace Research Institute
KFP: Korean Fighter Programme
KTX-1:   Korean Trainer eXperimental 1
LFV: Luftfartsverket – Swedish CAA
MND: Ministry of National Defence
MOCI: Ministry of Commerce and Industry
NBAA: National Business Aircraft Association
ONERA: Organisation National d'Etudes et de Recherches Aéronautique –
         National Office for Aeronautic Studies and Research
R&D: Research and Development
ROKAF: Republic of Korea Air Force
SGAC: Secrétariat Général de l'Aviation Civile – French CAA
SEA: Société d'Etudes Aéronautiques
STAe: Services Techniques de l'Aéronautique

Acknowledgements

Doing research is quite like solitary work, though in a team. It is lonely work because it involves countless hours and days of reading and writing, analysing and rewriting, until the book is finally completed. Nonetheless, it involves teamwork since research cannot be done without the continuous support from advisors, colleagues and friends.

I owe a great debt of gratitude to my first advisors Charles Edquist and Maureen McKelvey for their constant attention, care and interest in my work and my ideas. I would also like to thank Leif Hommen for his careful reading of the chapters and his great advice during all the work. Besides their role as advisors, they are great friends.

Other people have helped me and ought to be mentioned and thanked for their help at various stages of the study. Ove Granstrand gave me very detailed comments on the last manuscript of the book, spurring lots of new ideas and improvements. Hans Sjögren, Kajsa Ellegård, Lars Linkvist, Ingrid Schild, and many other colleagues read and commented all or parts of the manuscript. I am grateful for their help.

The environment of the Department of Technology and Social Change at Linköping University has also been a catalyst to the research process. I appreciate the help of Christina Lärkner, Eva Petersson and Margareta Nordstad in supporting the day-to-day administrative demands, and with a warm smile.

Research cannot be done without facts gathered in the real world. Many people have helped me dig up these facts. I cannot, unfortunately, thank all those I interviewed by name, but I am deeply grateful for the time they spent explaining their fascinating stories.

Some people ought, however, to be named. For the French case I would like particularly to thank René Lemaire, who shared with me his enthusiasm and fascination for the Falcon and gave me so much of his time. Luc Berger, from Dassault Aviation, also gave me his continuous support.

I am very grateful to Ulf Edlund, from Saab, who showed a constant interest in all my work and commented on all the empirical chapters.

The Korean case could not have been done without Chin-Young Hwang, who gave me a long and invaluable introduction to the Korean aerospace industry and on several occasions commented on the chapter. I am also obliged to Jean-Michel Lorne and Bae Jung-Eun from the French Trade Commission in Seoul for organising my interviews with representatives of the Korean aerospace industry, as well as to the Science and Technology Policy Institute (STEPI) in Seoul for hosting me during my Korean fieldwork.

Finance is also a crucial element in doing research. I am grateful to the Swedish Council for Planning and Coordination of Research (Forsknings-rådsnämnden, FRN), for integrally financing this work and to the Royal Swedish Academy of the Engineering Sciences (Kungliga Ingenjörs-vetenskapsakademien, IVA) for partly supporting my travel to South Korea.

Derrick Picha read the last manuscript and improved the language. I am grateful for his help.

During all these years of research, my parents, Marcel and Edith Texier, encouraged my efforts, and even though I was far from home, they were always there for me. Their love and affection was very precious to me. In addition, my father reviewed and corrected the language in several chapters.

My final thanks go to Marie, for her love and for her caring support during these years.

François Texier

francois@texier.net

✈

1. Introduction

When once you have tasted flight, you will
forever walk the earth with your eyes
turned skyward, for there you have been,
and there you will always long to return.
Leonardo da Vinci

Structural change towards growing industries is essential for economic growth, employment creation and firm performance. Swedish industry has, however, presented some rigidities with regard to its ability to renew itself from the mid-1970s to the mid-1990s. In particular, it has been observed that product innovations were too few, despite a high R&D intensity at the national level, and that high-technology and growth industries were under-represented in the Swedish industrial structure (Edquist and McKelvey, 1998; Edquist and Texier, 1996).[1]

Three main mechanisms can accelerate change in the production structure. These are:

1. diversification by firms into new industries;
2. emergence of new-technology based firms; and
3. foreign direct investment in advanced industries.[2]

The strategy of established firms moving into new, growing industries is not very common in Sweden (Granstrand and Alänge, 1995, p. 143),[3] but has been a very important engine of competitiveness and economic growth in East Asia (Lall, 1996; Pilat, 1994). This study will examine the diversification mechanism.[4]

1

The concept of diversification has been studied extensively, in terms of management as well as in terms of relationship between the strategy and the growth of the firm.[5] Although it is clear that during the process of diversification, firms interact with other organisations, such as the state, research organisations or any organisation concerned with innovative activities, questions remain as to the nature of these interactions and the kind of rules, later in this book called institutions, affecting these interactions. This is problematic because innovation policy and management design require a clear understanding of the process in all its complexity.

This work presents an empirical comparative case-study of diversification after first addressing the theoretical state-of-the-art in the field. It focuses on delineating what kind of institutions affect the process of diversification, and apply this perspective in a comparative case-study of the aerospace industry. To evaluate the importance of the national characteristics of institutions, diversification is studied in three countries with policies supporting strong military independence. Two cases belong to the European aerospace industry, i.e., Dassault Aviation in France and Saab in Sweden. The third case-study is Daewoo Heavy Industries, in the emerging South Korean aerospace industry. These three studies are used to reveal the kind of institutional structures and management strategies that are needed in order to facilitate industrial renewal through diversification. The conclusions drawn from the analysis of the comparison are intended to assist the design of government policy and firm strategy for economic growth and competitiveness.

1.   PURPOSE OF THE STUDY

The purpose of this study is to understand firm-level diversification within an institutional environment and to delineate the nature of the specific institutions affecting the process. The analysis focuses on the processes of firm diversification in relation to institutions, whether national or of another nature, and aims at understanding the phenomenon and its causes rather than its consequences. This implies that learning processes occurring during the diversification are also under scrutiny, as well as the interactions between the firm and other organisations. Thus, the research questions addressed in the study are:

- Why do firms diversify?
- What is the role of national institutions and organisations in the firm's choice of a diversification strategy?

- How is diversification implemented within firms?
- What kind of learning mechanisms are used by firms for the generation and exploitation of the knowledge needed for their diversification?
- How do firms and supporting organisations interact in the process of diversification?

2. THEORETICAL APPROACH

To address these research questions, one needs to clarify the theoretical concepts involved. What is diversification? What are the different perspectives discussed in the literature? The traditional approach of the literature on diversification is essentially concerned with firm-level management issues.[6] This approach attempts to understand why and how firms diversify, assuming that the management of the firm controls the destiny of the firm. Yet, external learning processes and an institutional environment broader than one defined by the market in which firms diversify are seldom, if ever, considered.

Taking institutional factors into account implies a broadening of the theoretical perspective. This can be done using a systems of innovation approach, allowing for an understanding of how innovation processes are affected by firms and other organisations. However, this approach does not systematically address the concept of diversification. It is therefore necessary to integrate the literature on diversification and on the systems of innovation framework if institutions affecting diversification processes are to be understood.

2.1. The Concept of Diversification

At the firm level, diversification is one of the strategies the management may apply to sustain the growth of the firm or simply to secure the firm's survival (Penrose, 1959). The strategy can result in a market diversification, a product diversification or both. It can also be a technological diversification. In the first case, new markets are identified for an already existing product. The firm can then use its existing competences, knowledge and technologies to reap benefits from the new opportunities. In the second alternative, new products enlarge the market in which the firm is already active and may also create new market opportunities (Ansoff, 1957). Finally, in the last alternative, the firm uses new technologies in already existing products, improving their performance (Granstrand, 1998). In this work, diversification is the process by which a firm enters a new market, without necessarily leaving its existing one(s), with a product new to the firm but not necessarily new to the world. The strategy requires an organisational change and the development of technologies within the firm.[7]

To explain why firms diversify, Penrose (1959) introduced the resource-based theory of the firm. In her theory, the firm is considered as a bundle of resources that can be used in the course of the firm's operations. The use of unused resources or the quest for economies of scope can be some initial explanations to diversification. Other explanations, such as taking advantage of new opportunities, are also brought forward to explain why the firm diversifies.

In the course of diversification, the firm has to embark on new activities, related or not to its original set of industrial activities. Hence, there are risks, technological and market-related, that should be evaluated before and during the diversification. However, risks might also be of an institutional kind. For instance, the differences between managing a military and a civil activity can be a barrier to diversification from one to the other (Feldman, 1997). As this example implies, the firm must be considered in its environment, including political and institutional dimensions as well as economic and technological dimensions.

2.2. The Firm, its Environment and Institutions

Diversification, it will be argued, must be understood within an institutional context broader than that of a market with buyers and sellers only exchanging information in the form of prices and quantities. The institutional environment in which the firm operates is discussed in relation to previous work in institutional economics.[8] This literature addresses the role of institutions in relation to economic performance. Institutions are defined by North (1990, p. 3) as 'the rules of the game in a society'. What in everyday language are called institutions, i.e., universities, research laboratories, and so forth, are hence referred to as organisations.

The firm interacts with a number of organisations existing in its surroundings. Differences in institutional environments can affect the behaviour of firms. In other words, similar firms might do things differently in different countries, and this can be empirically examined with regard to diversification involving product innovation.

The systems of innovation approach focuses on the interaction between firms and other organisations during innovation processes. Institutions affecting these innovation processes, whether technological or organisational, are also studied. This allows the analysis of firms at national or regional political-economic levels or within specific industrial sectors.[9]

The interactions of the different elements of the system imply exchanges of various types of knowledge, whether technological or market related, as well as the generation of new knowledge. The internalisation by firms of knowledge must also be considered. Hence, learning processes must be understood in relation to systems of innovation (Cohen and Levinthal, 1990; Lundvall 1992a).

Though the systems of innovation approach addresses problems of knowledge generation in a dynamic perspective, diversification as an innovation strategy or as an innovation policy instrument has hardly if ever been discussed. In this respect, management and systems of innovation perspectives can be seen as potentially complementing one another, as will be developed in the presentation of the theoretical framework in Chapter 2.

3.   STUDYING DIVERSIFICATION IN SYSTEMS OF INNOVATION

To be able to answer the research questions, a focused comparative case-study method has been chosen. Such a method is generally acknowledged as appropriate to spur theoretical developments in the field of investigation.[10] Besides, in this study, particular attention has to be paid to very specific aspects of the diversification process, i.e., the cause of the diversification, its implementation and the knowledge generated and used. The scope of the study is therefore not limited to the management perspective, but extends to the system of innovation in which the firm operates, allowing for an understanding of the process of diversification, including markets, government policies and university research.

In the study, three cases of diversification are designed to show why and how the firms diversified, whether or not they succeeded in internalising new knowledge and finally if and why they succeeded or failed in the venture. Conducting the studies in one industry but in three countries will allow for the separate analysis of management aspects from political, institutional and economic dimensions, indicating to what extent and in what ways governments were involved in the generation of product innovation.

The industry chosen for this work is the aerospace industry. National prestige and ideologies of military independence have long shaped the aerospace industries in Europe, in the United States and more recently in some Asian countries. Moreover, national institutions have supported the civil aircraft industry through subsidies, in Europe, or through defence procurement, in the United States.

The comparison is based on the study of three cases of aircraft development and production, the Dassault Mystère 20, in France, the Saab-Fairchild 340, in Sweden and the Daewoo KTX-1, in the Republic of Korea.[11]

The case-studies were carried out partly through reviewing existing written material, such as academic research, industrial analyses and annual reports. In a second phase, interviews with the main decision-makers in the diversification process were conducted.

4.   THREE CASES OF DIVERSIFICATION IN THE AEROSPACE INDUSTRY

In two of the cases, Dassault in France and Saab in Sweden, the first successful diversification from military to civil aircraft is investigated. This means that the studies concentrate on the first civil aircraft going into production in these two firms. The third case, in Korea, examines the first diversification from heavy industries into aircraft development by the firm Daewoo Heavy Industries.

Questions addressed during the studies were: How were technologies transferred between the military and the civil parts of the firm? What was the role of the government in the creation of the new activity in the firm? What types of cooperation were initiated between the different organisations of the aircraft industry or between firms, universities and research organisations? What institutions were involved in the process of diversification and how did they change over time? What management strategies were employed?

4.1.   The Case of Dassault Aviation in France

Dassault was a major organisation in the development of the French aircraft industry. The firm started before the Second World War and immediately afterwards engaged in military programmes. National institutional arrangements in France after the Second World War, attempting to support state-owned firms, reduced the possibilities for private firms to engage in large civil programmes (Carlier, 1983, p. 16). However, from 1945 to 1963, Dassault kept prototyping military freighters for the French forces. With limited transformations, some of these aircraft could also be used on the commercial market. This policy of prototyping was to maintain the competence of the firm in the design of transport aircraft at international level.

On the basis of these previous developments, the Mystère 20 made its first rollout in April 1963. It was a twinjet transport aircraft planned for transport of government officials and military officers. Knowledge previously developed for military aircraft was used to a large extent. For example, the wing's structure, as well as the control system, was directly transferred from previous military programmes. In July 1963, the American airliner Pan Am placed an order of 40 aircraft plus 120 options. Business jets were just emerging and Pan Am wanted to develop the market for small civil jets in the United States.

Since the Mystère 20, Dassault has developed a large range of business jets. More than 35% of the turnover of the firm came from its civil production in 1999, and although the competition is more and more severe, Dassault is among the leaders in the market for business jets worldwide.

4.2. The Case of Saab in Sweden

Saab was originally established as a military aircraft producer with the responsibility for providing the Swedish Air Force with advanced fighters. Several attempts to produce civil aircraft never worked out for different reasons and instead, Saab diversified into the car and truck industries (Dörfer, 1973). However, at the end of the 1970s, Saab managed to design and produce a civil aircraft in a joint venture with the American aircraft manufacturer Fairchild, namely, the Saab-Fairchild 340.

The survival of the firm had always been linked to orders from the Swedish Air Force. The reduction of Swedish military expenditures during the 1970s threatened the very existence of Saab as an aircraft manufacturer. In 1978, Saab engaged in the development of a new military aircraft, the JAS 39 Gripen, teaming up with Volvo Aero for the manufacturing of the engine and with Ericsson for the radar system. In parallel, the firm launched the development of a regional aircraft with the financial support of the Swedish government.

Survival, however, may not have been the only reason for diversification. At the end of the 1970s, the market for regional aircraft was growing very fast. There was a need for small and pressurised aircraft able to carry between 30 and 50 passengers. The American market for commercial passenger transportation was deregulated in 1978 and Saab could find a proper opportunity there to finally succeed in producing a civil aircraft. Saab had the right size for, and an appropriate experience in, designing small transport aircraft. Moreover, competences had been accumulated in military technologies that could be translated into civil use through the design of a new civil aircraft (Eliasson, 1995; Fölster, 1993).

The Saab 340 was a success during the 1980s, capturing more than a third of the US market of regional aircraft. However, Saab became locked into a technological choice with the use of turboprops instead of jet engines while developing a new regional aircraft at the beginning of the 1990s, the Saab 2000. The whole aerodynamics of the aircraft was dependent on this choice. Since the competition in regional aircraft had developed a focus on jet aircraft and because the Swedish aircraft did not receive government subsidies as competitors did, Saab had to stop its production of all civil aircraft in May 1999.

4.3.   The Case of Daewoo in South Korea

The aftermath of the Korean War, ending in 1953, was accompanied by industrial transformation in the new Republic of South Korea. The country's process of restructuring was dramatically accelerated in 1961 after the *coup d'état* of General Park Chung Hee. New policies and institutions favouring the development of export industries led by large family-owned conglomerates, the chaebols,[12] allowed a rapid growth in the country. General Park's desire for military independence pushed the development of defence industries at the beginning of the 1970s. Korean Air, the flagship of Korea, was selected to assemble the first helicopter in Korea, the Hughes 500, and later the F-5 fighter aircraft. Samsung was selected to assemble the engine for the latter aircraft.

During the 1980s, development of the aerospace industry became a national goal; not, as formerly, because of national military independence but because of the economic and technological benefits such an industry was expected to bring to the country. It was also decided, for reasons of prestige, that Korea had to belong to the narrow and exclusive group of aerospace nations.

Several national programmes started at that time and the chaebols were now willing to enter the industry. Daewoo Heavy Industries began with small-scale subcontracting of parts and components for the aerospace industry worldwide. In 1988 the firm lost a prestigious contract for the production of a Korean fighter aircraft and became disillusioned about its chances of strengthening its position in the industry.

During the 1980s, however, the Agency for Defence Development, the national military procurement agency, had launched a programme to develop a small trainer for the air force, the KTX-1. Korean Airlines, which had started the studies, withdrew in 1988, not willing to continue financing the development of the aircraft. Daewoo Heavy Industries was then selected as prime contractor for the programme.

The development of the trainer first involved the Swiss firm, Pilatus, which provided technical support. However, due to some misunderstanding between the firms, the cooperation rapidly collapsed. A consulting firm was then called on for support. After ten years of development and five prototypes, the aircraft was finally selected by the Korean government to equip the Korean Air Force and entered production in 1999.

5.   OUTLINE OF THE BOOK

The book is divided into three parts. The first part has two chapters and addresses theoretical and methodological issues. In Chapter 2, the theoretical framework is presented. It builds upon the literature on diversification and on the systems of innovation approach, thereby attempting to show how the diversification process can be understood in a systems of innovation perspective. Chapter 3 presents the method that was followed in carrying out the research. Along with a method description, the chapter describes the problems encountered and how they were solved. It also discusses how the sources were appraised and the limitations of the method.

The second part of the research includes the empirical material. It is divided into three chapters detailing the cases that were studied. These chapters are presented in chronological order, starting with Chapter 4, the case of the Dassault Mystère 20 in France (1960–1965), followed by Chapter 5, the case of the Saab 340 in Sweden (1970–1984) and finishing with Chapter 6, the case of the Daewoo KTX-1 in South Korea (1970–1998).

In the third part, the three cases are compared and analysed in relation to the theoretical perspective. This part is divided into two analysis chapters: Chapter 7 is concerned with why the firms diversified, and Chapter 8 addresses the question of how the firms diversified. Finally, Chapter 9 concludes the book, emphasising the nature of institutions and the learning dimensions affecting the process of diversification.

NOTES

1. Growth industries are defined as those industries that grew most rapidly in the 1975–1990 period in the OECD area as a whole. They are: Pharmaceuticals, Aircraft, Office and Computing Machinery, Electrical Machinery and Components, Plastic Products as well as Printing and Publishing. The overlap with high-technology industries is considerable. All except the last two are also high-tech industries, where high-tech industries are defined by the OECD as industries with a high ratio between R&D expenditures and sales. Note that the industries defined as growth industries, as well as high-tech industries, may change over time.
2. Combinations of these three mechanisms may also occur.
3. Zander (1997), for example, notes that the diversification trend in Swedish firms depends on the industry observed. Firms in the paper and pulp, iron and steel or chemical industries are less diversified in terms of technologies than firms in the telecommunication or electrical equipment industries.
4. The concept of diversification will be defined in Chapter 2, Section 1.1.
5. See, for example, the work of Ansoff (1957), Penrose (1959) and Rumelt (1974) and more recently Montgomery (1994) and Granstrand (1998).
6. See, for example, the work of Ansoff (1957), Amit and Livnat (1988), Ramanujam and Varadarajan (1989) and Very (1993).
7. This definition is discussed in Chapter 2, Section 1.1.
8. See for example the work of Freeman (1987) and North (1990).
9. The concept of systems of innovation has been developed in its different forms since the work of Freeman (1987). Lundvall (1992a) and Nelson (1993) concentrate on national systems of innovation. Edquist (1997a) develops a general taxomony of systems of innovation, while Carlsson (1992), Malerba and Breschi (1997) and Mowery and Nelson (1999) concentrate on sectoral systems. The concept of systems of innovation is more developed in Chapter 2, Section 1.2.
10. This argument is based on George (1979), Ramanujam and Varadarajan (1989, p. 544), Yin (1994) and Edquist (1997b).
11. The reasons for choosing these cases will be detailed in Chapter 3, Section 2.
12. The chaebols are the basis of the Korean industry. They are described in more detail in Chapter 6, Section 1.2.

Part I

Theoretical Framework and Methods

2. Diversification in Systems of Innovation

The airplane is just a bunch of sticks and wires and cloth, a tool for learning about the sky and about what kind of person I am, when I fly. An airplane stands for freedom, for joy, for the power to understand, and to demonstrate that understanding. Those things aren't destructible.

Richard Bach[1]

There exists a fairly wide consensus about the fact that increased welfare is closely related to economic growth. The question of the kind of economic growth needed is, however, more subject to debate, because the relationship between economic growth, increased welfare and employment needs to be better understood (Edquist, McKelvey and Hommen, 1998, p.128). The concept of jobless growth was, for example, introduced to describe the phenomenon in which industrial activities underwent a growth that did not affect employment (Edquist, McKelvey and Hommen, 2000, Section 5.1.3.).

Specific sectoral studies have shown that the concept of jobless growth did not apply to all industrial activities. For example, Edquist and Texier (1996) showed that at the OECD level, some industrial sectors experienced a growth both in terms of production and in terms of employment. Firms involved in product innovation, especially in industries with a high research and development intensity, were largely represented in these growing sectors.

13

Since some industrial sectors grow faster than others, in terms of both production and employment, firms locked into activities with a slow rate of growth might investigate the possibility of entering into growing sectors through diversification. How then does the process of diversification take place within firms?

At the firm level, the phenomenon of diversification had long been ignored by the economic literature, which concentrated on addressing mono-product firms, until the work of Edith Penrose (1959), *The Theory of the Growth of the Firm*. In this book, Penrose tried to understand the different aspects of the growth of firms, especially why and how firms could grow.

The literature on diversification which followed the work of Penrose (1959) focused, for a long time, on analysing the process of diversification from the firm's perspective. The main objective of this literature was to relate diversification to the growth of the firm.[2] This approach considered that the environment of the firm was defined in terms of a market with customers and suppliers, while the nature of information exchanged between firms was reduced to information on price or quantities. As a result, other types of external learning processes are ignored as well as other types of organisations and the institutional environment in which firms diversify.[3]

The more recent literature on diversification, such as Montgomery (1994) or Granstrand (1998), has not succeeded in clearly specifying the nature of the institutions of relevance during the diversification of firms. This literature is important as a starting point for this theoretical framework but needs to be complemented by stressing the prominent role of institutions in the diversification process. Using the conceptual approach of systems of innovation, this chapter attempts to broaden the perspective of the study of the diversification process.

The systems of innovation approach examines how innovation processes function, looking at the interaction between the various parts of the system in which the firm operates. Technical change is a central element of the approach, but little has been done to understand innovation strategies at the firm level. A number of empirical studies exist, but there are no systematic attempts to understand how a strategy such as diversification takes place in a system of innovation. Public innovation policies and firms' innovation strategies ought to be present in the systems of innovation framework, and so far the latter are not.

Therefore, the questions addressed in this chapter are why and how firms diversify in their respective systems of innovation. What are the incentives for firms to diversify? What are the risks of a diversification? What are the dynamics of the process of diversification?

Section 1 discusses some conceptual issues, defining the concept of diversification and the concept of systems of innovation. It attempts to show how diversification can be studied in a systems of innovation approach. Section 2 is concerned with the reasons for diversification as described in the literature on diversification and from a systems of innovation perspective. Finally, Section 3 considers the implementation of the diversification within the firm and examines the effects of institutional factors on the strategy.

1.   CONCEPTUAL ISSUES

The concept of diversification encompasses a lot of different aspects of firm management. The activities of firms comprise continuous transformations and changes in products, markets, technologies and organisations. How are these changes related to diversification? This section discusses the various approaches to the concept of diversification developed in the literature. Moreover, using conceptual frameworks such as network theory and innovation systems approach, the theoretical scope is widened to study the firm in its institutional environment.

1.1.   What is Diversification?

The concept of diversification implies that the firm engages in something new and faces various kinds of transformations. Three dimensions are usually discussed when defining diversification. These are *the product, the market and the technology* of the firm.[4] In this study a fourth dimension is introduced, namely the change in *organisation*.

Conflicting views exist in the literature as to which dimension should be focused upon while defining diversification and which should not. This section examines various definitions presented in the literature. Building on the different meanings of diversification, a new definition is given which will be used throughout the remainder of the study.

Analysing strategies spurring the growth of the firm, Ansoff (1957, p. 114) considers that growth through market diversification or through product diversification can exist separately, but should be defined individually as product development or market development. Market development is a strategy that aims at finding new usage for existing products, while product development seeks to improve what Ansoff (1957) calls the 'mission' of the firm, increasing the efficiency of specific products in a market already 'given' to the firm.

Ansoff (1957, p. 114), in trying to integrate market and product diversification, states that 'diversification calls for a simultaneous departure from the present product line and the present market structure'. This definition of diversification does not only refer to product development or market development, but to a combination of the two. This definition is also used by Chandler (1977, p. 473; 1990, p. 219), observing that, after World War II, large American firms expanded mainly by entering new markets with new products.

During the diversification process the firm has to acquire new competences, new skills and new techniques and this both for the new market and for the new product. Ansoff (1957) also introduces the idea that diversification implies some kind of organisational transformation of the firm. The latter idea is also developed by Rumelt (1974, p. 10), who, while focusing on the product and market dimension of the diversification, insists on the changing role of the management of the firm. However, it should be noted that the work of both Ansoff (1957) and Chandler (1977; 1990) referred mainly to post-World War II firms. The rapid technological development that followed the war introduced a new dimension to the phenomenon, i.e., the technology itself.

Thus, the technological dimension of diversification has been taken into account more recently. For example, Malerba, Breschi and Lissoni (1998) analyse the extent of technological diversification in various countries and how its direction is constrained by the previous knowledge base of the firm.

In the same line of thought, Granstrand (1998) defines technology diversification as a move in which the firm improves the performances or the number of functionalities of existing products through the use of new technologies. Although technological diversification can lead to product diversification, the two types of diversification are not necessarily related (Granstrand, 1998, p. 473; Granstrand, Patel and Pavitt, 1997, p. 24). This focus on technology diversification is due to the fact that the growth of technology based firms is related to their degree of diversification.[5] However, as Granstrand (1998, p. 466) points out, technology based firms are only a subgroup of the modern business firms, restraining the validity of the argument of growth.

Jacobsson and Ehrnberg (1997, p. 335) do not use the concept of technological diversification but instead discuss the concept of technological discontinuity, which in their words is 'a substantial change in the set of technological competences required to design and produce a product, often resulting in a significant change in the price or performance of a product, or indeed in a new product'.

This concept relates to the concept of product diversification with a focus on its technological dimension. It attempts to delineate the impact of technological change on a phenomenon that might become a product diversification, though this is not a necessary condition. However, this definition relates only to qualitative aspects of the product, such as its performance, and it does not indicate whether the discontinuity has some implications in terms of growth or improvement of the performance of the firm.

Diversification can be defined separately by its market and product dimensions and by its technological dimension. In her influential work *The Theory of the Growth of the Firm*, Penrose (1959, p. 144) defines diversification as being an impetus to the growth of the firm as well as a consequence of its growth. Other aspects, like market uncertainties, are taken into account but to a lesser extent. As the firm grows, it might choose to diversify. In Penrose's definition:

> [A] firm diversifies its productive activities whenever, without entirely abandoning its old lines of product, it embarks upon the production of new products, including intermediate products, which are sufficiently different from the other product it produces to imply some significant differences in the firm's production or distribution programmes (Penrose 1959, p. 119).

For Penrose (1959), diversification is very similar to carrying out product innovation in the firm, while all the divisions of the firm have to adapt to the new product through structural changes inside the firm, in particular, in terms of new production and distribution facilities. Penrose (1959, p. 119) considers the adaptation of managerial services to the novelty within the firm as a consequence of the diversification.

Difficulties arise in this definition since concepts such as 'intermediate products' or the idea of products being 'sufficiently different' are not specific enough.[6] Penrose (1959) focuses her definition on product diversification but does not specify if there is a technological change involved by this diversification. Moreover, it is unclear whether the 'distribution programmes' should be considered as new markets or if this is another issue such as the logistical organisation of the firm.

To clarify her definition, Penrose (1959, p.110) defines technology and market as being the 'areas of specialisation of the firm'. Since the focus of her definition is on product innovation, she identifies four types of diversification clearly defined by specific changes either in technology or market, the product dimension always being new.

1. In the first type of diversification, the firm diversifies in its area of specialisation. In other words, it develops a new product out of existing technologies for its existing market.
2. In the second kind of diversification, the activity of the firm shifts to a new market with a new product based on existing technologies. The firm can then use its competences, knowledge and technologies to reap profits from the new market opportunities.
3. Alternatively, the firm may engage in a diversification of its existing market, with a new product and new technologies. In this alternative, new products are developed for an existing market to the firm.
4. Finally, the firm can change its orientation completely, with a new market, a new product and new technologies.

Thus, diversification is here defined around three main dimensions, i.e., markets, products and technologies. While this definition always implies the emergence of a new product, markets and technologies can either be old or new depending on the type of diversification considered.

Ramanujam and Varadarajan (1989, p. 525) add another dimension in their definition of diversification. They insist on the organisational changes occurring during the process, in particular in the transformation of the administrative structure of the firm. In their words, '[d]iversification is defined as the entry of a firm or business unit into new lines of activity, either by processes of internal business development or acquisition, which entail changes in its administrative structure, systems, and other management processes'.

The definition provided by Ramanujam and Varadarajan (1989) reduces the scope of the process of diversification. The unit of analysis is the firm and the process of diversification implies a transformation of the structure of the firm at the different levels of the organisation. This in turns sets some limits on the concept of diversification. For example, a firm buying shares of another firm would not be considered as diversifying its activities if the investment did not imply organisational changes inside the diversifying firm.

In the above discussion, various dimensions of diversification have been addressed. These were *the market, the product, the technology and the organisation* of the firm. Changes in the market and the product dimensions are important because they imply that the firm will leave its existing field of activity. The technology dimension is problematic because it relates to the technological competences on the basis of which the firm can make new products and enter new markets. However, this is an important dimension as it indicates that the firm engages in technical innovative activities. The organisational dimension must be included in the definition so that holding companies and firms buying shares in other companies, and thereby not being involved in innovation processes, can be excluded.[7] On these bases, the following definition will be used in this study:

> Diversification is the process by which a firm enters a new market, without necessarily leaving its existing one(s), with a product new to the firm but not necessarily to the world. The strategy requires an organisational change and the development of technologies within the firm.

This definition does not indicate whether, in the diversification process, the transformation of one dimension is more important than the other. However, it points out that the transformation of the firm is general since the changes affect product, market, technology and organisation, and that changes in these four dimensions together constitute a sufficient criterion to define a diversification. It should be clear that none of these dimensions need to be new to the world. It is the renewal of the firm as a whole that is considered. Diversification is seen as a deliberate effort by the management to renew the activities of the firm.

The definition does not consider the extent to which the diversification is related to the previous activity of the firm. The concept of relatedness, as described for example by Rumelt (1974), implies that the firm can use its existing skills, technological, managerial or otherwise, and apply them in the new division. When the firm is not able to use its existing skills, the diversification is defined as unrelated (Rumelt, 1974, p. 29; Rondi, Sembenelli and Ragazzi, 1996, p. 181).[8]

This definition does not provide any indication as to how the diversification process is implemented; this will be dealt with in Section 3 of this chapter. In addition, this definition does not take the institutional environment of the firm into account, even though as the coming section will show, the environment matters to the firm's strategic choices. It is in the terms of the definition above that diversification has to be understood in the coming discussion, and that further analysis will be conducted.

1.2.   Systems of Innovation, Institutions and Organisations

In their review of research on diversification, Ramanujam and Varadarajan (1989, p. 525) described the general environment of the firm as being the 'legal-political-economic-technological-social-ecological milieu in which the firm operates'. This definition does not help much since it barely provides a list of potential dimensions without clarifying what they are, how they relate to each other and how they affect the firm. Furthermore, Ramanujam and Varadarajan (1989, p. 544) criticised the lack of understanding in the literature on diversification of the role of the institutional environment in the implementation of diversification by firms.

The reason why the environment of the firm appears to be somewhat neglected in the literature on diversification can be understood in the words of Penrose (1959, p. 215), who considers that 'it is not the environment "as such", but rather the environment as the entrepreneur sees it, that is relevant for his action'. More specifically, Penrose (1959) considers that the environment matters to the firm in the form of the image that the management constructs out of specific and selected information regarding external parameters. These can be, among others, the market structure, the coming demand for new products or the available supply of material. It is on the basis of these elements of information that the management can act and form a strategy.

One major deficiency in the literature on diversification is the failure to broadly consider the role of the environment of the firm in the strategy. It reduces the environment to a market with buyers and sellers, while recognising that the firm develops in an environment including 'people, other organisations, social and economic forces, and legal constraints' (Nadler and Tushman, 1997, p. 163). However, these elements, defining the environment, are not separated from a 'market' definition of the environment. Precisely defining the environment of the firm is important since it provides the firm with both incentives and obstacles for its activities (Granstrand, 1998, p. 475).

The environment of the firm relates to the various elements existing in the milieu in which the firm is active (not necessarily geographically speaking). These elements, on account of their very existence, influence the way the firm operates. They can be organisations such as other firms, universities and research laboratories, and also institutions such as laws, norms and cultures, regulating or simply affecting the way the physical elements of the environment interact.[9]

The traditional analysis of diversification can thus be broadened through the investigation of how firms are affected by their environment. This section introduces environment concepts through which diversification can be studied. After a review of network and system theories, this section concentrates on the concept of systems of innovation. This introduces the idea that firms with similar characteristics will behave differently in different institutional environments. In other words, similar firms might do the same things differently in different countries. Therefore, this section defines the concepts of institutions and organisations and how these concepts relate to the systems of innovation framework. Finally, the concepts of competences and of learning are discussed.

1.2.1. The concepts of network and systems of innovation

The literature on diversification provides us mainly with an understanding of the process of diversification from within the firm. The firm is described as a unit with a management team acting for its growth defined in economic terms such as profit or production. The basic type of relations the firm may have with its surroundings are with its customers, suppliers or competitors. Richardson (1972) points out that this simplification is not acceptable considering the fact that it ignores too many important elements of influence in capitalist economies. Richardson (1972, p. 883) then asserts that firms are part of a 'dense network of cooperation and affiliation'.

Following this line of reflection, the network theory, as developed by Håkansson (1989; 1990) focuses on the relationships between firms and other organisations. According to Håkansson (1990), firms are embedded in their industrial networks, and changes in the network affect the behaviour and the activity of the firm. The network theory emphasises the importance of considering events from a historical perspective. However, it is limited in its scope by the lack of attention to institutional phenomena. Interactions between firms are taken into account only in the meaning of interfirm relations. Moreover, the attention of the network approach is reduced to some specific organisations such as firms and research organisations.

In order to acknowledge the existence of organisations other than firms and research organisations, as well as to integrate the institutional environment in the framework of the study, the concept of systems of innovation has been developed.[10] In the words of Lundvall (1992b, p. 12), systems of innovation can be defined as 'all parts and aspects of the economic structure and the institutional environment affecting learning as well as searching and exploring – the production system, the marketing system and the system of finance present themselves as sub-systems in which learning takes place'.[11]

This definition, Lundvall (1992b) recognises, is broad and needs to be detailed while analysing specific cases. Moreover, its focus is not on innovations but on the processes leading to it, i.e., learning, searching and exploring. These three functions are, however, clearly reducing the scope of Lundvall's definition. It is not the production system as a whole, or the marketing system as a whole that matters, but these parts that are concerned with learning, searching and exploring.

As such, the system of innovation must encompass all organisations involved in innovation processes as well as the relationships between these organisations. This includes not only firms and their research divisions but also other types of research organisations, such as universities or national research laboratories. Since the different elements of the system interact they exchange different types of knowledge. Consequently, learning, searching and exploring processes must be understood since generation and transfer of knowledge between organisations of the system are important in diversification processes. Finally, the financing aspects of innovation are taken into account. Above all, the institutional environment regulates the system through the coordination of the relations between the elements (Lundvall, 1992b, p. 10).

1.2.2. Sectoral and national/regional aspects of systems of innovation

An extensive debate is going on concerning the boundary of systems of innovation. The question lies in what should be considered in the analysis and what should be omitted. Depending on the case studied, the limits of the system can be sectoral or technological, if the boundary is defined by the technologies themselves, or local, regional or national, if the boundary is geographic.

While the systems of innovation approach focuses on the relationships between economic change and innovation processes in general, the concept of technological systems concentrates on the specific technologies around which the system develops (Carlsson, 1992; Jacobsson and Ehrnberg, 1997). Focusing on technological discontinuities, i.e., dramatic technological changes affecting the firm's economic activities, Jacobsson and Ehrnberg (1997) assert that four units of analysis have to be borne in mind to analyse the transformation. These units are the technology, the firm, the industry and the technological system. The first two units are concerned with the firm's capacity of reaction to technological change and with the nature of the technological discontinuity (Jacobsson and Ehrnberg, 1997, p. 336). As each industry is specific in terms of competition and dynamics, technological discontinuities are seen to differ according to the industry in which they occur. The final element of analysis is the technological system, which is defined around a specific technology, with three main elements. These elements are the economic competence in the system, the network of firms and their relations and finally the institutions regulating the system (Jacobsson and Ehrnberg, 1997, p. 330).

In their taxonomy of sectoral systems of innovation, Malerba and Breschi (1997) consider only the firms that are involved in innovative activities within an industrial sector. The focus is only on firms and on their different capabilities and performances in innovative activities. The capabilities of firms is here central to understand the selection processes that are involved in such activities.[12] This taxonomy differs from the technological system approach since the latter considers organisations linked to innovation processes, both vertically and horizontally (Malerba and Breschi, 1997, p. 131). Moreover, in sectoral systems, geographical boundaries have a role only for specific technologies or when parameters such as trust intervene. In other cases, specific industrial and technological characteristics are the structuring element of the system.

Although focusing on the firms involved in innovative activities to define a sectoral system of innovation, Malerba (1999, p. 15) includes other organisations affecting innovation processes. These organisations can be universities, government agencies and other research organisations. Moreover, he insists on the impact of the institutional environment regulating the system.

Enright (1994) takes up the analysis of innovation processes at the regional level. The concept of regional clusters combines a sectoral analysis and a regional analysis. It defines groups of firms closely related, both in terms of geography and type of activity. Innovation processes benefit from the proximity between firms. Needs for technical solutions to specific problems in neighbouring firms can be rapidly identified and taken care of by other firms in the cluster. Saxenian (1994) also makes this argument in the comparison she makes between Silicon Valley and Route 128 in the United States. Proximity between firms and trust relations are seen as very important factors of success for Silicon Valley.

To justify the national character of a system of innovation, Freeman (1995) points to the fact that technology has national characteristics even in a world economy where multinational companies (MNCs) have a great importance. In other words, Freeman (1995, p. 15) claims that technology is national but concedes that science is global. However, this argument is now questioned for many industries and is, to some extent, contradicted by the work of Cantwell (1995), considering that MNCs have opened the internationalisation of both science and technology.

Technology is not, however, the only aspect of the system that justifies the concept of national systems of innovation. Institutions, as 'rules of the game,'[13] also have national characteristics. They define the relations between firms within a system of rules. Nelson (1993) comprises a collection of descriptive articles of 15 national systems of innovation. In this book, national systems are seen to differ in their degree of specialisation, whether it be in terms of technologies, competences or institutions.[14] Moreover, policies are still formed mainly at the national level.

The concept of 'nation' is of course problematic, particularly at a time when globalisation and internationalisation of the economy appears to be of increasing importance. However, globalisation does not eliminate the fact that nations still matter and that firms are organised differently in different nations. For Lundvall (1992b, p. 2), the idea of national systems of innovation

> . . . presumes the existence of nation states and this phenomenon has two dimensions: the national-cultural and the étatist-political. The ideal, abstract, nation state is one where the two dimensions coincide, i.e. where all individuals belonging to a nation – defined by cultural, ethnical and linguistic characteristics – are gathered in one single geographical space controlled by one central state authority (without foreign nationalities).

This definition by Lundvall is particularly interesting since it identifies the two main characteristics of a nation.[15] How these dimensions, i.e., national-cultural and étatist-political, interact and may influence the diversification process and the choice of a new industrial orientation is unclear, however. Indeed, some industries can be identified as more prestigious than others. They reflect the technological level of a nation-state, while their economic prospects place them as priorities in industrial policies. For example, the aerospace industry has been, all through its development, an object of prestige for industrialised countries, and has also become an object of economic war.

The two concepts of sectoral systems and national systems of innovation are different perspectives that are not mutually exclusive. Indeed they can have intersections, especially when studying a specific industry like the aerospace industry. Some industries obviously present some national characteristics and are particularly sensitive to national institutions. Decisions regarding trade, norms or research and development orientations are, to a large extent, taken by national governments and as a result influence the way firms develop.

1.2.3. Institutions and organisations

The foregoing section insisted on the deliberate focus on innovation taken by the systems of innovation approach. However, it was also seen that the system is composed of organisations and that these operate within an institutional environment. The following discussion details the concept of institutions, organisations and their relations to innovation processes.

Departing from traditional neoclassical economics, North (1990, p. 3) defines institutions as 'the rules of the game in a society or, more formally, the humanly devised constraints that shape human interactions'. Despite its conceptual vagueness, since it encompasses all rules affecting the interactions between individuals or organisations, this definition is a useful starting point to understand the internal regulations within systems of innovations.

The main focus of North (1990) is on defining how firms interact within the market in order to reduce their transaction costs. This focus is also taken by Hodgson (1988, p. 174), stressing that the market is 'a set of social institutions in which a large number of commodity exchanges of a specific type regularly take place, and to some extent are facilitated and structured by these institutions'. Thus, the market is embedded in a broader institutional environment encompassing institutions which are not necessarily connected to the market.

There exists a wide range of institutions affecting systems of innovation and shaping learning processes between organisations. Edquist and Johnson (1997) present a taxonomy of institutions in which they identify a number of dichotomies describing institutions. These dichotomies are formal and informal institutions, basic and supporting institutions and finally hard and soft institutions. Formal institutions are characterised by codified rules, for example laws, while informal institutions are simply habits or social norms.[16] Basic institutions constitute the ground rules of economic processes, such as property rights, whereas supporting institutions enforce the basic institutions.

Finally, hard institutions are policed while soft institutions need not necessarily be obeyed (Edquist and Johnson, 1997, p. 50).

This categorisation of institutions allows the identification of the kind of institutions providing constraints or incentives to innovation processes in a system of innovation. However, it does not allow an explanation of how single strategies of firms are affected by institutions and which specific institutions are concerned. Only empirical work can provide answers to these questions.[17]

In relation to this concept of institutions, North (1990, p. 5) defines organisations as 'groups of individuals bound by some common purpose to achieve objectives'. Consequently, what is commonly considered as an institution, for example universities or research units, will here be defined as an organisation.

What are then the relations between institutions and organisations? North (1990, p. 7) considers one-way relations where organisations are created as a response to the opportunities opened by institutions. According to Edquist and Johnson (1997, p. 59) institutions and organisations are related in a complicated two-way association. Some organisations, like firms, are influenced in their strategic choices by institutions. Conversely, other institutions are embedded in organisations, for example in the form of routines. Moreover, some organisations generate institutions while some institutions generate organisations. Accordingly, these complicated relations between institutions and organisations need to be detailed from case to case.

The state is characterised by Hodgson (1988, p. 153) as structuring interactions within the society, including the market and firms as well as people's behaviour. Some elements of the state can be described as organisations creating institutions influencing innovative processes within systems of innovation (Edquist, 2000). Through public policy making, institutions can be created to influence the way innovative activities are conducted.

1.3. Competence of the Firm and Learning

As the definition of diversification implies some transformations of the competences of the firm, it is important to discuss the concept of competences and its relation to the concept of learning in a system of innovation.

The core competence of the firm relates to the set of competences defining the activity of the firm in terms of technology, market or production.

According to Teece et al. (1994, p. 19), the core competence has two dimensions; an organisational/economic dimension and a technical dimension. The organisational and economic competence includes competences about what to produce, for who and at what cost as well as about how to design the most efficient organisation. The technical competence of the firm defines the technological base on which the firm builds its development and production activities.

The concept of learning is used to define the increase of competence within an organisation. Learning processes occur within firms, through their research and development activities, for example, or between firms and other organisations. Learning processes are collective and not individual (Teece et al., 1994). Routines, as an example of institution, are established in order to facilitate these learning processes and to memorise their results within the firm (Johnson, 1992, p. 30). As such, routines have a high tacit content, which makes them not easily transmittable. It is then the role of the management of the firm to define routines efficiently, in order to enhance the capabilities of the firm to the utmost (Teece et al., 1994). Hence, the single most important competence for the development of a firm lies in the skilful management of the learning capacity within the firm.

Both concepts, i.e., competence of the firm and learning processes, must be borne in mind in analysing diversifying firms because to succeed in the diversification the firm engages in a venture which implies the generation of new competences through learning processes.

2.   REASONS FOR DIVERSIFICATION

This section attempts to understand what induces the management to choose to diversify the firm's activities. The management works out a strategy for the future of the firm taking stock of the information it can get from the firm on the one hand and, on the other hand, from the environment of the firm. This implies that the boundary of the firm must be understood. Granstrand (1998) proposes to define the interior and the exterior of the firm by the physical separation between the firm and its environment. This, Granstrand (1998, p. 468) reckons, poses some difficulties as the physical boundary of the firm is a vague notion. Besides, it might be more useful to consider the field of action controlled by the management team as being internal to the firm, and conversely the field of action that cannot be controlled as being external. The borderline is here again very vague, and therefore, the following study will combine the notions of physical boundary and of control to describe the process of diversification.

The management exerts extensive control over what happens inside the firm. It follows that the decision to diversify hinges upon an accurate assessment of the resources of the firm coupled with the prospects of growth in new specific sectors. Section 2.1 aims at clarifying the motives that, according to the literature, induce the management to launch out on a diversification venture.

The environment of the firm is in constant transformation, however. The firm has to adapt to these transformations if it wants to stay in business. The transformations may be slow or rapid. They can be characterised by strong or weak changes in technologies, markets or institutions, or in the three together. In this sense, the environment of the firm can be seen as constraining or providing incentives for the development of the firm. The management has no control over what is happening but must take action in order to keep the firm in business. Section 2.2 attempts to describe how the environment of the firm can impel a diversification.

2.1.   Reasons Internal to the Firm

The management team, by its awareness of the present state of the firm, is able to formulate strategies aiming at an improvement of this state. This improvement can be in terms of the growth of the firm or even a better use of its existing resources. This section investigates the growth of the firm as a reason and a consequence to the diversification. It then describes how economies of scope, use of unused resources and new opportunities can constitute incentives for diversification.

2.1.1. Growth of the firm

Chandler (1990, p. 230) identifies four major strategies of growth for American firms. These are mergers, vertical integration, expansion in new geographical markets and finally diversification. The relationship between the growth of the firm and diversification is also presented by Penrose (1959).

Small firms may choose to keep their size for various reasons. The founder may want to keep the entire control over the activity of the firm (Penrose, 1959, p. 28). This implies that the firm has to stay small so that no new management competences need to be introduced in the firm. Another reason might be the lack of ambition of the owner and his or her will to keep business growing at its own rate.

Penrose (1959) confronts these hypotheses with an argument about the attraction of power and money for both owners and managers of firms. The larger the firm, the more power and rewards for the manager. The manager of a small firm is mainly interested in the product he or she produces. However when the firm starts growing, a need for professional management arises in financing, human resources and so on. This means that professional managers, whose aim is not the product in itself anymore but making money and increasing their own wealth, will replace the manager-entrepreneur (Penrose, 1959, p. 29). This argument is supported by Mueller (1969) who argues that since managers' compensation is directly related to the size of the firm, managers have strong incentives to find ways to increase the size of the firm. However, according to Teece (1982, p. 42) this hypothesis is rejected by most empirical evidence.

As the main argument for growth is profit, Penrose (1959, p. 30) considers that growth and profit 'become equivalent as the criteria for the selection of investment programmes'. The management's will to maximise the profits can turn to a diversification to satisfy the firm's own internal capacity of growth. Therefore, the firm might diversify in order to satisfy its own need of expansion when its existing line of activity cannot absorb the existing profits of the firm.

Conversely, diversification can also be a policy inducing the growth of the firm. Whenever the possibility of growth is better in a new sector, the management of the firm will then have an incentive to diversify assuming that the resources of the firm, both financial and managerial, allow such a strategy (Penrose, 1959, p. 144).

The relationship between the growth of the firm and diversification is not clearly established, however. Montgomery (1994, p. 172) stresses that diversification is not a 'direct road to success'. In that she follows the argument of Rumelt (1974, p. 94), emphasising that it is more the way in which the firm diversifies that matters than the diversification *per se*. Firms engaging in related diversification perform better and are more prone to grow than firms engaging in unrelated diversification.[18] In addition, Granstrand (1998, p. 472) and Granstrand et al. (1997, p. 8) argue that stress should be put on technological diversification as being more likely to promote the growth of the firm. This argument is limited, however, by the nature of the firm studied, since the firms studied were technology-based.

As the argument of growth is difficult to establish, Teece (1982, p. 43) observes that it can only be part of the explanation of why firms diversify. A stronger incentive is that firms diversify in order to use their resources more efficiently. This is the resource-based theory of the multiproduct firm, as will be discussed in the following section.

2.1.2. Resource-based theory of diversification

The underlying question addressed here is why a firm diversifies instead of reinvesting in its existing line of product or giving dividends to its stockholders. The traditional neoclassical perspective reveals no ground for explaining why a firm diversifies.[19] The emergence of multiproduct firms is possible in neoclassical theories, but only by accident.

Moving away from the neoclassical analysis, Teece (1982, p. 46) considers that the theory of the multiproduct firm needs to be a dynamic one involving disequilibrium. Diversification may be considered as a strategy for the firm in order to achieve economies of scope. In other words, diversification permits a more efficient use of the productive resources of the firm.

Economies of scope

The idea of economies of scope can then be summarised as follows: the cost of the joint production of both products A and B is lower than the cost of production of the product A plus the cost of production of the product B. In other words, there are some complementarities in production that can be used to reduce the global cost of production (Teece, 1980, p. 226). Though the focus is on production, other areas of the firm may benefit from economies of scope, for example, development, marketing or logistics.

Economies of scope are however not enough to explain why firms diversify, because the combined production of several products and the appending marketing and logistics services needed is not necessarily more efficient in a firm without subcontractors than in a firm with subcontractors. Besides, economies of scope may be more a consequence of diversification than one of its causes. Production complementarities as well as synergies can be found in a diversified firm but not in a monoproduct firm. Nevertheless, if economies of scope are not enough to explain the process, they can be part of the explanation.

Use of unused resources
According to Penrose (1959), a major incentive for firms to grow has to do with the fact that resources within the firm are never fully used. By resources is meant:

> ... the physical things a firm buys, leases, or produces for its own use, and the people hired on terms that make them effectively part of the firm. Services, on the other hand, are the contributions these resources can make to the productive operations of the firm. A resource, then, can be a bundle of possible services (Penrose, 1959, p. 67).

Teece (1982, p. 47) extends the resources to the financial assets of the firm. He considers diversification as a means for the firm to use the resources that are not fully used. Diversification is then a means to keep these resources inside the firm, for example, by providing employment to a competent workforce in new areas of activities, by reducing the profits of the firm, and thereby its taxation, or through new investments in new ventures. If the firm does not diversify, it can sell the unused assets to another firm and reinvest the benefits in existing activities or increase the dividends of the stockholder.

Montgomery and Hariharan (1991) as well as Malerba, Breschi and Lissoni (1997) investigate these hypotheses and find that firms diversify into industries in which they can use the resources they already have. Montgomery et al. (1991, p. 87) indicates that it is not necessarily the technologies that are important, as argued by Malerba et al. (1997), but that other aspects, such as the level of capital intensity, the level of selling intensity or the level of R&D intensity, are similar to the resource profile of the firm.

This latter argument is confirmed by Teece et al. (1994) in their analysis of why firms diversify in a 'coherent way', i.e., in relation to their original line of production. The diversified firms studied by Teece et al. (1994) were all characterised by the fact that they were multiproduct corporations with a non-random composition of their portfolio of products.

2.1.3. Taking advantage of new opportunities
Diversification can be triggered by the emergence of new opportunities. Systematic research and development activities create new opportunities for the firm, as existing products can be improved and new products developed. However, as argued by Granstrand et al. (1997, p. 13), opportunities opened by new technologies cannot be predicted and therefore can push the firm in unexpected directions. Thus, another form of opportunity stems from the

emergence of new markets in which the firm can enter using its existing resources or new technologies it has developed.

The latter argument is supported by Penrose (1959, p. 116) who adds that opportunities can also stem from the selling activities of the firm. An established firm has built up relations with its customers. These relations imply a degree of trust between the partners. The firm can then either create or respond to new demands from its customers, building upon the existing relations.

According to Penrose (1959, p. 114), it is the vision the management of the firm has of its environment that triggers the decision to diversify. By vision is meant the understanding of relevant factors for the growth of the firm, such as the state of competition in the existing business, the prospects of growth in the incoming technology or the possibilities for the firm to be a first-mover in a new business.

New opportunities are seen as coming both from the internal activities of the firm, through, for example, organised research and development, and from the environment of the firm. In terms of management of the firm, one difficulty with this hypothesis is that opportunities have to be identified and properly managed. It also implies that a potential market exists or can be developed at the same time as the firm diversifies. Unfortunately, opportunities do not emerge in short time periods and cannot be monitored (Gambardella and Torrisi, 1998, p. 488). As for the resource-based theory of diversification, this theory can only be a partial explanation of the reasons for diversification.

2.2.   Reasons External to the Firm

So far, reasons for diversification have been seen as stemming from the will of the management of the firm to sustain the growth, to better use the internal resources or to take advantage of opportunities. The management has some control over the future activities of the firm, being aware of the existing potentials of the firm in terms of competences, market or finances. However, the choice of diversification may be influenced by factors external to the firm, in relation to which the management can only adapt its strategy. In this section, the external aspects of diversification are discussed, starting from the need for firms to reduce their vulnerability through diversification, then describing how institutions can trigger the strategy. Finally, public technology procurement is analysed as one policy that can influence the choice of the firm to diversify.

2.2.1. Spreading risks

Penrose (1959, p. 138) presents spreading risk as a major reason for diversification, in particular for firms with cyclical activities. If the environment of the firm is unstable, the firm faces uncertainties leading to vulnerabilities in its specific line of activities. Spreading the activities of the firm is hence seen as a minimising of the risks for the firm as a whole. However, Penrose (1959) considers that it is more a question of relative profitability than one of risk which matters. For the firm to diversify, '[i]t is not necessary that existing markets become less profitable in themselves, only that they become *relatively* less profitable for any new investment the firm wants to undertake' (Penrose, 1959, p. 105).

The role of risk as a trigger for diversification is then only a matter of how the firm can find the best, or most profitable, way to invest its financial resources. This leads back to the previous arguments of the resource-based theory of diversification. By identifying activities more profitable than the one in which it is engaged, the firm is able to reduce its exposure to risks and promote its potential growth in new areas.

2.2.2. Institutions forcing the firm in specific directions

The systems of innovation approach focuses on innovation processes and their role in economic development. Firms are hence seen as interacting with each other and with other organisations in an institutional environment. Relations do not only exist among the various organisations of the system, but as Edquist and Johnson (1997) emphasise, there are also complex relations between organisations and institutions.

Two types of relations can be observed; a passive and an active one. In passive relations, the firm is affected by institutions and reacts to these by adapting its own activity. As such, the firm follows the transformations of its own environment. In an active perspective, McKelvey and Texier (2000) have argued that the system of innovation as such is not important for the firm, but that it is the way the firm takes advantage of institutions to create its own system that matters. Here, the relationship between the firm and the institutional environment is dynamic because the firm chooses and determines the way relations with other organisations develop.

Passive perspective

In a passive perspective, the firm can be seen in its system of innovation as interacting with other organisations of the system. Network theory considers that the firm is embedded in a network of relations with other firms and organisations (Håkansson, 1990). Furthermore, this theory considers that transformations of the network imply transformations of the organisations in the network because of their interdependencies. Consequently, the firm may have to diversify in order to adapt its activities to a new network. However, the theory only considers inter-firm or firm–organisation relations though other types of interactions may exist and provide the firm with impulses to change.

Following the reasoning discussed in the network theory, the firm can be considered as being embedded in the system of innovation in which it operates. The institutional environment provides rules regulating the relations between the firm and other organisations of the system. As a result, institutional changes of the environment should affect the strategy of the firm.

According to North (1990, p. 89), institutional change can occur in two ways, i.e., as radical or incremental transformation. He considers that most institutional changes occur incrementally and over a long period of time, providing stability to the system. Radical changes take the form of revolutions and are rare. Although all institutional changes do not affect the firm, some are of direct importance to its strategy. Both radical and incremental changes imply transformations within the system of innovation. The nature and extent of these transformations induce new strategies within firms in order for them to adapt their activity to the new rules.

Transformations of the institutional environment affect the firm by providing either incentives or constraints to new strategies. In other words, some institutional changes may provide the firm with new opportunities, in the form of new markets or new use of technologies. On the other hand, other changes may constrain the firm by reducing a market or forbidding the use of some technologies. Both constraints and incentives may lead the firm to diversify.

Diversification from military to civil activities can be seen as an example of a strategy triggered by institutional changes. Feldman (1998), as well as Mowery and Rosenberg (1989), have shown that the military aircraft industry in the USA was highly dependent on military procurement from the government.[20] This dependence on governmental demand and credits had some direct consequences for the strategies of firms. Changes in public opinion with regard to the allocation of government credits had a direct impact on the industry, spurring changes in industry and diversification.

Taking the example of Boeing-Vertol's diversification from helicopters to electric trolleys for public transportation during the 1970s, Feldman (1998) shows that the firm was forced to find new uses for its know-how and personnel in order to survive. Other examples of institutional changes driven by public opinion might be the rejection of products that are not environmentally friendly. In order to continue its activity, the firm may have to change its line of products radically and adapt it to the new market.

Institutional change can also provide the firm with new incentives. As Samuels and Whipple (1989) argue, the aerospace industry in Japan was developed both for industrial reasons and for the prestige of the nation. The Ministry of International Trade and Industry (MITI) already wanted an aerospace industry at the beginning of the 1970s and considered it as being as important as the nuclear and the information technology industries (Samuels and Whipple, 1989, p. 275). The reason for this was that the aerospace industry was seen as providing the nation with international status, military independence and new technologies that could be useful for other sectors. To succeed in this effort, MITI pushed the heavy industries to diversify and start the production of aircraft. In a first step, the production was done under subcontracting to foreign firms, until the country was allowed to conduct its own R&D in military sectors. The second step implied stand-alone programmes in cooperation with US firms.

Active perspective
Taking the example of the development of mobile telecommunication in Sweden, McKelvey and Texier (2000) showed that firms can diversify their activities by taking advantage both of specific institutions of their environment, and of technological opportunities.

Originally, the firm Ericsson was producing telecommunication systems for the fixed telecom network. When mobile telecommunication started to become a reality in the 1970s, Ericsson cautiously started to engage in this new activity. At the beginning, the firm was dependent on the Swedish system of innovation to develop mobile telecommunication technologies. This implied that the firm was in constant interaction with small firms developing specific technologies for the telecommunication network. Intimate relations between firms, Swedish university research and the Nordic national telecommunication organisations (the Nordic PTTs) provided a stable institutional environment to establish the technologies. It also resulted in the establishment of telecommunication standards such as the NMT (Nordic Mobile Telecommunication) in 1982 and the GSM (Global System for Mobile Communication) in 1991, which were decisive institutions for the establishment of the mobile telecommunication industry.

However, as Ericsson grew bigger and expanded its activities abroad, the importance of the Swedish system of innovation decreased for the firm. Ericsson started R&D laboratories in various countries and developed tight contacts with foreign universities. Thereafter, it was not the Swedish system of innovation that mattered to Ericsson but the dynamic system of innovation the firm was developing. The first diversification of Ericsson, from fixed to mobile telecommunication was triggered by institutions in the Swedish system of innovation. In the second diversification of Ericsson, from analogue to digital technology, the firm was active in the creation of the new digital telecommunication standard. The firm contributed to the creation of institutions and was pro-active in its institutional environment. The interactions between firms and other organisations can also lead to new institutions fostering diversification as is the case with the creation of new standards.

2.2.3. Public and private technology procurement

The previous discussion has focused on how the transformation of the institutional environment of the firm could initiate its diversification. One particular type of innovation policy, public or private technology procurement, is here analysed as a tool that might foster diversification.

According to Granstrand (1984), technology procurement is

> ...the procurement by a buyer of products, services or systems, which at the time being are not available on the market and for which some element of technical development is needed. The buyer, which is almost always an organisation rather than an individual, may be a public body . . . as well as a private firm with domestic or foreign origins (p. 9).

As this definition indicates, there are some elements of novelty in the product ordered by the buyer, and these imply a technological development within the producing firm. This suggests that a firm can diversify because it was invited to do so by another organisation procuring the new product or because it was able to offer its competences to the buyer. The relations between the buyer (the user of the product) and the seller (the producer of the product) imply a certain degree of common competences between them. If the buyer has insufficient competences, it can either rely on the producer's competences, build up its own competences or involve a third party, a procuring agency, that can substitute itself to the buyer (Granstrand, 1984, p. 10).[21]

The fact that the buyer can be either a public agency or a private organisation implies that technology procurement can be used as a technology policy by a government to develop new products (Edquist and Hommen, 1999, p. 5). Although technology procurement can initiate a diversification in a firm, its efficiency as a policy instrument is still not clearly established, both for the development of new technologies and technological spillovers in industry. While the US civil aerospace industry has largely and successfully developed on behalf of the Federal expenditures for military airplanes (Mowery and Rosenberg, 1989), other projects have failed to provide the technologies expected, as was the case of the computer for schools developed in Sweden during the 1980s (Kaiserfeld, 1999).

3. IMPLEMENTING DIVERSIFICATION

When the management of the firm has evaluated the possibilities of diversification and assessed the viability of the strategy, the problem of its implementation remains. How do institutions affect the management of the diversification? How do firms interact with their environment (institutions and other organisations) to develop new technologies and new products?

Implementation of diversification can be done both through internal and external development. External development mainly means acquisition of other firms in order to gain access to new competences. Another way to acquire new competences is via subcontracting technologies with other firms. Internal development implies that the firm uses its own resources, for example, in the form of personnel or research potential, to implement the diversification. Specific management capabilities are required in order to diversify successfully. These are discussed in the following Section, 3.1.

The diversification process implies that the firm must engage in learning processes involving its own resources and other organisations. Section 3.2 discusses the learning dimensions involved in the process of diversification and how the firm is able to learn in interaction with other organisations.

Various factors affect the development of the diversification strategy during its implementation. Some are external parameters that can affect the development of the strategy. The educational system, as well as the organisation of R&D at the national level, has an impact on the way the diversification process takes place within the firm. Moreover, other infrastructures, set up for example by government policies, can also provide a useful support to diversifying firms. These issues are discussed in Section 3.3.

3.1. Management Capabilities

The diversification process implies a development of the firm's assets. By assets is here meant both physical assets and personnel. If the firm does not give up its existing line of business, then it has to grow outside its original physical boundaries in terms of facilities and machinery. New plants have to be built, in which new machinery will be installed and operated by newly employed personnel. Even though some of the resources may already exist in the firm, they may not be sufficient, possibly creating a need for new investments in order for the firm to carry out its diversification. These new investments may lead to the acquisition of existing firms within the sector into which the firm diversifies or to the subcontracting of another firm to develop the technology or the product.

3.1.1. Acquisitions
Following the definition of diversification given in Section 1.1 of this chapter, the acquisition implies the integration of the acquired firm. It goes beyond a participation in the ownership of the firm through the purchase of shares.

The acquisition of another firm can be seen as a simple strategy for the diversifying firm. The buying firm knows what it is going to buy, or at least has a relatively precise idea of the capacity of the acquired firm. In this sense, the acquisition enables the diversifying firm to launch a new product and enter a new market without having to abandon its existing one. The assets of the acquired firm come under the management of the diversifying firm.

This type of acquisition raises some difficulties for both firms. Utterback (1994, p. 227) argues that acquisitions of small firms by large ones can fail because large firms might just buy an 'empty box'. In other words, the competent personnel leaves the acquired firm and what is left is the 'physical' firm with production facilities and blueprints. Another problem comes from the difficulties of managing the acquired division. Trust between management teams has been shown as being difficult to develop, creating conflicts and ultimately leading to a failure of the diversification (Feldman, 1999b, p. 1808).

Granstrand and Sjölander (1990, p. 370) observe that, for technology-based firms, diversification through acquisitions risks failure if the acquired firm has not already started to market the new product. However, even if acquisition is a risky strategy, acquisition of small technology-based firms by large technology-based firms has been common, for example in Sweden, as a way for diversifying firms to acquire new knowledge and resources (Granstrand and Sjölander, 1990, p. 372).

McKelvey, Texier and Alm (1997) have shown that in the case of the development of the mobile telecommunication industry, the large and established firm Ericsson profited largely from the purchase of small firms. In the 1970s, Ericsson was a supplier of telecommunication systems for fixed networks. At that time, only a small division of Ericsson was involved in the development of equipment for mobile telecommunication. The technologies necessary for mobile telecommunication had mainly been developed in small development firms, contracted by the Swedish PTT, while the NMT standard had been set up by the Nordic PTTs. Through the purchase of these small firms, Ericsson was able to upgrade its competences and became a leader in the business of mobile telecommunication.

Diversification by acquisition can be a rapid strategy for the firm provided that it is able to secure the proper resources in the acquired firm for the success of the new venture. However, it implies some risks that the firm has to carefully assess. As an alternative to acquisition, the knowledge needed can also be obtained from other firms through contractual relationships.

3.1.2. Contractual relationships with other firms

In order to gain access to the missing knowledge necessary for its diversification, the firm can contract it from other firms and thus avoid the problems that an acquisition can raise. As such, the knowledge and the technologies necessary for a successful diversification can partially exist within the firm, but some elements may be lacking. Contracting another firm to develop these technologies can be seen as a possibility for the diversifying firm, since this strategy may not involve the high costs and risks of an acquisition.

However, contracting also implies some risks, mainly concerning the ownership of the new technology and its implementation within the diversifying firm. Concerning the ownership of the new technology, the contracted firm may use the knowledge it has produced under the contract for its own development and hence market the technology on its own account. Moreover, the technology transfer can raise problems if the tacit knowledge it entails is not easily transferred (Teece, 1980). As a result, the integration of the contracted technology in the diversifying firm can fail. Avoiding this outcome requires a clear assessment of the relations between the contracting firm and the diversifying firm (Granstrand et al., 1997, p. 19).

Feldman (1998) has shown in his study of Boeing-Vertol's diversification from helicopters to electric vehicles that contracting the knowledge necessary to the diversification is not an easy process. In this case, the contracted firm, a consulting agency, developed the vehicle on the basis of very unclear specifications from Boeing. The technical solutions had not been properly tested and the system as a whole was over-engineered. It resulted in repeated problems in the vehicle and the relative failure of the diversification. The contracted firm must, therefore, be clearly aware of the detailed needs of the buying firm, otherwise the knowledge gap may induce the contracting firm to develop a solution of its own that may not fit into the requirements of the diversifying firm.

The contractual relationship, involving knowledge generation, can also be between the diversifying firm and the user of the new product. In the case of private technology procurement, the buyer's competence, in terms of market or technology, is very important for the success of the process. By sharing its experience with the producer, the buyer allows for a development of the internal capability of the diversifying firm. Similarly with the contracting of a consulting firm, this involves a number of problems with regard to the ownership of the technologies, as well as in cases where delays are not respected or if the performance of the product does not meet the specifications. Granstrand (1984, p. 11) argues that this should be clearly formulated in the contract between the firms.

3.1.3. Internal development

The R&D activity of the firm and its diversification effort are related, the findings of the R&D department not necessarily being connected to the existing business of the firm (Penrose, 1959). Moreover, the R&D activity can provide the firm with new knowledge during the diversification. This argument is supported by MacDonald (1985, p. 590), who indicates that firms base their diversification on their R&D activities, and that the intensity of R&D within a firm is directly related to the propensity of the firm to diversify. However, little is said on the role of R&D as a tool to implement the strategy.

Once the management has made the decision to diversify, actions have to be taken in order for the diversification to succeed. The competences of the firm in the new business area are limited, by definition, and have to be adapted to the new business. New competences have to be developed in terms of both technologies and management. Whether the diversification is related or not, an R&D effort has to be pursued in the direction of the area of diversification.

If the diversification was the result of previous R&D activities, new activities would build on previous experiences and competences, thus continuing along the same technological trajectory. Difficulties occur when the diversification is not related or if there is a technological discontinuity.

The diversification may introduce a disruption in the traditional activity of the firm. Tushman, Andersson and O'Reilly (1997, p. 9), as well as Jacobsson and Ehrnberg (1997), present the concept of technological discontinuity to describe the technological disruption between the old activity and the new activity of the firm. Technological discontinuities can be either competence-enhancing, if the technology builds on existing know-how, or competence-destroying, if the technology suppresses existing competences (Utterback, 1994, p. 207).

Although there exists a consensus in the literature regarding the idea that successful diversification is more likely to be successful in cases of related diversification,[22] some studies have shown that unrelated diversification could succeed. McKelvey et al. (1997) have shown, for example, that the large established firm Ericsson had succeeded in diversifying from fixed to mobile telecommunication during the 1980s.[23]

As seen previously, a firm can get access to new competences through acquisition or through subcontracting. These strategies have drawbacks and the firm may prefer to invest in its own competence through investments in R&D. There is one limitation to this strategy, especially regarding high-tech industries. Firms entering new industries may do so at a stage where the technology in itself creates a barrier to new entrants. In other words, the R&D effort necessary for the firm to enter the new business may be too high. As a consequence, a frequent reason for failures in diversification is the insufficient level of investments the firm makes in R&D (Utterback, 1994, p. 226). The balance between R&D for the traditional activity of the firm and for the new activity is too often weighted in favour of the traditional activity because of the uncertainties of the new business.

This does not preclude the possibility that a firm may succeed in a diversification using internal development. However, it seems that it is the combination of both external and internal development that is the most efficient approach. McKelvey et al. (1997) show that this was clearly the case in the development of mobile telecommunication in Sweden. The firm Ericsson was shown to succeed in its diversification by using a combination of both acquisitions and heavy investments in R&D.

3.2.   Learning Dimensions in the Diversification

The management of a diversifying firm faces a new situation in which different kinds of new knowledge have to be integrated. In order to succeed in the diversification, the management has to understand the risks involved by the absence of specific types of knowledge, to try to estimate their effects on the strategy and to know how to learn about the missing competences.

The management of new knowledge should hence be associated with the management of the risks raised by the diversification. The risks encountered by the diversifying firm can be reduced by a thorough investigation of the various types of competences the firm needs to acquire. Then, there is a process of learning regarding the new knowledge needed to go through the diversification. The management of the new knowledge should also involve a degree of implementation or practice. In other words, there is a degree of 'learning by doing' in the learning process in which the firm engages.

Teece et al. (1994) consider that the degree of success for a diversifying firm is directly related to the firm's capacity to learn in both market and technology dimensions. Failures to learn in both ways generally implies failure of the diversification strategy. As argued by Gambardella and Torrisi (1998, p. 449), knowledge about market and technologies might not be the only forms of new knowledge the firm must learn during the diversification. In this study, the following learning dimensions are identified as important for the management of diversification:

1. development of the new technology;
2. understanding of the new market;
3. learning how to finance the new venture and the size of the investment;
4. understanding of the new management capability of the firm; and
5. understanding of the new institutional environment in which the firm engages.

These five learning dimensions related to diversification are not independent from one another and can overlap.

3.2.1. Development of the new technology

The first learning dimension to be managed concerns the technology. As the diversification progresses, a concern of the management is the firm's success in turning out the new product. The technologies used in the new product can be new to the firm but known outside, or they can be new to the world. If the technology is new only to the firm, it can be managed either through internal or external development. When the technology is acquired, the firm has to integrate it into the new activity and start its new production.

However, the diversification process implies that the firm leaves what Teece (1988) calls its natural trajectory or core business. While the core competences of the firm are known to the management, there remains a question as to the nature of the new technology in relation to the old technology. The problem is that the firm knows what it can expect from its core competence, but does not know what can be expected from the new technology. The degree of relatedness between the technologies has to be taken into account by the management, even though the extent of the relatedness cannot be known.

3.2.2. Understanding of the new market

The new market into which the firm penetrates can have characteristics that differ from the old market. The type of relations between the organisations within an industry differs from industry to industry, and new customers as well as new suppliers have to be found. Establishing these new relations and making them work properly may require periods of time longer than expected.

The relations between the various partners differ from market to market. The firm risks entering a new market without having enough knowledge about it. It may, for example, lack information about the structure of this new market (Detrie and Ramanantsoa, 1986, p. 35).

For example, a firm diversifying from military to civil markets must learn the similarities and differences between the two. A military market is characterised by few governmental customers, while a civil market is more open and with different regulations.

3.2.3. Learning how to finance the venture and the size of the investment

According to Detrie and Ramanantsoa (1986, p. 35), an underestimation of 60% of the financial resources needed is common in diversifying firms. This leads to poor results of the strategy (Feldman, 1999b, p. 1809). Established firms have already invested heavily in their specific activity, plants have been built, machinery installed and loans may have been taken. Evaluating the size of the financial investment that the firm should place in the new venture is arduous.

The balance between maintaining the old activity and investing in the new one is very difficult to achieve. According to Utterback (1994, p. 226), this is a common reason of failure for established firms. However, this is not to deny the fact that established firms can succeed in their diversification, as shown by McKelvey and Texier (2000). The mobile telecommunication firm Ericsson was able to succeed in going through two major technological discontinuities, i.e., from fixed to mobile communication and from analogue to digital signalling, and, consequently, became a world leader in the mobile communication business. However, this was done through very heavy investment in R&D especially in the case of the diversification from analogue to digital mobile communication (McKelvey and Texier, 2000).

If the financial resources of the firm are not sufficient to conduct the diversification, there must be an investigation of other possible sources of financing. This requires that the firm has the possibility to convince the potential financial partner about the probability of success of the venture and hence allow for profit sharing, for example, through a percentage of the royalties earned on the product.

3.2.4. Understanding of the new management capability of the firm

Growth through diversification also implies a growth of the management service in the firm. Thus, new management has to be found. According to Penrose (1959, p. 46), if the firm grows but cannot find the resources to manage its growth it will then run into difficulties. To this problem, which is merely an internal problem to the firm, is added another one which has to do with the hiring of new managers who are not used to the specific functioning of the firm.

Another common reason for failure in diversification is due to the non-separation of the management of the traditional activities of the firm and that of its new activities (Detrie and Ramanantsoa, 1986; Utterback, 1994). The management of the new activity must be given a free hand by the general management of the firm. This does not imply a clear cut separation between the various activities of the firm. The relations between the management of the old activity and the management of the new activity must be well defined so that the diversification is made in terms of cooperation between management services and not in terms of competition.

Even if the spheres of action of the old and the new management are well defined, synergies between the activities of the firm can occur and have to be managed. The role of the management is to evaluate the possible synergies between the different departments of the firm so that resources – financial, physical and managerial – can be optimised. New management capacity may be necessary in order for the strategy to succeed. Moreover, the management of the new venture must be given space and finance to be able to promote the diversification (Rumelt, 1974, p. 138).

Assessing the risks taken by the management is tricky as these are easily underestimated. The management division associated with the old activity may be reluctant to reduce its controls over the firm as a whole. This can result in situations where potential synergies are disregarded or neglected.

3.2.5. Understanding of the new institutional environment

The institutional environment is closely related to the market, but should be discussed separately since it can affect both the new technology and the market. Institutions can be understood here at different levels. At the market level, the firm must take into account institutions governing the relations between the various organisations of the market, such as the rules of contracting or of establishing trust relations between firms. At the technology level, institutions regulate the way the product is designed as well as the production of new products. Institutions specify how technologies and products should operate, in terms of safety, standards and environment. Hence, they constrain how the firm can develop and produce a new product.

Relations between firms are established by routines and common practices and are constrained by the institutional environment. Lundvall (1992b) describes these relations in terms of trust and opportunities. Llerena and Cohendet (1997, p. 236) argue that institutions provide the system with incentives for interactive learning between the elements of the system. Even in a conducive institutional framework, learning relations are based on trust and therefore take time to build. Diversification efforts dependent on trust may not succeed if the diversifying firm usually conducts its relationships in an opportunistic manner.

Other institutional and relational difficulties can occur when the firm enters a market strongly dominated by national political interests. The difference between managing a military and a civil company may, for example, hinder diversification from one to the other. Secrecy is required of military industry and during official commercial negotiations there may be intense political games backstage.

Knowledge about informal institutions is difficult to acquire since it is based on experience and hence on the time spent to develop relations between different partners.

3.3.   External Inputs in the Implementation of Diversification

The development of the firm necessitates the building up of competences within the firm. However, the support of external organisations, such as universities, may also be needed. In the case of external development, institutions may intervene, for example, in the form of laws regulating acquisitions.

Consequently, despite the fact that the success of the diversification process is related to the type of management capability of the firm some aspects are outside its control. These aspects can be considered as constraints or incentives to the development of the firm and can be found in the system of innovation in which the firm operates.

Following the definition given in Section 1.2.3 of this chapter, institutions are the laws, rules, and standards governing the system of innovation. Moreover, the firm diversifies in the system of innovation in which it operates. Hence, some institutions have an effect on the process of diversification. This indicates that the state can have a role in the implementation of the diversification; through the educational system, as will be discussed in Section 3.3.1, through the development of the technological infrastructure, as presented in Section 3.3.2 and through specific institutions created by the state, as outlined in Section 3.3.3.

3.3.1. Education and national/regional research and development

Management of new knowledge was seen in Section 3.2 as central to the success of the diversification. If new knowledge, such as management capability, can be developed inside the firm as part of the programme of diversification, other new knowledge, for example, knowledge about the new technologies, may have to be found outside the firm. If the firm wants to grow, it needs to have some personnel with competences related to the new area of activity. Hence, there is a need for a labour market with resources related to specific industrial needs.

McKelvey et al. (1997) show in their study of mobile telecommunication that one of the roles of the Swedish State was to provide university education in scientific domains related to the new technologies. The organisations involved in the public education system have to evaluate the future human-resource needs of an industry so that the firms can hire competent personnel. The relations between the firms and the system of innovation provide information about these needs. The organisations of the system mutually create incentives for the development of education programmes. In the case of Ericsson, education programmes in Swedish universities were designed specifically for the needs of the firm. Ericsson was active in various boards of these universities and financed new research programmes.

In the case of the software industry, Mowery (1999, p. 158) argues also that the shortage of skilled workforce in Europe and Japan was a direct drawback to the development of their industry. In parallel with education programmes at universities, the development of a national research capacity is important. The development of specific R&D laboratories, at universities or in specialised organisations, provides some long-term prospects for the development of new technologies and new products. This supports not only the existing firms that are diversifying but also gives incentives for the creation of new firms. The building up of the national competences not only sustains the national economy but also exerts a favourable influence upon the creation of new standards at the international level.

In his study of the South Korean industry, Kim (1997, Chapter 2) considers that the South Korean government was a 'learning facilitator'. The government provided the industry with laws and incentives to accelerate the learning rate of Korean firms and also created government R&D institutes and industry-specific institutes. These two kinds of organisations were oriented towards specific industrial and technological areas (Kim, 1997, p. 47).

3.3.2. National infrastructure support
The role of the state in the diversification process is exemplified in the work of Lall (1996). Addressing the development of the so-called Asian Tigers, Lall (1996) analyses the different policies implemented by the governments of the respective Asian countries to foster technological progress. The technologies and the industrial sectors, in which the states were willing to enter, were selected according to their prospects of economic growth and welfare. Spillovers from high-technology industries into other industries were also considered. This led to the creation of targeted R&D development programmes.

The South Korean government did not want to develop foreign direct investment policies, since these were considered as undermining the independence of the country. In order to access technologies and facilitate the diffusion of information, the government created online databases, providing firms with information on sources and prices of technologies. An agency whose aim was to provide firms with industrial contacts was also created. Reverse engineering was also encouraged (Lall, 1996, p. 75).

In order to support the diversification process, the industrial infrastructure of the country can be adapted to the requirements of the new technology. In South Korea, the government created centres of excellence and science parks, in which companies were invited to develop their activities. Both tax deductions and proximity to other firms were instrumental in facilitating the diversification of firms into new high-tech areas (Lall, 1996, p. 76).

3.3.3. Specific institutions

A variety of institutions can facilitate the process of diversification. These include:

1. standardisation;
2. patent and other intellectual property rights law; and
3. grants and tax incentives.

Standardisation

New standards can provide a framework in which new technologies can be developed. The extent of the diversification can then be limited by the standard, as it reduces the range of technologies available for a specific product. The standard can also be beneficial for the firm if it has developed its technological base with regard to the standard or if it has been involved in the creation of the standard.

The story of mobile telecommunication shows that the emergence of the NMT standard during the 1970s was crucial for the development of the industry. This standard was set up by the Nordic PTTs and established the technical characteristics and functionalities of all the elements of a mobile telecommunication infrastructure. The firms willing to diversify in the new industry had to comply with the standard specification in order to be able gain market shares (Meurling and Jeans, 1994, p. 39).

Standardisation can be organised both by governmental organisations and firms. In the case of the videocassette recorder (VCR) industry, Japanese firms were competing with European firms to enforce a standard for the industry. Despite the effort of the European governments to protect the European firms, the market adopted the Japanese standard VHS (Tyson, 1992, p. 219). In this case, the European firms then had to adjust to the new standards and make the necessary technological changes to their products in order to be active on the VCR market.

Patent and other intellectual property rights laws

Rules regarding patents and intellectual property rights are other types of institutions that intervene during the process of diversification. They can affect the success of the strategy positively, in the event that the firm possesses the patents, or negatively, if the patenting system does not enable the firm to take advantage of a given technology (Llerena and Cohendet, 1997, p. 236).

However, patents and other intellectual property rights laws are not useful if the firm is in a country that does not comply with international regulations. South Korea used reverse engineering as a tool to learn about western technologies. This practice permitted an accelerated pace of learning in South Korean firms and was stopped only when the first legislation to maintain intellectual property rights in South Korea was voted through in 1986 (Kim, 1997, p. 38).

Grants and tax incentives

Entry into new technological areas is often hampered by huge requirements for R&D investments. The diversifying firm is constrained by its own budget and present activity. Evaluating the size of the investment in a new R&D programme is difficult because of the uncertainties related to the returns of the investment, both in economic and technological terms.

One type of policy that can be used is to give tax incentives to firms investing in targeted R&D programmes (Lall, 1996, p. 63). Another possibility is to facilitate the investment by giving firms loans and grants (Lall, 1996, p. 80). Through these tools, the burden of the financial risks of the diversification is reduced, supporting the effort of the firm in its strategy.

4. SUMMARY

In this chapter, diversification has been defined as a strategy resulting in changes in four dimensions of the firm. These dimensions are the firm's product, its technologies, its market and its organisation. Thus defined, the diversification process implies a renewal of the competence base of the firm. The reasons for diversification stem from various factors, either internal or external to the firm.

The need to grow is seen as a general reason for the firm to design new strategies, but as such is not enough to explain the decision to diversify. Other strategies can be designed with the same aim. Economies of scope can be a reason for diversification, but these are not enough, since the firm can still subcontract part of the production at a lower cost. This theory points out the fact that the firm can use its resources more efficiently, providing that the unused resources can be identified.

New opportunities emerging from the research and development of the firm are seen as important for the decision to diversify. However, new opportunities arise not only within the firm but also from the system in which the firm operates or from other systems. This is the case of market opportunities.

The firm is seen as an element in a system of innovation, whose boundaries are defined in terms of both geography and type of industry, depending on the type of analysis. The institutional environment governing the relations between the elements of the system affects the strategic behaviour of the firms and their learning capacity.

Reasons for diversification can therefore also be seen, from an external point of view, as flowing from constraints on or incentives in the firm that are created by the institutional environment. Specific policies, such as public procurement policies, can trigger the diversification of the firm in directions planned by public authorities in close cooperation with industry. Institutional changes in the system of innovation can also be an input. They can create a risk for the firm or induce new incentives for the development of new products.

New knowledge is needed for the implementation of the diversification strategy. Five learning dimensions have to be managed. These are: learning about the new technologies to be used in the new product; learning about the new market in which the firm engages; learning how to manage the new division of the firm in interaction with other organisations; learning about how to finance the venture and finally learning about the new institutional environment of the sector in which the firm diversifies. Every aspect of the diversification process is plagued with its specific risks, and this should be taken into account by the management of the firm.

The role of the system of innovation in diversification is twofold. On the one hand, it can impose constraints or provide incentives triggering diversification in firms. On the other hand, it can support the diversification process. The firm has to find a labour market suited to its needs. Otherwise, no activities are possible. This implies a commitment of both the firm and the state. The system of innovation includes institutions that constrain the firm in its technological choices and in its possibilities for growth. The legal system, concerning acquisition, for example, has to be taken into account when implementing the strategy.

The relations between the firm and the different elements of the system of innovation are numerous and their influence on the firm's behaviour has been demonstrated. The firm is therefore to be viewed as diversifying within its system of innovation. Incentives and constraints or threats to the diversifying firm arise from both inside the firm and from its environment.

NOTES

1. Pilot and novelist Richard Bach is famous mainly for the novel *Jonathan Livingston Seagull*.
2. See, for example, the detailed survey of Ramanujam and Varadarajan (1989).
3. The institutional environment of the firm will be addressed in Section 1.2 of this chapter.
4. In this chapter, technology and product are two different dimensions. Different technologies might be used for similar products, as well as different products might build on the same technology. Moreover, a product may combine several technologies. For example, a camera can use film or it can be digital. Similarly, digital switching technology can be used either to switch telecommunications or as routers for computer networks.
5. A technology-based firm is a firm 'reliant or based upon technology in exploiting business opportunities' (Granstrand, 1998, p. 466).
6. Penrose (1959, p. 109) rules out the question of the precision of her definition because of the 'futility of attempting to measure the "extent" of diversification as such, for there is no single all-purpose measure'.
7. For example, the investments of the Swedish car and truck manufacturer Volvo in the pharmaceutical industry or in the food industry during the 1980s would not be considered as a diversification according to this definition since the strategy did not entail any organisational change within the firm.
8. Scherer (1990, p. 93) defines the relatedness of the diversification with regard to the statistical industrial classification of the firm. A firm engages in a related diversification if the move occurs in the same two-digit industry but in a different four-digit industry according to the SNI classification. However, such a definition is too orientated towards product diversification and does not include changes in markets, technologies or organisations.
9. Section 1.2.3 of this chapter goes deeper into the definition of the concepts of institutions and organisations.
10. See for example the work of Lundvall (1992a), Nelson (1993) or Edquist (1997a).
11. It should be noted that in this definition, Lundvall refers to a national system of innovation, as does Nelson (1993). Edquist (1997a), however, introduces the concepts of systems of innovation *per se*, not defined by its geographical boundaries. In this study, Lundvall's definition is considered as valid for a system of innovation in general, defined by geographical or sectoral boundaries. Hence, a system of innovation may be regional, national or even sectoral as will be seen in Section 1.2.2.
12. The concept of 'selection' draws from evolutionary economics. Nelson and Winter (1982) propose that the selection environment can be specified by four elements: '(1) the nature of the benefits and costs that are weighed by the organizations that will decide to adopt or not to adopt a new innovation; (2) the manner in which consumer and regulatory preferences and rules influence what is "profitable"; (3) the relationship between "profit" and the expansion or contraction of particular organizations or units; and (4) the nature of the mechanisms by which one organization learns about the successful innovations of other organizations and the factors that facilitate or deter innovation' (Nelson and Winter, 1982, p. 262).

13. This definition is based upon North's definition (1990) and will be developed in Section 1.2.3.
14. In particular, the article by Edquist and Lundvall (1993) on the differences between Denmark and Sweden further shows the role of history in the formation of national systems.
15. However, we may remark that the idea that both dimensions may somehow coincide is far from what can be observed in almost all the so-called nation-states. France for example has several regional cultures and (unofficial) languages but only one central authority.
16. The distinction between formal and informal institutions can be difficult to assess, as the rules of society, for example politeness, have been established not only as non conscious rules slowly developing over time, but also as codified rules learnt at school or at home. However, this distinction will be useful for the analysis of the coming empirical work of this study.
17. The Conclusion Chapter of this book attempts to precisely describe these institutions of relevance for the diversification process.
18. Performance is here measured in terms of return on equity, return on capital and price-earning ratio (Rumelt, 1974, p. 94).
19. See, for example, the work of Teece (1982, p. 40) and Montgomery (1994, p. 163).
20. The concept of technology procurement is developed further in Section 2.2.3 of this chapter.
21. The question of the competences of the buyer is developed further in Section 3.1.1 of this chapter.
22. See, for example, the work of Very (1993), Teece et al. (1994) and Malerba et al. (1998).
23. This diversification cannot only be considered as a technological diversification since the original market targeted by Ericsson was a market of professional users, as doctors on call or firemen. It is only later on that mobile telecommunication became a mass market.

3. A Case-Study Approach to Analyse Diversification in Firms

Learning the secret of flight from a bird was a good deal like learning the secret of magic from a magician. After you know what to look for you see things that you did not notice when you did not know exactly what to look for.

Orville Wright[1]

The purpose of this research is to understand the process of firm-level diversification within an institutional environment and to delineate the nature of the specific institutions affecting the process. It focuses on two very specific aspects of the diversification process, i.e., the reasons for the diversification and its implementation, the latter involving knowledge generation through learning processes.

This chapter details how a method was chosen so that the research questions could be properly addressed and describes the way the research was conducted as well as how problems were solved.

1. METHOD SELECTION

Studying the process of diversification in firms can be done using different kinds of tools. Surveys and statistical analysis could for example show the extent of the technological diversification in a firm or group of firms. However, they would not allow for an understanding of the institutional phenomena related to the process of diversification.

An important aspect of the theoretical discussion was concerned with the learning processes activated during diversification and how institutions affect their outcomes. Here again, we need to be able to identify how firms learn and manage the knowledge that is necessary for the diversification. This knowledge is not necessarily related to technologies, but is here considered in a broader sense, covering non-technical phenomena ranging from institutions to markets and to the organisation of firms. Following the processes through which knowledge is acquired is difficult because they generally involve the interactions of the firm with several organisations.

The identified centrality of institutions and learning processes for understanding the process of diversification in firms, suggests that a case-study methodology is the most appropriate. Such an approach makes it possible to follow all the steps of the process of diversification, from its beginning to its accomplishment.

This choice of method follows the reasoning of Ramanujam and Varadarajan (1989, p. 544), who identified in their review of research on diversification a need to understand how firms actually implement their diversification strategies from a perspective encompassing the firm and other organisations. These authors point out that it is necessary to carry out case-studies in order to understand processes to which the traditional diversification perspective is blind. Furthermore, following Eisenhardt (1989, p. 532), developing theories, or building new ones, requires intimacy with the empirical reality through in-depth case studies.

The need to carry out case studies in order to develop theories is also recognised by researchers within the systems of innovation tradition (Edquist, 1997b, p. 27). Since the systems of innovation approach builds on a large number of abstract concepts, such as institutions and organisations, there is a need to define them accurately through theoretical reflection. Consequently, empirical work is needed either to foster theoretical reflection or to test the validity of theories. Conceptual clarity is required in order to increase the coherence of the approach, raising its theoretical integrity, and allowing for a better understanding of innovation processes.

Researchers on case-study methodology emphasise that carrying out focused comparative studies can promote theoretical development in the field of investigation (George, 1979; Yin 1994). George (1979, p. 60) stresses that case studies can be a useful tool for theory development, even if the number of cases is not 'representative in the statistical sampling sense'. It is not the number of cases which matters, but their variety and the way they are designed. According to George (1979, p. 60), 'the investigator in designing the study will either seek cases in which the outcome of the dependent variable differed or cases having the same outcome but a different explanation for it'.

Furthermore, a limited number of cases is needed so that it is possible to handle the complexity of the data provided by each case (Eisenhardt, 1989, p. 545). Too many cases would only allow for a superficial gathering of data, missing the 'deeper social dynamics' of the process studied (Dyer and Wilkins, 1991, p. 615).

Finally, the use of comparative case studies is advocated in order to be able to scrutinise characteristics of cases that would otherwise be hidden (Feldman, 1985, p. 165). Hence, a comparative case-study method allows for a more thorough investigation of the cases with respect to the normally 'hidden' variables that are of interest for the study. The observation of one phenomenon in one case can raise questions as to why the same phenomenon did not occur in the other cases. This will facilitate further developments of the theoretical framework of Chapter 2.

An essential argument of the theoretical framework is that some specific institutions, especially national ones, are important for the process of diversification and need to be analysed. This argument implies that case studies need to be chosen in different countries. Observing similar cases of diversification in different countries with differing institutions can illuminate the national characteristics of the relevant institutions. Studying diversification in different countries will therefore make it possible to address the role of organisations interacting with the firm during the process of diversification, from an institutional perspective. The role of national management traditions can be investigated in the same way. A comparative analysis can also indicate the extent to which, and in what way, governments may be involved in an industrial process.

Understanding the evolution of the firm within its system of innovation will permit a clear separation between the strategic management aspects and the political, institutional as well as economic aspects of the different cases. Applying the system of innovation approach entails structuring the comparison around a number of themes identified as important for understanding the cases and for developing the theoretical framework. Such themes are, for example, the role of institutions in the implementation of diversification and interaction between the diversifying firm and other public or private organisations. This allows for a focused comparison of the cases, as will be done in Part III, Analysis and Conclusions.

2.   SELECTING THE CASES

One difficulty that emerges while carrying out comparative case studies is that the scrutiny of too many variables reduces both the accuracy and the validity of the results (Feldman, 1985). It is therefore important to select cases that are similar in terms of variables which are not the main focus of the research, but that are different with regard to the variables investigated. According to Feldman (1985, p. 167), 'rigorous case selection across countries can maximise similarities and enable intelligent explanation of differences'.

Since this study will examine the kind of institutions that are relevant in the process of diversification, a variable such as institutional differences between industries should be eliminated. For example, some institutions in the telecom industry are not found in the dairy-product industry, and vice versa. While cases should be chosen in different countries in order to capture national institutional differences, they should be chosen in the same industry and present many similarities. Thus, it will be possible to identify the kind of institutions that made a difference and whether these institutions were of a national or a sectoral nature.

2.1.   Choice of the Industry

The choice of the industry should be determined by the research questions. Choosing an industry with 'strong' institutions, in terms of policies and also in terms of regulation of the industry, will allow a magnification of their possible role during the diversification. The aerospace industry is thus particularly apt in relation to the theoretical framework developed for this study. Many of the most economically advanced countries have struggled to establish their own aerospace capability, implementing numerous institutions to support such efforts against international competition. This has certainly been the case in such European countries as France, Sweden and the United Kingdom. Although aerospace is a growth industry at the OECD level, the development of the European aircraft industry has been under constant competitive pressure from American firms. More recently, the emergence of Asian aerospace firms has created a new source of competition.

National prestige and ideologies of military independence have shaped the European aircraft industry, which is now led by a number of 'national champions', although smaller than their American counterparts. At the same time, specific institutions supporting both military and civil aircraft industries have been designed on both sides of the Atlantic.[2] Newly industrialised countries, with a desire to declare their independence from the United States and Europe as well as to improve their economic power through investments in high-tech sectors, have also designed programmes to sustain their aerospace industries.

In the aerospace industry, firms and firm strategies might be expected to be strongly supported by their institutional environment, raising the question whether such institutions are predominantly national or sectoral. If, as suggested in Chapter 2, institutions influencing the diversification process have mainly national characteristics, then it may be concluded that the firm diversified within its national system of innovation. If, on the contrary, no national characteristics can be identified, then the national system of innovation was of no consequence for the diversification, so that only the sectoral system mattered.[3]

2.2.   Choice of Firms and of Countries

Continuing from the choice of method and industry, appropriate countries and firms also have to be selected, bearing in mind that the cases must be possible to study within the time available, allowing reliable and rapid access to information. Moreover, this information must not only enable the research to follow the process in which the firm engaged, but also to understand the historical and cultural contexts in which the cases are embedded.

Three major criteria of selection of the cases can now be defined. The cases should be chosen in the aerospace industry in three different countries. Secondly, the diversification in the firms should be as similar as possible in terms of products and competences of the firms. Finally, access to information should be efficient and allow the connection of the case with its historical and cultural context.

Perfectly matching all the criteria of a comparative case-study methodology is often not possible, and in this study, some of the original selection criteria had to be relaxed. Two cases following almost all of the criteria were identified: Dassault Aviation in France and Saab in Sweden.

Sweden is a neutral country and this neutrality has had important consequences for the development of its industry, while France, though not a neutral country, has pursued policies of military independence, especially in relation to NATO. The defence policies of these two countries have contributed greatly to the shaping of their aerospace industries. In Sweden and France, two cases of diversification from military to civil aircraft were identified. The existence of written material showed that these cases would likely offer rapid access to information.

A third case was selected in the Republic of South Korea, at Daewoo Heavy Industries. Essentially, the rationale for selecting a case in South Korea relates to the assumption that East Asian countries and firms have conducted aggressive diversification policies as a means of economic growth (Amsden, 1989, p. 128; Whitley, 1992, p. 42). Studying a case there could improve the level of understanding of the process of diversification.

In Korea, the predominant role of the state in all industrial activity and the risks presented by the cold war with North Korea have also influenced the industry. As for the two European cases, Korea has had policies of military and technological independence. However, no case of diversification from military to civil aircraft in Korea was identified. It was only possible to study a diversification into military aircraft production, albeit one with civil applications. Thus, the criterion concerning the similarities in terms of product and competences had to be relaxed. As will be seen in the coming section, the third criterion about rapid access to information also had to be relaxed.

3.   IMPLEMENTING A COMPARATIVE CASE-STUDY METHOD

The implementation of a comparative case-study method implies the collection of evidence that will allow for the identification of the facts of relevance for the research questions. In order to achieve validity, it is important to use multiple sources of information, such as written documents, whether from archives or from previous research, and interviews. This implies a complex research process but also an improved quality of the result and of the narrative (Yin, 1994, pp. 84 and 103).

3.1.   Gathering the Material

The case studies were carried out partly through reviewing existing written material, such as academic research, industrial analyses and annual reports. In a second phase, interviews were conducted with the main decision-makers in the diversification process. These interviews were carried out with persons both inside and outside the firms, i.e., at the higher and lower management level of the firm, and at the government level, including senior civil servants and deputies in the relevant countries. Interviews were also carried out in civil and military research organisations.

Using the existing literature to identify people to be interviewed, two pilot studies were carried out in Sweden (September 1996) and in France (November 1997) in order to facilitate the construction of a thorough interview protocol relevant to the cases.[4] For reasons of cost, it was not possible to do the same in Korea. The pilot studies indicated names of relevant people to interview. Using a so-called 'snowball technique', in which further sources are identified during the course of the interviews, it was possible to get access to new respondents.

The pilot studies were also used as an empirical basis for constructing the theoretical framework as well as for developing a detailed interview protocol. One interview protocol was designed for each group of respondents: higher and lower management personnel and civil servants. Although the protocols always followed a similar framework, the focus of the questions varied. Civil servants were thus not asked engineering-related questions while engineers were not asked about national technology policies.

The interviews were not conducted by going through the protocols mechanically, question after question. The protocols were used more as a guideline. This approach allowed spontaneous follow-up questions to be asked in order to clarify specific details of the case. The interviews lasted between one and three hours and were generally tape-recorded, while notes were also taken during the entire time. After the interviews, the notes were typed and completed, if necessary, by listening to the tapes.

In France and Sweden the interviews were conducted in French and Swedish respectively. In Korea the interviews were conducted in English, except for two interviews which had to be done with the help of a translator. A total of 38 people were interviewed, sometimes twice: eight in France, eleven in Sweden and nineteen in Korea. Informal and 'return' visits for further interviews were possible in France and in Sweden but not in Korea, and as will be explained in the next section, the absence of written material in Korea required a larger number of interviews.

The research in Sweden was carried out in September and October 1998. The Korean case was studied in January 1999 and the French case in May 1999.

3.2. Problems Encountered and Solutions

Language was not a problem during the interviews, except when a translator was used. The interviews were in these cases slower and lacked the spontaneity of the other sessions. Moreover, the translator acted as a 'filter'. Due to time constraints, he or she had to summarise what the respondent said and therefore selected information.[5] Fortunately, only two interviews in Korea were done with a translator. Otherwise, as the common language of the aerospace industry is English, all the Korean respondents were able to communicate well in English.

With regard to specific cultural characteristics, there were again no difficulties either in France or Sweden.[6] However, problems emerged in Korea. Carrying out interviews in a completely unfamiliar socio-cultural environment is difficult because the interviewer is largely unable to relate the responses to the relevant cultural context. This was solved in two ways. First, the research in Korea was done with the help of the French Trade Commission in Seoul. Using their existing network of connections and using the names I was able to give them, they set up interviews in accordance to my requirements.[7] Secondly, I was able to have long discussions with researchers at the Science and Technology Policy Institute (STEPI) in Seoul, where I had an office during the fieldwork. These discussions often shed new light on the interview data.

Another problem with the Korean case was that quite often the respondent was willing to talk but did not want to be quoted. Answers of the kind 'I'll tell you this, but don't write my name', were relatively frequent. Thus, in order to be able to write the Korean chapter, I had to protect the identity of the respondents. Respondents are therefore identified by a random letter of the alphabet, which is used as a reference in the chapter. Moreover, I do not name the respondents in the reference list, but indicate the firm or organisation in which they work. For the two European cases, I name the respondents in the reference list.

Last but not least, as I am the first non-Korean researcher to conduct an academic study of the Korean aerospace industry, there is very little relevant written material (not even in Korean). Therefore, interview data are the main source of information for the Korean chapter.[8]

The French and the Swedish fieldwork did not raise any specific technical difficulties. I encountered great openness in all the interviews and a lot of written material exists on both cases. However, the openness of the respondents was at times accompanied by a tendency to romanticise stories.

This raises the question about the appraisal of the sources which is done in the following section. Finally, it should be noted that while both the French and the Swedish cases are historical, the Korean case is current. As a result, the two European cases did not involve any secrecy as did the Korean case.

4. APPRAISING THE SOURCES

Being an industrial engineer in a dominantly social sciences department is not always easy. However, my engineering background proved to be a great advantage in conducting the interviews. Studying the process of developing new aircraft was facilitated by the fact that I already knew the terminology of the aerospace industry and the technologies relating to it. This often allowed me to gain the confidence of the respondent and to concentrate on asking questions on the management of the technologies instead of having to ask questions on 'how things work'. As a matter of fact, it also enabled me a couple of times to avoid being misled on technological issues.

The selection of respondents was always done in such a way that they were as close as possible to the case or to a particular event related to the case. An appraisal of the quality of my sources was achieved through data triangulation, involving double-checking all information in at least two interviews and when possible checking with a written source printed at the time of the event. Data triangulation reduces the risks of describing 'facts' from the sole perspective of one respondent (Nilsson, 1973). Time and other parameters tend to introduce a bias in the descriptions of facts by respondents. This is especially important to bear in mind when two or more firms are involved in the same venture (Schild, 1996, p. 139).

While data triangulation has been used to appraise sources, it was not always possible to double-check all the information. Especially in Korea, I often felt the suspicion of the respondent and his consequent reluctance to give names of possible new respondents. Written sources have been used to fill information gaps and confirm existing information but also to guide towards new questions.

In France, Monsieur Lemaire granted me access to an impressive archive with a number of documents produced during the development of the Dassault Mystère-Falcon 20. In particular, I was able to read the logbooks of the technical director of the project, Monsieur Paul Déplante. These logbooks, covering the period of 1962 to 1970, included the documentation of day-to-day technological development of the aircraft as well as remarks, notes and comments of all kinds. In Sweden, I had the opportunity to study some of the archive material at Saab in Linköping – in particular all the minutes of the management board of the joint venture between Saab and Fairchild (later referred to as MMB in the text).[9]

For language reasons, it was not possible to conduct this kind of archive research in Korea. The lack of documented sources in languages other than Korean creates an opening for more research in this field by Korean-speaking researchers.

A final way to validate the sources was to send the empirical chapters to respondents for comments. Although this is not a remedy for many of the problems discussed in the previous paragraphs, it does improve the quality of interpretation of interview data. The technique gives an overview of the case to the respondent, often stimulating new memories and providing the opportunity to make corrections. This technique has proved effective in this study, leading to several important corrections. Finally, the three empirical chapters were reviewed by independent experts in the national aerospace fields that were studied.[10]

5.   LIMITATIONS

A narrative can only be as good as the quality of the material it builds upon, and the existence of problems in the research method do represent limitations. Although constant awareness of these problems has been maintained throughout the research process, it is still possible that a knowledgeable reader might find discrepancies with what he or she feels is a more accurate account of events. This is often a question of interpretation, or an opening for further studies in the field, as has already been noted for the Korean case.

Besides technical and descriptive limitations, there are some theoretical limitations to this study which are worth mentioning at this point. The strategic value of the aerospace industry, in technological, economic and even military terms has shaped the relationships between the state and the firms in a peculiar way. The industry is regulated very strictly, while firms are under the constant control of the state. Finally, the firms studied are large corporate entities producing a very limited number of massive and extremely complex products for only very few customers. The conclusions that this study draw from the cases might not be valid for firms producing mass-market types of products. Despite these limitations, this book provides an up-to-date account of the history of the three programmes developed by these firms.

NOTES

1. On 17 December 1903, Orville Wright made the world's first successful sustained and controlled flight of a man-operated, motor-driven airplane, at Kitty Hawk, NC. The airplane flew over a distance of 40 metres in 12 seconds (http://www.aerofiles.com/chrono.html, viewed 4 December 1999).
2. See, for example, the work of Mowery and Rosenberg (1989), Tyson (1992) or Feldman (1997).
3. Sectoral and national systems of innovation were defined in Chapter 2, Section 1.2.2.
4. The interview protocol is enclosed in Appendix A of this book.
5. Note also that the price of a translator is very high, while the outcome of the interview is by definition unsure. Deciding whether or not to do an interview with a translator can be really problematic.
6. I am French by birth, citizenship and education but have lived in Sweden since March 1993 and am fluent in Swedish.
7. These initial names were given to me by Mr. Ulf Edlund, Vice President of Strategic Planning at Saab, and Mr. Chin-Young Hwang, PhD student at SPRU, University of Sussex.
8. In the text, to separate references to published material from interviews and letters to the author, interviews are referred to with the name of the respondent, followed by the letters 'int.' and the year of the interview. Letters and fax are referred to with the name of the sender, followed by the letters 'p.c.' (for personal communication) and the year when the letter was sent. Both interviews and letters are listed in detail in the reference list at the end of the book.
9. These minutes were useful in identifying tensions between the two firms, as they accurately describe the course of the management meetings and the comments of the people participating in the meetings.
10. Professor Claude Carlier, Director of the Aeronautic and Space History Centre in France, reviewed the French chapter. The chapter about Saab was reviewed by Professor Anders Blom, Head of the Structures and Materials Department of the Aeronautical Research Institute of Sweden. Mr Chin-Young Hwang, who has worked for ten years at the Korean Aerospace Research Institute in Taejon, South Korea, and is currently PhD candidate at the Science Policy Research Unit (SPRU), University of Sussex, reviewed the Korean chapter. I am grateful for their help.

Part II

Empirical Research

4. From Military Aircraft to Business Jets in France: The Case of the Dassault Mystère-Falcon 20

> *I have often said that the lure of flying is the lure of beauty. That the reasons flyers fly, whether they know it or not, is the aesthetic appeal of flying.*
>
> Amelia Earhart[1]

This chapter addresses the diversification from military to civil aircraft by the private firm Dassault Aviation at the beginning of the 1960s, in the institutional context of the French aircraft industry of the time.[2] It will investigate how the institutional environment, in which Dassault acted, affected the diversification process and the generation of knowledge within the firm.

The firm is described as embedded in a system of innovation, involving organisations such as some elements of the state, other firms and research organisations. Formal and informal institutions regulate the functioning of the system (North, 1990). These institutions can spring from government policies, such as laws, or can emerge informally, for example, as rules of behaviour between firms (Edquist and Johnson, 1997). Thus, this chapter does not solely concentrate on the management of the firm, but enlarges the perspective to the institutional environment of the firm, be it national or sectoral.

In other words, understanding why and how Dassault diversified will be achieved through analysing the interactions between the firm and its system of innovation. For example, the relation between the French state and

Dassault is one element in the explanation of the strategy and its implementation. The interactions between Dassault and the state-owned aerospace firms are other explanatory factors.

In order to understand the institutional environment of the firm and why it affected the firm's strategy, it is necessary to have some knowledge of the evolution of the industry over time and to place the diversification process in its historical context. This will be the subject of Section 1 of this chapter. We shall see how the firm's diversification into civil aerospace was hampered by its national institutional environment. Section 2 examines the firm's successive abortive attempts to diversify against the backdrop of these institutional hurdles. During the late 1950s a new type of civil aircraft emerged – the business jet – answering new needs for rapid transportation, especially in the United States. This is described in Section 3 and introduces Section 4, which contains a description of how Dassault was able to diversify and develop a civil aircraft for the international market. Section 5 describes the final stages of the development process of the aircraft, including the certification process and the organisation of production.

1. DASSAULT IN THE FRENCH AIRCRAFT INDUSTRY AFTER WORLD WAR II

In 1917, after producing propellers for some years on behalf of the 'infant' French aircraft industry, Marcel Bloch started the firm Société d'Etudes Aéronautiques, SEA, to build aircraft for the French Air Force. The venture came to a halt when World War I ended, and a new firm was created in 1928 – the Société des Avions Marcel Bloch. The firm was bought by the French state on 16 January 1937, following the 1936 law of nationalisation of all war industries (Carlier and Berger, 1996a, p. 16). Most of the assets of the firm were then used to set up the Société Nationale de Construction Aéronautique du Sud Ouest (SNCASO). Four other state-owned firms were formed out of other private aircraft manufacturing firms.[3] The law allowed private firms to design new aircraft but not to manufacture them.

Marcel Bloch was asked by the state to administer his nationalised company. In the meantime, on 12 December 1936, he started a new development firm, the Société Anonyme des Avions Marcel Bloch. That company was, in its turn, partly integrated into SNCASO in February 1937 and Marcel Bloch stayed in the firm until the outbreak of World War II.

Before the war, Marcel Bloch had been a leader in the development of both military and civil aircraft. Among other achievements, the pride of

SNCASO had been the development of a civil aircraft called the Languedoc. Following the Second World War and his dramatic experience in a concentration camp during 1944, Marcel Bloch bought what was left of his factories confiscated during the war and returned to developing aircraft. He changed his name to Marcel Dassault, and the firm was renamed Société des Avions Marcel Dassault on 20 January 1947 (Carlier and Berger, 1996a, p. 20).

The post-war period in Europe witnessed large-scale industrial reconstruction and reorganisation. Five years of war had profoundly deteriorated all national economies in Europe, and decisive political actions were needed to promote industrial development. During these years, new institutions meant to foster economic growth in Europe sprung up. Some industries were identified as being more important than others, on account of the prospects for economic growth and technological development they offered, but also on account of the prestige they carried.

Early on, the aircraft industry was seen as satisfying these criteria by the French government. The production means available were outdated, competences had disappeared and the risk of mass-unemployment in the plants was a threat to social peace (Carlier, 1983, p. 18). Meanwhile, the overwhelming domination of the American and British aircraft firms, a result of their war efforts, gave them the *de facto* status of sole producers of military and civil aircraft in the western world (Carlier, 1983, p. 56).

The post-war restructuring of the aircraft industry was carried out under the leadership of the communist minister of aviation, Charles Tillon.[4] Priority for production was still given to the state-owned firms. The nationalisation programme initiated in 1936 was extended to private airlines which were consolidated into one state-owned civil airline, Air France. Finally, the government granted financial support for the development and production of large programmes of new airliners to state-owned firms, as the Caravelle in the 1950s and the Concorde in the 1960s. As the international market for civil aircraft was dominated by American and British firms, French private firms were in actual fact almost excluded from civil aircraft development (Carlier, int., 1997).

Furthermore, the activity of private firms kept being restricted to designing aircraft, be they military or civil, and to producing prototypes. While funding for large civil programmes was blocked by the Caravelle and later by the Concorde, private firms mostly focused on the design of military aircraft during the 1950s. The military market was larger that the civil one, and the granting of the military programmes was based on open competition between private and state-owned firms (Carlier, p.c., 2000). All aircraft production had to take place in the state-owned firms. However, owing to their organisational difficulties, part of the production gradually went to the private firms (Carlier, 1983, p. 16; Carlier and Berger, 1996a, p. 22).

As a result, after World War II, a new division of labour between private and state-owned firms slowly emerged in the French aircraft industry. Civil aircraft and helicopters were developed and produced by the state-owned firms, while military aircraft were developed by the private firms. This situation was to affect the organisation of the industry for the coming decades.[5]

In that peculiar context, Marcel Dassault stuck to his idea of producing a civil aircraft while asserting his presence in the military sector. The flourishing market for military aircraft in the 1950s gave the firm the opportunity to highly specialise in the development of state-of-the-art military aircraft. Consequently, Dassault won most of the procurement competitions for new equipment on behalf of the French Air Force.

The first aircraft developed by Dassault for the French Air Force was the Flamant, a passenger aircraft for military purposes. Between 1949 and 1953, 325 units of the aircraft (including the prototypes) were produced. The success of the aircraft enabled the firm to develop and produce a number of military jet fighters during the 1950s. Consequently, it boosted the firm's self-confidence and strengthened its financial position. Moreover, Marcel Dassault gradually acquired a flair for anticipating the air force needs, through permanent contacts both with politicians and military officers. Thus, the firm repeatedly found itself in a position to propose finely tuned solutions when competing for military programmes (Carlier, p.c., 2000). Among Dassault's major achievements during the 1950s, the Ouragan, of which 350 units were built from 1952 to 1954, must be mentioned, as well as the Mystère II, the first French supersonic fighter aircraft, the Mystère IV, of which nearly 600 units were produced from 1954 to 1958, and the Super-Mystère, with 180 units produced from 1957 to 1960 (Carlier and Berger, 1996a, p. 63).

However, owing to the government's desire to give priority to state-owned firms with regards to the development and production of civil aircraft, Dassault was barred from entering the civil market. This created an institutional environment which made it impossible for the firm to diversify, reducing its opportunities to compete with state-owned firms.

2. THE FIRST TRANSPORT AIRCRAFT DEVELOPED BY THE GENERALE AERONAUTIQUE MARCEL DASSAULT

The post-war period radically transformed the structure of the French aircraft industry. New firms and new institutions were set up, giving the industry a new start. As shown in the previous section, it was on the basis of an informal division of labour between state-owned and private firms that Dassault engaged in the prototyping both of transport aircraft and fighter aircraft for the military market.

During the 1950s, the increased specialisation of the firm in the development and production of fighter aircraft reduced the importance of transport aircraft programmes. However, transport related competences and experience remained inside the firm through a prototyping policy. These aircraft were aimed at the military market, but Marcel Dassault had some hopes that they could eventually be sold on the civil market.

The present section describes the development of the various transport aircraft which preceded the Mystère 20, the latter is the proper subject of this chapter. The experience accumulated during these years provided a solid foundation on which the Mystère 20 could be developed.[6]

2.1. The First Transport Aircraft – the Flamant

In 1946, the government organised a competition between state-owned and private firms to design a small twin-propeller transport aircraft. The aircraft was to be used in the French colonies both as a rescue or a police aircraft and as a liaison aircraft (Estèbe, int., 1997). Using his personal assets, Marcel Dassault had launched the development of the MD 303 Flamant, on the basis of previous aircraft designed before the war and the firm's knowledge of the needs of the French Air Force for a so-called 'colonial aircraft,' or 'counter-insurgency aircraft' (Lemaire and Parvaud, 1995, p. 18). The prototype developed by Dassault won the competition against the aircraft developed by SNCASO, the SO 94. A total of 319 Flamants were sold to the French Air Force. This first large contract turned out to be essential for the relation between the firm and the air force. It also assured the financial stability of the firm, because of the cash inflow generated by the contract. Though the aircraft was categorised as military for its rescue applications on battle fields, its functions could be civil as well.

One condition of the state for the fulfilment of the contract was that the aircraft should be produced jointly by state-owned and private firms; Dassault being the integrator of the aircraft. This type of agreement was new in the industry, but was to become increasingly frequent in the coming programmes procured by the French government. The Flamant opened new financial possibilities for the firm and also opened the door to a deeper involvement in the development of fighter aircraft.

Meanwhile, Marcel Dassault retired from his position as executive director on 10 February 1954, but kept the ownership and financial control of the firm (Carlier and Berger, 1996a, p. 42). This ownership was to enable him to concentrate on networking activities at political and military leadership levels, as well as on prototyping new aircraft (Carlier, int., 1997). His influence on the management of the firm remained very important. Leaving the operational management of the firm was a way for him to avoid the administrative worries of a firm while continuing to do what, to him, was interesting – prototyping new airplanes (Carlier and Berger, 1996a, p. 79).

2.2. Following Projects – the Communauté and the Spirale

While the firm was increasing its specialisation in jet fighters, transport aircraft were still on the drawing boards, but most of the projects never went further than wooden mock-ups. The prototyping strategy aimed at avoiding the loss of competences in a domain for which new markets might emerge. In a continued effort to meet the needs of transport aircraft for the army, the firm designed the twin-turboprop MD 415 Communauté in 1958, first flying in 1959. Following one year of flight tests, the programme of the Communauté was finally given up in January 1960, as the French government purchased another aircraft (Lemaire, 1992).

The Communauté was directly replaced by another aircraft, the MD 410 Spirale I, which in turn was replaced by the Spirale III. Again, the latter was geared towards transportation purposes for the French Army, at the time fighting the war of independence in Algeria. After the firm won an initial contract in May 1959, the aircraft was due to go into production in cooperation with Sud Aviation. However, with the end of the Algerian War the need for this type of aircraft disappeared and none were produced. The cessation of hostilities was not, however, the only reason for this setback. During the 1950s, the technological development of jet engines had opened up new possibilities for military aircraft, and by the end of the decade, a growing number of firms were seeking civil applications for the technology (Carlier and Berger, 1996a, p. 59).

Convinced that propeller-driven aircraft were becoming obsolete, Marcel Dassault ordered the development of a twinjet liaison aircraft, the

Méditerrannée. As it happened, the aircraft never left the stage of full-scale mock-up (Carlier, 1992, p. 262). At this stage, the firm had come to be more and more specialised in the design and production of state-of-the-art fighter aircraft.

2.3. Contrasted Results in the Development of Transport Aircraft

With an eye on the needs of the air force and the army, Dassault engaged in the development of a number of propeller-driven transport aircraft during the 1950s. The success of this development campaign was very limited, however, as only one type of aircraft was sold to the government. In addition, after the Algerian War was over, the potential market for this kind of aircraft no longer existed. However, Marcel Dassault's determination to develop a military transport aircraft remained unchanged.

Notwithstanding the law establishing a division of labour between state-owned and private firms, the financial and organisational difficulties of the former had induced the government to authorise the production of aircraft in Dassault's plants (Carlier, int., 1997). The firm had developed a production capacity which would allow new ventures. Moreover, the various prototyping efforts meant the building up of invaluable experience for further projects, but the lack of a market for transport aircraft was acute, as the French government was reluctant to buy any new aircraft. Contemporaneous with these industrial developments in Europe, a whole new industry was emerging in the United States – the business jet industry.

3. THE EMERGENCE OF THE BUSINESS JET INDUSTRY

After World War II, the growth of economic activities in the United States spurred a new transportation need for top executives. Airlines had focused their routes around hubs in specific regions and did not cover smaller airports around the country. More efficient communications required the development of a new type of aircraft, smaller than airliners, needing shorter runways, and yet much faster than small propeller-driven aircraft. This section describes the first steps in the emergence of the business jet industry in the United States and Europe.

3.1. Business Jets in the United States

During the 1950s, the need for small, all-weather civil aircraft became pressing in large American corporations. The National Business Aircraft Association (NBAA) was created in 1953 out of the former Corporation Aircraft Owners Association. Early on, the NBAA expressed the desire to see the existing obsolete fleet of corporate aircraft replaced by modern jets. Since the end of World War II, transportation using corporate aircraft had more than tripled and the prospects were ever-growing. However, the aircraft industry was not responsive to the demand for business jets, as it considered the market to be too small and too risky. Nonetheless, the NBAA was not alone in its discontent. The US Air Force was also looking for a small jet passenger aircraft both for training and for liaison (Phillips et al., 1994, pp. 16–17).

As the need for smaller aircraft powered by jet engines was emerging, the commercial aircraft industry was entering one of its most important revolutions, the changeover to jet-powered airliners. The new technology allowed faster speeds and improved reliability, as compared to traditional piston engines. Jet engines had been used to power military aircraft since the immediate post-war period but had not yet made their way into the civil aircraft industry. Both in Europe and in the United States, firms were trying to develop jetliners. The British firm de Havilland came first with the Comet, which first flew in 1949, and later with the Comet IV in 1958. The 27 May 1955, the French Caravelle, developed by the SNCASE, flew for the first time (Carlier, p.c., 2000). None of these aircraft became real commercial successes. The Comet IV suffered a number of accidents and encountered fierce competition from the American Boeing 707 and Douglas DC8 (Phillips et al., 1994, p. 19).[7]

In August 1956, the US Air Force launched a competition for a new transport aircraft which could receive a civil certification. The request was for 300 small twinjet aircraft for eight to ten passengers. The two major competitors for the programme were the Lockheed Jet-Star and the North American Sabreliner. Although the Jet-Star was the winner of the competition, the Sabreliner, smaller and cheaper, was in the end bought by the US Air Force (Lemaire and Parvaud, 1995, p. 24).

Large airlines were also more and more interested in increasing the number of services they could offer to passengers. In particular, Pan American World Airways or Pan Am, at that time a very prestigious airline, was starting to investigate the possibilities of having a business jets division and was looking for suitable aircraft.

3.2.   The Situation in Europe

In Europe, a number of firms were also starting to develop corporate aircraft. In France, for that matter, the firm Morane-Saulnier had succeeded in converting its two-seater military jet-trainer into a four-seater civil jet. The MS-760 Paris, of which a first prototype had already flown in January 1953, was followed by the MS-760B Paris II, developed in 1960. A total of 219 units of the Paris II were built (Porter 1985, p. 1; Phillips et al., 1994, p. 52). The aircraft was used as a liaison aircraft for the French government and some official services. It was then realised that this type of aircraft could enhance transportation efficiency between smaller airports and also for specific missions (Delacroix, int., 1999). A similar attempt to convert a small jet-trainer into a business jet took place at Saab with the Sk 60, but it eventually fell through. In England, the firm de Havilland was developing the DH 125, a small twinjet aircraft.

At Dassault, the interest for such an aircraft was very limited. The twinjet Méditerrannée had not led to a prototype and although one American executive, Don Peyton, had shown some interest in the twin turboprop aircraft Communauté, Marcel Dassault did not want the firm to abandon its military activities. Actually, Marcel Dassault wanted to enter the civil market and leave his name to an airliner, but he was reluctant to take the risks involved without a firm backup from the French government. The first tenet in his commercial strategy remained the selling of aircraft to the French Air Force (Lemaire, int., 1997; Estèbe, int., 1997; Carlier, int., 1997).

In Autumn 1961, Jean Delacroix, director of the Secrétariat Général de l'Aviation Civile, the French civil aviation authority, visited the plant of Dassault in Mérignac, in the vicinity of Bordeaux, with an intention of assessing the various prototypes of small transport aircraft developed by the firm. Several small transport aircraft prototypes with twin propellers or jet engines had been developed, but none had resulted in commercialisation, with the exception of the Flamant. As other French firms had also started to develop similar aircraft, Delacroix confirmed Marcel Dassault's opinion that the time had come for the firm to begin the development of a twinjet (Lemaire and Parvaud, 1995, p. 33). The idea for such an aircraft was not new, and Marcel Dassault thought that the government would buy the aircraft for its higher civil servants and military officers (Carlier, int., 1997).

The technical department of Dassault in Mérignac was contacted and asked to start the project. On 15 November 1961, the project Mystère 20 was launched. It would be an aircraft with a fuselage two metres in diameter and a capacity of six to eight passengers (Lemaire and Parvaud, 1995, p. 33). Under the technical direction of Paul Chassagne and Paul Déplante, René Lemaire was assigned responsibility for the development of the prototype (Carlier and Berger, 1996b, p. 223).

Despite Dassault's reluctance to embark upon a civil venture, market studies were carried out in the United States. Bernard Waquet, head of Dassault's marketing department, and Serge Dassault, studied the potential market for the aircraft in the United States at the beginning of the 1960s and kept an eye on its development. The need for small civil jets was identified, and a number of contacts were made with potential customers. However, the French government did not seem very enthusiastic, since a study carried out in December 1962 by the Institut des Transports Aériens (ITA or Airborne Transportation Institute) had produced almost completely opposite results, with a global market estimated at roughly fifty aircraft during the 1960s (ITA, 1962, p. 15).

The Airborne Transportation Institute based its study on the project Horizon, a market forecast carried out by the American Federal Aviation Administration, which evaluated the number of corporations that might need a business jet over the coming decade. Dassault was not the only firm developing a business jet, and the price tag of the Mystère 20 was considered too high to be competitive, especially against the British DH 125. As a result, according to the ITA study, the only chance of success for the aircraft was a sale of the Mystère 20 to the French Air Force or the government as a liaison aircraft (ITA, 1962, p. 17).

3.3. A New Emerging Business

A number of firms in the United States and in Europe were attempting to develop a small passenger jet-powered aircraft. The use of the aircraft was, however, not clearly defined. In the United States, the aircraft was thought of as a civil transport for top executives as well as for military officers. In Europe, the structure of the commercial airline industry did not put the same stress on executives, and the demand for small aircraft was therefore more orientated towards military officers or higher civil servants, as a liaison aircraft.

From the mid-1950s onwards, projects started on both sides of the Atlantic. The competition was not well-defined, as the real needs were not clearly identified. It was not clear as to which firms could really afford to purchase an executive aircraft. Sticking to its traditional commercial strategy, Dassault was still focusing on the development of an aircraft for the military market and the government. In the face of all the uncertainties, the firm started the development of the Mystère 20 in late 1961.

4. THE DEVELOPMENT OF THE MYSTERE 20

The development of the Mystère 20 started in the context of a new emerging market with new technological opportunities.[8] The new aircraft had to meet exacting requirements – it had to be faster than all the prototypes previously developed by Dassault, and it had to offer a much higher standard of comfort than military passenger aircraft, while being more efficient and economical. On the basis of the initial estimations concerning the future use of the aircraft, the range was established at 1,500 km, and it had to be powered by jet engines, as propeller-driven aircraft would be obsolete in this market. The latest jet engine industry developments had resulted in several models of small and reliable engines which could now equip a civil aircraft.

The Mystère 20 project started, nevertheless, amidst many uncertainties. At that time, in 1962, it remained unclear whether such a market even existed, and if it did, whether it would be a civil or a military market. Although Dassault was under high working stress with the production of three military aircraft (Mirage III, Mirage IV and Etendard IV) ordered by the French Air Force and the Navy, a small team in Mérignac was given the order to develop the Mystère 20. As mentioned above, Marcel Dassault had retired from the leadership of the firm in order to devote more time to developing new prototypes of airplanes. The Mystère 20 was one of these 'amusing' aircraft Marcel Dassault liked to develop and the team working in Mérignac would often be referred to by the staff in Saint Cloud, nearby Paris, as 'Marcel Dassault's ballet dancers'. The fact that the development team was located in Mérignac, 600 kilometres from the central management of the firm, would also give the development team the freedom it needed to develop the new aircraft. The coordination of the work between Saint-Cloud and Mérignac, as well as between Dassault and the certification authorities, was, nevertheless, maintained from Saint Cloud by André Etesse, Vice CEO of the firm.

This section describes the early development phase of the aircraft. It relates the first difficulties encountered by the development team and how they were solved. During the early stage of prototyping, an unexpected customer signed the first contract. The second part of the section shows how Pan Am and Dassault established their initial commercial agreement. Finally, the financing of the project is described at some length.

4.1.   Designing the Prototype

The planned cruising speed of the new aircraft implied the use of jet engines. However, the wing previously developed for transport aircraft prototypes was meant for much lower cruising speeds. It follows that achieving the targeted speed required the development of a new wing, enlisting technologies perfected for the subsonic military aircraft designed by Dassault. Marcel Dassault's philosophy in developing new aircraft was to always avoid dramatic technological changes, thus limiting the inherent risks. This strategy was known in the firm as the 'small-steps policy' and had far-reaching consequences for the design of new aircraft. If a wing was to be innovative in any way, the engine had, of necessity, to be of a duly proven design; conversely, if the engine was of a new type, then the designers had to fit a wing previously developed inside the firm (Lemaire, int., 1997; Estèbe, int., 1997). In order to comply with the small-steps policy, some compromises had to be made. The first engine selected by the development team was the Pratt and Whitney JT12, already being used by Lockheed on the Jet Star and by North American on the Sabreliner (Carlier and Berger, 1996b, p. 223). The fuselage was developed on the basis of previous prototypes of transport aircraft. The aircraft rapidly took shape, with a swept wing and podded engines placed at the aft on both sides of the fuselage.[9]

4.1.1. Selecting an engine and positioning it

When the Mystère 20 project was launched, only one well-tested engine was available on the market; the Pratt and Whitney JT12. Another engine was under development at General Electric, the CF700, a so-called bypass engine. The CF700 was the first small bypass engine available on the market. The core of the engine was the J85 engine, widely used on military jets, and a fan had been added at the aft of the engine to improve performance, especially in terms of thrust.[10] This type of engine permitted noise reduction and fuel saving, while providing more thrust than engines like the JT12.

In 1962, the CF700 engine had already been discussed as an alternative to the JT12. The fact that it was the first of its kind made it an attractive engine, but it had two drawbacks – it was a relatively recent engine, and its casing required larger pods, covering the aft-fan. Such a configuration would result in what Marcel Dassault called 'the big barrels', which he did not consider to be aesthetic! The CF700 was therefore dropped and the JT12 engine was installed instead, as originally planned (Leroudier, int., 1999; Lemaire, int., 1999; Carlier, int., 1997).

Another reason for the early choice of the JT12 lay in the fact that the French aero-engine manufacturer, SNECMA, was to produce the engine under licence from Pratt and Whitney (Déplante, December 1962). Giving work to a state-owned firm would facilitate claims for financial support from the French state.

Nonetheless, the choice of the JT12 was criticised by people external to the firm, such as some engineers from Boeing, on visiting the plant in March 1962, and the head of the SGAC, Secrétariat Général de l'Aviation Civile, the French civil aviation authorities, in December 1962. According to the SGAC, since the Mystère 20 was to have much better performance than its direct competitor, the de Havilland 125, it ought to be equipped with the CF700, allowing for a cruising speed of Mach 0.82 instead of the planned 0.76 (Déplante, December 1962).[11]

Despite these claims, the programme continued with the JT12. During the studies of the twinjet Méditerrannée, the engines had been placed under the wings of the aircraft. This configuration was changed for the Mystère 20, and the engines were placed in the aft of the fuselage. However, the same configuration had been patented by the state-owned firm Sud Aviation for the design of the Caravelle. A licence agreement was first discussed between the two firms, but as Sud Aviation and Dassault were to share the workload for the production of the Mystère 20, the agreement was later considered as void (Etesse, int., 1999 and Lemaire, int., 1999).

4.1.2. The development of the wing
When designing the supersonic fighter Mystère IV, Dassault had adopted a swept wing, for aerodynamic reasons. On account of their lower speed, civil aircraft were still fitted with a wing perpendicular to the fuselage or at a small angle to the perpendicular. However, this perpendicular configuration was not adapted to subsonic speeds. The wing of the Mystère 20 was, therefore, developed on the basis of the wing of the Mystère IV military fighter.

Nonetheless, some problems were encountered in the control of the aircraft, particularly at high stall angles in the case of in-flight situations such as the low speed flights required when landing on short runways.[12] To solve these problems, high-lift devices were needed on the leading edge of the wings. Similar difficulties had appeared on the Etendard IV, a subsonic military aircraft for the French Navy. For this aircraft, Dassault had installed mechanisms in the leading edge of the wing. These devices improved the behaviour of the aircraft by changing the shape of the wing at low speeds. The mechanism, now known as a dropped leading edge, had already been used on military aircraft but had never been utilised on a civil aircraft before. Paul Chassagne and Jacques Estèbe, engineers responsible for the design of the Etendard IV also happened to be responsible for the design of the Mystère 20, thereby facilitating the transfer of technology from military to civil aircraft.

Despite the shape and the high-lift devices, developing the wing turned out to be a long and difficult process. Studies in a wind tunnel, in cooperation with the National Office for Aeronautics Studies and Research (Office National d'Etude et de Recherche Aéronautique, ONERA) had not been successful, and most of the development work was to be done by testing the wing directly in flight. As René Lemaire (int., 1997) recalls it: 'We would take off during the morning. I would look through the windows to see how the wool strings, taped onto the wing, were behaving. Then we would land...discuss with the technicians, ask them to change this or that on the wing, which they did during the next couple of days, and then we would fly again.' It took three months and 68 flights to find the right shape of wing.

4.1.3. The control surfaces

Other technologies were taken from military aircraft. By the end of the 1950s, a lot of military aircraft had their control surfaces actuated by servo-actuators. The mechanism used consisted of a hydraulic system in which hydraulic pressure was transmitted through tubes to the servo-actuators, helping the mechanical linkage to move the control surfaces (Barnard and Philpott, 1989, p. 291). This technology was gradually superseding the traditional systems of pulleys and wires of older aircraft.

There were two main reasons for the need for servo-actuators. The first was that at transonic and supersonic speeds, the pressure on the control surfaces was very high. In order to be able to manoeuvre the aircraft, the pilot needed the hydraulic help of the servo-actuators to supplement his own physical strength in the case of the aircraft only having a mechanical control.

The second was that at transonic speed, the risk of a reverse of the commands could make the aircraft practically impossible to fly. For example, when the pilot wanted to turn left the aircraft might instead turn right (Barnard and Philpott, 1989, p. 298). Dassault had been developing hydraulic servo-actuators for its military aircraft. The Mystère 20 was fitted with the actuators of the Mystère IV and became, in effect, the first civil jet aircraft equipped with this type of technology (Chassagne, int., 1997; Lemaire, int., 1997).

4.2. Pan Am

While the Mystère 20 was being developed during 1962, work was being carried out by Dassault in the United States to find potential customers for the aircraft. The first responses from the market were positive as the need for business jets existed. Despite the fact that Marcel Dassault wanted first and foremost to get a contract with the French government, he was pushing the concept of an exclusive executive aircraft in the development team. In September 1962, a first potential customer, Youngstown Airways, visited the plant at Mérignac and commented on the aircraft (Déplante, September 1962). The small airline wanted to buy only six aircraft, which was too small a number for Dassault to start the production. At that time, another, much larger, airline was starting to diversify into business jet services: Pan American World Airways.

4.2.1. A short description of Pan Am
Under the leadership of Juan Trippe, Pan Am was probably the most outstanding airline in the world until the 1970s. It opened virtually all major overseas routes between the United States and the rest of the world during the 1930s and the 1940s. The entrepreneurship of Juan Trippe, and his visionary attitude, was the driving force behind the commercialisation of the jetliner Boeing 707. Later, in 1967, he contracted Boeing to develop the Boeing 747, virtually buying an aircraft which did not even exist on paper. Twice as big as the 707, the 747 would allow substantial savings on transatlantic flights (Kuter, 1973; Gandt, 1995).

The fantastic success of the firm was, however, bound to slow down with the emergence of new competition during the 1970s. As the market for overseas flights was deregulated in the United States, new airlines could offer flights to Europe or China. Moreover, the oil crisis of 1973 dramatically reduced the number of passengers. As a consequence, the firm started to experience difficulties in continuing to support the development cost of the

Boeing 747. At a time when the airlines were already in a deep financial crisis, a Pan Am Boeing 747 was blown up by terrorists over the Scottish village of Lockerbie in 1991. This event signalled the end of Pan Am. After several attempts to save the firm during the 1980s, it was finally bought by Delta airlines in 1991 (Gandt, 1995).

However, while in the glorious days of the 1960s, the idea that top executives should be constrained by airline timetables was not appealing to Juan Trippe, and neither was he content with the idea of executives travelling in small, noisy propeller-driven aircraft. Trippe, among others, thought that smaller jet aircraft should be made available to these executives. Following the general trend at the beginning of the 1960s, Juan Trippe set up a team to investigate what manufacturers around the world could offer. His intention was not to operate the aircraft from Pan Am, but to sell it to large corporations on the American market.

4.2.2. Looking for a business jet

In 1963, Juan Trippe sent a delegation from Pan Am to see the business jet developed by the British firm de Havilland. The delegation was led by Franklin Gledhill, and Charles Lindbergh was its technical advisor. The American business jets were too heavy and too expensive for Pan Am. Although the de Havilland 125 seemed to fit most of the requirements of Pan Am, the negotiations ceased when Pan Am asked for some technical changes. The major change consisted in replacing the British engine with an American engine, namely the General Electric CF700. In order for the company to be allowed by the American government to buy a European aircraft, the aircraft had to be fitted with American engines (Déplante, May 1963). De Havilland turned down the request, leaving Pan Am to continue its quest for a business jet elsewhere.

While the Pan Am delegation was in England at the beginning of May 1963, the Mystère 20 was getting ready for its maiden flight in Mérignac. Besides looking for a business jet, Pan Am was also one of the first airlines interested in buying the supersonic airliner, Concorde. After visiting de Havilland, Pan Am's delegation arrived in Toulouse to see the first steps of the development of the Concorde.[13] Bernard Waquet, marketing manager of Dassault, had previously contacted Pan Am and took then the opportunity to invite the delegation to visit Dassault's plant in Mérignac after their visits in England and Toulouse.

It is unclear, however, under what circumstances the contacts between the two firms were made. Through its marketing division, Dassault knew that

Pan Am was looking for a business jet. For example, in Paul Déplante's notes from April 1963, it was indicated that the fuselage of the Mystère 20 lacked headroom, Pan Am's CEO, Juan Trippe, being 1.75 metres tall while the diameter of the fuselage was 1.70 metres (Déplante, April 1963).[14] Dassault was convinced that Pan Am would not buy a European aircraft, as the US regulations would make such a deal very complicated (Leroudier, int., 1999). On the invitation of Bernard Waquet, head of the marketing division, the Pan Am team came to Mérignac.

During their stay in Mérignac, the Pan Am team saw the production line for the fighter aircraft Mirage III, as well as for the Mirage IV. The visit ended during the morning of 4 May 1963 with the presentation of the Mystère 20. The aircraft had not yet performed her maiden flight, and a hydraulic failure of the nose wheel was being fixed. The Pan Am team was seduced by the aircraft and Charles Lindbergh is said to have phoned that night to Juan Trippe in the United States to tell him: 'I've found your bird!' Later that day, the aircraft flew for the first time (Lemaire and Parvaud, 1995).

However, although the 'bird' was found, some profound modifications were required by Pan Am. Among other things, the engines were to be General Electric CF700 instead of the Pratt and Whitney JT12, implying an upgrading of the technology and a 25% range increase. Moreover, the nose wheel was to be doubled, and the avionics were to be American. From May 1963 to July 1963 the relations between the two firms were extremely intense. Pan Am wanted a contract to be signed in July 1963. That same month, a team of five Pan Am engineers, led by John Borger, arrived at Mérignac to detail the technical specifications of the aircraft (Chassagne, int., 1997; Lemaire, int., 1997).

On 25 June 1963, Benno-Claude Vallières, Dassault's CEO, Paul Chassagne, technical director of Mérignac's plant, Pierre François, spokesman of the board of Dassault, and Bernard Waquet, marketing manager, flew to the United States to meet Juan Trippe and discuss the contract. The negotiations over the technologies and performance requirements were rapidly replaced with harsh discussions over the price per unit of the aircraft. Having been promised an order for 40 aircraft plus 120 options, Benno-Claude Vallières finally agreed to the deal, despite the risks involved, since the aircraft was still at an early prototype stage and production was not yet organised. One condition from Dassault, to which Pan Am agreed, was that the contract could be broken if the French state did not support the production of the aircraft financially (Déplante, June 1963). The contract was finally signed at the beginning of July 1963.

4.3. Financing the Project

The success of the project was consequently subject to the financial support of the French state. Help was essential to finance the development and production of the aircraft. Despite the ongoing negotiations between Pan Am and Dassault, the first call for support was turned down by the government on 28 May 1963. The government still relied on the market estimations of the Airborne Transportation Institute, which indicated an insufficient demand for business jets. However, after the contract between Pan Am and Dassault was signed, it became more difficult for the French government to refuse to financially support Dassault.

The pressure on the government to support the programme was now coming from many directions. The head of the SGAC, Jean Delacroix, a strong believer in the Mystère 20, repeatedly promoted the aircraft at the Ministry of Transportation (Delacroix, int., 1999). Moreover, on 31 July 1963 the Directorate of Airborne Transportation (DTA: Direction du Transport Aérien) backed Dassault in a letter to the Minister of Finance and Industry. The letter emphasised the prestige that the deal with Pan Am would give the French aircraft industry, its importance for the trade balance of the country as well as the possibility of creating new jobs within the industry (Carlier and Berger, 1996b, p. 231).

In parallel with the action of the national organisations, the SGAC and the DTA, both Marcel Dassault and André Etesse, Vice-CEO of Dassault, were lobbying various ministries to obtain the necessary financial help (Leroudier int., 1999 and Etesse, int., 1999). On 1 August 1963, the government granted Dassault a loan of FRF48 million. This sum amounted to about half the total cost of the aircraft's development. This loan was to be shared in equal parts between Dassault and Sud Aviation, the subcontractor of the production of mainframes for the Mystère 20. The deal with the government also implied that Dassault had to pay the state 1% of the export price for each exported Mystère 20 and 5% on all exported spare parts (Carlier and Berger, 1996b, p. 231).

4.4. Early Design and First Customer

According to Jacques Estèbe (int., 1997), director of production, the prototype of the Mystère 20 could be described as being the result of the blend of three elements: the wing of the Mystère IV, the high-lift devices of the Etendard IV and the podded-engine design as on the Caravelle. Although being a simplification of what the first prototype really was, this shows that the Mystère 20 clearly followed the development of military aircraft previously carried out in the firm. The technologies could be used in the new aircraft without any restrictions. To a large extent, the engineers were able to use the competences they had previously developed, provided that they kept performance high but at a relatively low production cost.

Pan Am's decision to buy 40 aircraft and place 120 options, at a stage when the aircraft had practically not flown, may be surprising. It is to be remembered, though, that Pan Am's strategy was very aggressive and did not shun risk-taking. The venture of the Boeing 747, starting in 1967 at a time when the aircraft did not even exist at all, is a good reminder of the risk-taking strategy of the firm (Gandt, 1995).

The civil aircraft administration SGAC unflinchingly supported the Mystère 20 in the Ministry of Transportation. Regarding the technological aspects, the SGAC constantly followed the development of the aircraft and participated in a number of meetings with Dassault. This early involvement was to be very important for the following phase of the development of the aircraft and for its certification.

By August 1963, the project of the Mystère 20 had overcome a host of difficulties – a serious customer had been found, the funding of the aircraft was now secured and the SGAC was backing up the aircraft. However, the constraints imposed by Pan Am for a new definition of the aircraft now had to be taken into consideration by the engineers and the aircraft had to be certified by both the French and the American civil aviation administrations.

5. FROM MYSTERE 20 TO FALCON 20

One of Pan Am's first requirements was to change the name of the aircraft so that it would sound as if the aircraft was American. The Mystère 20 therefore became the Fan-Jet Falcon 20, later shortened to Falcon 20. The list of the other required technical changes was very long, as Pan Am had a very definite idea of the kind of product they wanted to sell in the United States. A new delegation of five engineers from Pan Am was, accordingly, sent to Mérignac between July and October 1963 in order to redefine the technical characteristics of the aircraft. The group stayed with the French engineers to control, explain and coordinate the work between Pan Am and Dassault. In September 1963, the final design of the aircraft was completed. The main modifications between the Mystère 20 and the Falcon 20 were as follows (Carlier and Berger, 1996b, p. 231):

- Replacing the Pratt and Whitney JT12 engines with the General Electric CF700 bypass engines;
- Transforming the engine platform;
- Increasing the surface of the wing, from 36 to 41 square meters;
- Increasing the length of the fuselage by 60 centimetres;
- Replacing the mono-wheel nose gear with a double one with low-pressure tyres;
- Installing American avionics; and
- Increasing the range from 1,500 km to 2,600 km so that, in the United States, the aircraft could fly from coast-to-coast with only one stop for refuelling.[15]

The most problematic of all these transformations consisted in adapting the new engine and achieving the range required by Pan Am. The first part of this section describes the work undertaken to meet these requirements. The second part of the section presents the certification process of the aircraft which, thanks to the efficiency of the SGAC, went relatively smoothly. The third section outlines the organisation of the aircraft's production between Dassault and Sud Aviation.

5.1. Achieving the Required Range with a New Engine

The replacement of the engine had been Pan Am's most immediate requirement. It was known that the CF700 engine would theoretically permit a 25% decrease in fuel consumption while giving 20% higher performance than the Pratt and Whitney JT12. Despite the fact that the CF700 was not a proven engine, Marcel Dassault agreed to have it installed, given the scale of the contract with Pan Am. Fortunately, the wing had already been designed during 1962 and was now yielding very good performance to the aircraft. Thus, the 'small-step policy' of Marcel Dassault was not completely ignored after all.

Problems were bound to arise nevertheless. For example, it happened that the first prototypes of the engine CF700 were delayed and did not arrive before March 1964, thus constraining Dassault to continue the flight tests with the JT12 (Déplante, July 1964). The second major problem lay in the aerodynamics of the engine casing. General Electric had designed special pods for the CF700, so-called horse-shoe pods. The design was such that the core engine had its own casing and the aft fan had an extra casing shaped like a horse-shoe following the core. The aesthetics of the design were seriously questioned by Marcel Dassault. However, as the solution would allow the aircraft to comply with the requirements of Pan Am, it was accepted (Lemaire and Parvaud, 1995). Contrary to all expectations, the aerodynamics of the horse-shoe design was so poor that the engine lost 10% of its power, as compared to the JT12. Within a period of three months, the design team had to find a solution, and several new designs were tested. Finally, an integral casing was adopted and the engine reached the required power (Leroudier, int., 1999).

The range of 2,600 kilometres was a compulsory requirement of Pan Am. Despite the fuel saving achieved with the CF700, the range remained too short. The only solution likely to allow the range consisted in adding extra fuel tanks. Having external pods at the tips of the wing was not a satisfactory solution. The surface of the wing in that case had to be increased, from 36 to 41 square metres, in order to accommodate the new tanks.[16] The previous design of the wing could, however, be kept. This period was most critical for the firm, as the engineers were uncertain as to whether they would reach their objectives or not.

5.2.   The Certification of the Aircraft

The certification of an aircraft is a compulsory stage in the development of all civil aircraft. It implies that one or several civil aviation administrations enforce the compliance of the aircraft with a number of safety requirements. The certification is taken care of by civil aviation administrations in the countries where the aircraft is developed and sold. The requirements regard every aspect of the aircraft, from its flight behaviour, to the nature of the materials used. The regulations are especially concerned with the safety of the aircraft and constrain its technological characteristics. When new technologies are used on an aircraft, new certification procedures have to be designed to demonstrate the compliance of the aircraft with the safety regulations. As such, the certification rules are institutions, while the certification authority is an assessment and control organisation.

As the Mystère 20 was originally developed for military or governmental purposes it was not submitted to certification requirements. From the moment when the aircraft was to be sold as a civil aircraft, however, it had to comply with the regulations formulated by civil aviation administrations and hence be certified.

Jean Delacroix, head of the French civil aviation administration, the SGAC, believed that the aircraft had a strong potential as a civil aircraft. He had followed the first phase of the development of the aircraft and commented on the design (Déplante, February, July and September 1962). Meanwhile, he had taken steps to ease the certification procedures for the firm. After the contract with Pan Am was signed, it was clear that the aircraft had to be certified according to both French and American regulations. As Dassault had not developed civil aircraft since the Second World War, nobody within the firm had any experience of the certification process (Delacroix, int., 1999).

In order to certify the aircraft and hence implement the diversification, external support was needed. This support was to be found mainly in the very staunch commitment of the SGAC, supplemented by the participation of the FAA as well as that of an engineer from Boeing.

5.2.1. The support from Boeing

While the Mystère 20 was at an early stage of development, discussions started between Boeing and Dassault. Informal as it may have been, some kind of cooperation was being discussed regarding the future of the Mystère 20. A larger aircraft was envisaged, the Mystère 100, with a capacity of 40 seats.[17] With that perspective in mind, the Mystère 20 was then summarily discussed between the two firms. It was to serve as a kind of test and be, so to speak, the forerunner of a larger civil aircraft to be produced jointly by Dassault and Boeing (Déplante, January 1962). Although the Mystère 100 never followed the Mystère 20, Boeing kept alive its interest in the project.

Pan Am also had close relations with Boeing. For example, the first commercial transatlantic route had been opened by Pan Am on a Boeing 314 in the late 1930s, and Pan Am had been the launch customer of the commercial versions of the Boeing 707 in 1955 and later of the Boeing 747.[18] On Pan Am's advice, an exchange of engineers was initiated between Boeing and Dassault to accelerate the certification.

Robert Schroers, the Boeing engineer who had been manager of the certification for the Boeing 707, was then sent to Mérignac. The selection of Schroers had been made by John Borger, a Pan Am executive who had managed the certification for the Boeing 707 on behalf of the airline. In exchange, Jacques Alberto, an engineer from Dassault specialised in vertical take-off military aircraft, was sent to Boeing. Although Schroers did not provide any technological expertise, he was in a position to support Dassault in explaining the philosophy of the certification. In other words, he advised Dassault engineers on how to tackle the so-called 'big book' in which all the details of the certification were presented, and on how to convince the certification authority that the solutions chosen were safe and complied with the requirements (Lemaire, int., 1997; Leroudier, int., 1999).

5.2.2. The work with the FAA and the SGAC

Both the French and the American civil aviation administrations were involved in the certification process of the Falcon 20. In the mid-1950s, when the jetliner Caravelle was to be certified, the French civil aviation administration had translated the existing American regulations CR4B in order to simplify the certification of the Caravelle in the United States. That led to the creation of the French certification number 2051, relevant for all aircraft weighing more than 5.7 tons (Delacroix, int., 1999).

The certification was then organised around two certification administrations, i.e., the SGAC and the FAA office in Brussels. Flight tests were carried out both by the Dassault test pilots and by the CEV (Centre d'Essais en Vol, the French national flight test centre). For specific issues, flight tests were to be done compulsorily by the CEV. The STAe (Services Techniques de l'Aéronautique, a state-owned aerospace development laboratory) was in charge of the control of the technological solutions employed by the firm. Furthermore, a private firm, the Bureau Veritas, was in charge of the quality control of the production of the aircraft (Leroudier, int., 1999).

Thus, the certification of the Falcon 20 involved the participation of two foreign private firms, Pan Am and Boeing; one foreign administration, the Federal Aviation Administration, three national organisations, the SGAC, the CEV and the STAe, and finally one private French firm, the Bureau Veritas. It must be pointed out that flight testing and control of the production between these French organisations already functioned very smoothly, as they had been fine tuned earlier on during the development of military aircraft. What was new was the interaction with the certification authorities.

5.2.3. Hydraulic servo-controls

The certification of the Falcon 20 was not likely to raise too many problems for the firm, as the technologies used had already been tested in the military programmes. At least, this was the opinion commonly held, but some of the technologies had never been used in any civil programme whatsoever. As a result, these technologies were not even mentioned in the certification procedures.

One of the major problems encountered lay in the certifying of the use of hydraulic actuators for the command of the control surfaces. Powered actuators had been used previously in military aircraft. A few civil aircraft used the technology but only as an assistance to the mechanical devices and to reduce the load for the pilot, as in the case of an assisted steering wheel in a car (Lemaire, int., 1999). On the Falcon 20, the actuators did not only provide assistance to the pilot, but they took over full control of the aircraft without mechanical actuators (Leroudier, int., 1999). These hydraulic actuators had been developed for the military fighter Mystère IV, from which the Falcon 20 had inherited the wing and hence the actuators.[19]

The technology was overlooked, because unmentioned in the 'big book' of the certification, until 1965 when the American federal aviation administration interrogated Dassault regarding the consequences of having a metal chip trapped in the hydraulic circuit, thus blocking the actuators. The concern was about the capacity of the aircraft to land in case of a failure of the system (Leroudier, int., 1999). New tests had to be designed to show that the chip would not compromise the safety of the aircraft.

The FAA came up with even further requests, worried about the effects of a total hydraulic failure in the system. The firm answered that there existed two hydraulic circuits as well as an electric pump, providing a triple redundancy for the control of the aircraft. This was, however, not enough for the FAA, and the firm was required to show that in the event of total hydraulic failure the aircraft would be able to land in safe conditions. In order to demonstrate the compliance with this request, the pressure was gradually dropped in the hydraulic circuits, and it was finally shown that it was possible to land the aircraft even in the event of total hydraulic failure. Obviously, the manoeuvrability of the aircraft would then be extremely limited as the command would only use the gaps in the hydraulic system to allow control, but above a speed of 200 knots – 370 km/h – the aircraft could be landed safely (Leroudier, int., 1999; Delacroix, int., 1999).

This example illustrates the problems the firm could encounter during the certification of the aircraft and how the certification regulation as an institution could influence the choice of technology. Had the firm not been able to demonstrate the safety of the system, the certification authorities would have required a mechanical device and hence stopped a technological innovation on a civil aircraft. On 9 June 1965, the aircraft was finally certified, just a few months before the first delivery.

5.3. The First Steps of the Production

As the development of the aircraft was moving forward with the certification process, production of the aircraft also had to be prepared. The production facilities of the firm were already overloaded with the production of the military aircraft ordered by the French government.

However, the contract between the government and the firm implied that the production of the aircraft should be shared with the state-owned firm Sud Aviation. Dassault was to be responsible for the whole design and the final assembly of the aircraft while the state-owned firm would be involved in about half the production. The former relations between Marcel Dassault and Georges Hereil, CEO of Sud Aviation, facilitated the coordination between the firms. As a matter of fact, this type of collaboration between state-owned and private firms had become more and more common in the industry.

In October 1963, a division of labour was established. Sud Aviation was to manufacture the fuselage in its plants in Saint Nazaire, and Dassault was to manufacture the wing and the tail of the aircraft, as well as integrate the whole aircraft in Mérignac and then test it (Lemaire and Parvaud, 1995, p. 55). The cooperation between the two firms worked well, although each had to meet very narrow deadlines. The Sud Aviation plant in Saint Nazaire was under great social pressure since the Caravelle did not sell very well. Consequently, the deal with Dassault was a godsend. It seems, however, that that collaboration was not as efficient as it could have been, since Sud Aviation only manufactured parts of the aircraft and was never involved in the design of the aircraft in any way (Estèbe, int., 1997).

The first aircraft was delivered on time to Pan Am in September 1965. However, during the two years of development a number of changes had occurred and the first aircraft did not meet Pan Am's requirements completely. A company was then started in the US in order to upgrade the aircraft with the latest technical solutions. The first aircraft arriving in the United States went through a 'clean-up' before going to their respective buyers (Estèbe, int., 1997).

5.4.   Marketing the Aircraft

As has been described earlier, Pan Am did not want to use the Falcon 20 in the same way as it operated its jetliners. Right from the outset, the firm was more interested in selling the aircraft to other corporations on the American market. This had already influenced the design of the Falcon 20 and was to simplify Dassault's marketing task in the United States tremendously. Pan Am's image there was vastly more impressive than Dassault's. Besides, the requirements for American avionics and engines also facilitated the marketing of the aircraft on the US market. Pan Am created a business jet division to organise the sale of the Falcon 20 on the American continent.

It was only in April 1967 that Dassault decided to start its own marketing division, aimed basically at selling the aircraft to the rest of the world. As the number of aircraft sold around the world increased, especially in the United States, it was felt that a new maintenance division had to be created. As a result, in November 1972, a joint-venture was set up between Pan Am and Dassault, called the Falcon Jet Corporation in Little Rock (Carlier and Berger, 1996b, p. 237).

5.5.   Completing the Diversification

Between 1963 and 1965, the amount of work required from the engineers and technicians of Mérignac was extreme. The deadline imposed by Pan Am was excessively short, and the technical requirements often seemed out of reach. Besides the development of the aircraft, the certification process was an extra burden which was greatly simplified owing to the entrepreneurship of the members of the SGAC, the French civil aviation administration.

It followed that the success of the programme depended on the intervention of external organisations, such as the SGAC or Boeing and Pan Am. The close relations that were established between these organisations allowed a rapid identification of the problems of the aircraft and opened the way for developing adequate solutions. Moreover, these organisations enabled Dassault to understand the institutional environment of the civil aircraft industry.

The production of the aircraft was also dependent on another firm, Sud Aviation, as was required by the contract between Dassault and the French state. Besides, Dassault did not have the production capacity necessary for the manufacturing of the aircraft as the firm was overloaded with the production of two military aircraft.

6. CONCLUSIONS

The venture in which Dassault engaged at the beginning of the 1960s was, to a large extent, unplanned. Even if the owner of the firm, Marcel Dassault, wanted to leave his name to an airliner, he was not willing to take the risk of completely leaving the lucrative military market. Risks were to be carefully evaluated before starting a new project. This was illustrated by the 'small-steps policy' of the firm, which indicated that new projects should never be too innovative. Besides this aversion to risk, the firm was limited in its actions by the institutional environment, limiting the entrance of private firms on the civil market.

Through the development of transport aircraft prototypes, Dassault was able to keep its competences in the development of passenger aircraft and freighters. A number of factors triggered the diversification of the firm. First of all, the poor performance of the state-owned firms opened new possibilities for private firms. Agreements between the state and the private firms could be achieved, provided that the workload for the production of aircraft be shared with some state-owned firm. Thus, institutional arrangements could be arrived at even at the national level to support the industry in general. Secondly, the emergence of a new market in the United States opened up a whole range of new opportunities. However, the new market, in itself, was not sufficient. The firm needed a customer capable of absorbing a large quantity of aircraft in order to secure the investments. The fact that Pan Am was at that time looking for a business jet and chose the Mystère 20, was a key factor in the diversification.

Diversification was not only a matter of opportunities, however. As the programme went on, the firm needed to use its competences and expand them in order to develop an aircraft. In addition, Dassault had to finance the development and the production of the aircraft. The technological aspects enlisted all of Dassault's available resources and at the same time required the support of external organisations. Technologies existing internally could later on be used to accelerate the development of the new aircraft, while relations with Pan Am and with certification authorities completed the programme. Regarding the financial side, the government's role consisted in granting the firm a loan covering half the development cost of the aircraft. Without this loan, the firm would not have continued the programme.

The Falcon 20 was a very successful aircraft for Dassault. It has led to a whole family of aircraft, which has placed the firm in a leading position on the business jet market. The firm has been able to adapt its competences in military aircraft to develop a whole new family of civil aircraft, using national institutional arrangements together with opportune relations with other organisations.

Table 4.1: Chronology of the Main Events Before and After the
Diversification of Dassault

Year	Events
1917	Start of the firm by Marcel Bloch (later Dassault)
1936	Law of nationalisation of all military industries
1937	Creation of the state-owned firms
1945	Priority is given to state-owned firms for civil production; Incorporation of the Société des Avions Marcel Dassault
1949	Start of the production of the Flamant
1951	Purchase of the Ouragan fighter aircraft by the state
1952	Production of the Ouragan; Sound wall in a Mystère II First flight of a jetliner, the de Havilland Comet
1954	Start of the production of the Mystère IV
1956	Emergence of the business jet market
1958	Draft of the Communauté
1959	Draft of the Spiral I and III
1960	Draft of the Méditerrannée
1961	Launch of the Mystère 20 programme on private funding; First exchange of engineers with Boeing
1962	Studies by ITA show that there is no market for business jets
1963	Negotiations with Pan Am and first contract, 40 aircraft plus 120 options; Financial support from the French state; Division of labour established between Dassault and Sud Aviation for the production
1964	Change of engines; Last technical development
1965	Certification of the aircraft and first delivery to Pan Am

NOTES

1. Amelia Earhart was the first female pilot to fly solo over the Atlantic Ocean, on 20 May 1932.
2. In this chapter, the firm will be referred to as 'Dassault,' although the full name of the firm during the period covered by this study was the Générale Aéronautique Marcel Dassault, or GAMD. The name 'Marcel Dassault' is used only to refer to the person who founded the group.
3. Those private firms were as follows: Farman Henriot, which became the SNCAC; Potez, which became the SNCAN; Dewoitine, which became the SNCAM; and Loire et Olivier, which became the SNCASE (Thornton, 1995, p. 186). In March 1957, the state-owned firms from the south of France (SNCASO and SNCASE) were integrated into one sole entity, Sud Aviation, while the state-owned firms from the north and the centre of France (SNACAN and SNCAC) became Nord Aviation.
4. The Ministry of Aviation was created in May 1928 in order to organise the development and the production of aircraft in France. Though this ministry was independant from the Ministry of War, it was concerned with the planning of the production of military and civil aircraft. It is not to be confused with the air force, which was concerned with the use of military aircraft.
5. In this division of labour, the state-owned firms attempted to develop military aircraft with limited success. This increased the specialisation of both state-owned and private firms.
6. This chapter deals with the post-war history of the firm and not with the previous activities of the various firms created and owned by Marcel Dassault before the war. It is, however, recognised that some of the engineers employed by Marcel Dassault since the first years followed him into the new firm after the war.
7. The development of the Boeing 707 had started at the beginning of the 1950s as a military jet tanker, the Boeing 367-80, later the KC 135. The Boeing 707 first flew on 15 July 1954.
8. The name of the new civil aircraft, Mystère 20, directly indicates its origins in military aircraft at Dassault. Since the Second World War, the best seller of the firm had been the Mystère IV, the first French supersonic fighter.
9. Jet engines are completely covered by a casing or pod, hence the term podded engine.
10. Originally, General Electric had developed this engine for a lunar vehicle which needed high thrust for vertical take-off.
11. 895 km/h instead of 825 km/h.
12. The stall angle is the angle of attack at which the aircraft loses lift, provoking its fall.
13. The Concorde would however not fly before 2 March 1969.
14. The nature of the contacts must have been very lax as the note mentions the name 'Juan Trop' instead of 'Juan Trippe'. Moreover, the question of the diameter of the fuselage was also criticised by the Institute of Airborne Transportation, arguing that since 90% of male Americans measure between 1.75 and 1.90 metres, the Mystère 20 was to have a fuselage large enough to accommodate American passengers (ITA, 1962).
15. The 'dimensioning' mission for the range of the Falcon 20 was New York to Texas, or 2,600 kilometres (Leroudier, p.c., 2000).
16. Most of the fuel in an aircraft is always tanked in the wings.
17. The Mystère 100 was to have a capacity of 40 passengers. As the smaller aircraft would have only 8 passengers, or five times less, the name became Mystère 20 (100 divided by 5) (Lemaire, int., 1997).
18. The 707 and 747 were practically procured by Pan Am. In the 1950s, Juan Trippe was convinced that jet airliners were the ideal technology for transatlantic routes. He played on the rivalry between Boeing and Douglas to accelerate the development of the Boeing 707

and Douglas Dash 80. He then bought both aircraft, and Pan Am became the first airline to operate jetliners on transatlantic routes. Later, in the mid-1960s, Juan Trippe procured the Boeing 747 (Gandt, 1995).

19. When Jean Delacroix, head of the SGAC, asked Marcel Dassault why he persistently wanted to have the powered actuators, which actually were not necessary on this type of aircraft, Marcel Dassault answered: 'Monsieur Delacroix, my Cadillac has some hydraulic actuators.' The Mystère 20 was to be an exclusive aircraft for exclusive personalities (Delacroix, int., 1999).

5. From Military to Regional Aircraft in Sweden: The Case of the Saab 340

> *It is hard enough for anyone to map out a course of action and stick to it, particularly in the face of the desires of one's friends; but it is doubly hard for an aviator to stay on the ground waiting for just the right moment to go into the air.*
>
> Glenn Curtiss[1]

At the beginning of the 1930s, the aircraft industry in Sweden was just emerging. The idea of a strong air force was becoming accepted by the Swedish armed forces, the Swedish government and the parliament. In October 1936, the government approved a programme proposed by the Swedish Air Force to buy 297 military aircraft. About a third of these aircraft were to be produced in Sweden, while the rest were to be imported. This followed a parliamentary decision underlying the need for the Swedish industry to acquire competences in the aircraft industry (Andersson, 1989, p. 14).

Two main firms were at that time developing aircraft, Bofors, with its experience in military activities, and ASJA – AB Svenska Järnvägs-verkstäderna, an established aircraft manufacturer controlled by the Wallenberg family. In order to reduce the cost of development of new aircraft, and to profit from the competences of both ASJA and Bofors, the government insisted on the need for the firms to cooperate. After some negotiations, this led to the incorporation of the firm Svenska Aeroplan AB – Saab – on 2 April 1937. The creation of Saab would then satisfy the Swedish

97

government's twin objectives of having a national aircraft producer and military aircraft for the Swedish Air Force. The government guaranteed orders for Saab for the period of time between 1937 and 1943. This guarantee was to expire on 1 July 1943 (Andersson, 1989, p. 18).

Initially Saab produced aircraft under licence from German, American and English manufacturers. The firm became rapidly independent from such licensing after accumulation of enough knowledge to design aircraft. In May 1940, the first aircraft fully designed and produced in Sweden was flying, the Saab 17. The air force grew considerably within the Swedish armed forces. As of 1970, the Swedish Air Force had more squadrons of fighter aircraft than any European country. The Swedish Air Force as a whole was at that time similar in size to the British, the German or the French Air Force (Dörfer, 1973, p. 41).

This chapter investigates diversification at Saab,[2] from military to civil aircraft, at the end of the 1970s. It specifically describes the development of the regional aircraft Saab 340.[3] Having the state as its main customer, Saab did not have any real incentives or even needs to diversify until the early 1970s. This will be described in Section 1. Despite several attempts on the part of the firm to diversify from military to civil aircraft, the institutional environment of the firm did not provide any incentives to support or spur a diversification. Section 2 of this chapter will address the institutional shift of the 1970s, leading to incentives for diversification in the firm. Stemming from the understanding of this institutional shift, Section 3 describes the case of the Saab 340, identifying the reasons for diversification at the firm level. In Section 4, the diversification process is described.

1.   PREVIOUS DIVERSIFICATIONS AT SAAB

The incorporation of Saab had been the result of the Swedish government's insistence on having only one major firm in the Swedish aircraft industry. These origins affected the relations between the Swedish government, the Swedish military command and the firm. The development of the company, its strategies and technological choices have also been affected by these relations.

The Swedish state was and remains the main customer of the company. Although Saab attempted, and still attempts, to export its military aircraft, export figures have always remained very low. The aircraft most sold abroad has been the Saab 35 Draken, with 88 aircraft exported,[4] for a total production of 604 aircraft (Sehlberg, 1988, p. 19). In order to gain some independence from the state, Saab had to find new markets in which the control by the government and the air force would be lower.

This section reviews the attempts of the firm to diversify into the civil aircraft industry.[5] It goes through the various projects of the firm to develop a civil aircraft and explains why most of the time these projects failed.

1.1. The First Projects of Diversification in the Civil Aircraft Industry

1.1.1. The Saab 90 Scandia
At the end of World War II, the company faced a serious dilemma. When the company was set up, a special clause had been included in the agreement between the state and the firm. According to that clause, the company was to be dismantled in the event of dramatic changes in the world situation (Sehlberg, 1988, p. 14). The end of the war was considered such a situation, and the firm therefore had to be divested. The only other alternative for Saab was to begin to produce civil aircraft.[6] The government was ready to help Saab diversify its activities and in November 1946, the first civil aircraft produced by Saab was flying, the Saab 90 Scandia. With a range of up to 1,000 kilometres, this aircraft was to replace ageing DC-3s and to transport up to 32 passengers.

Since 1948, however, the tensions from the cold war and the emergence of the Korean War in 1950 had triggered a new need for a strong air force in Sweden. The Swedish Air Force and the Swedish government pressed Saab to stop the production of the Scandia to devote all its resources to the production of more than 600 military aircraft, the Saab 29 Tunnan (the so-called 'Flying Barrel'), all for the Swedish Air Force.

A total of 18 Scandia aircraft were produced, six out of which were produced by Fokker in Holland (Andersson, 1989, p. 35). To compensate for the lost investments, Saab received heavy compensations from the Swedish government in the form of bonuses on each Tunnan delivered on time to the Swedish Air Force (Andersson, 1989, p. 90).

1.1.2. The Saab 91 Safir
In parallel with the production of the Scandia, Saab started the production of a simple sport and training propeller aircraft, the Saab 91 Safir. This aircraft could carry four persons and was powered by one engine. It was produced from 1945 to 1963. It has been a great success for the company both in Sweden and abroad, having been exported to 21 countries. The reason why

the production of this aircraft could continue, despite the difficulties encountered with the Scandia, might be that the Saab 91 Safir was mainly bought by air forces all over the world and used as a training aircraft. Moreover, it was a small and fairly simple aircraft for which development and production costs were small in comparison to these of military aircraft (Andersson, 1989).

1.1.3. The Saab 105
In 1961, Saab started the development of a twinjet aircraft with four seats, the Saab 105. The aircraft was designed as a trainer for the Swedish Air Force, which eventually bought 150 aircraft, 40 of which were sold to Austria. During the development phase of the aircraft, studies were conducted to see if a business jet could be built onto the structure of the trainer. The aim was to build a small and inexpensive business jet (Phillips et al., 1994, p. 56). However, because of its military origins, the structure was over-engineered for a civil aircraft and it would have carried only two passengers since the certification rules at that time required two pilots in a jet aircraft. As a result, the aircraft would have been too expensive for the civil market and the idea was dropped (Rodling, int., 1998).

1.2.   The Long Way to a Civil Aircraft

Saab seemed to lose its interest in civil aircraft during the 1960s. As a matter of fact, the military aircraft Saab 37 Viggen required the involvement of the firm as a whole. At the beginning of the 1970s, the development phase of the Viggen came to an end. The firm had to find ways not to lose the competences of its development engineers. Some studies were carried out to develop a new version of the Viggen and turn it into an attack aircraft, but a lot of uncertainties reigned in the firm as to what the government wanted. During that time, several studies were carried out to see what the firm could do in the civil market. These studies would eventually result in the Saab 340.

Although the tradition of the company was the production of military aircraft, the management of the firm, in the early 1970s, became gradually aware of the necessity to develop a civil aircraft. Some first sketches of civil aircraft appeared in the annual report of 1970. Between 1971 and 1973, an international joint venture was envisaged to develop a civil aircraft. Finally, from 1974 to 1978, the annual reports continually insisted on the need to develop civil aircraft. In the meantime, these annual reports showed a more and more precise description of the projects.[7]

1.2.1. The Europlane
In the 1960s, aircraft transportation had grown very fast and the need for large airliners like the French Caravelle, developed by Sud Aviation, or the Boeing 707 was growing. Saab as well as other aircraft manufacturers in Europe were trying to establish alliances in order to compete with much larger American manufacturers (Edlund, int., 1996). In the middle of 1971, the German aircraft manufacturer MBB, British Aircraft Corporation and Saab held discussions investigating the possibility of a joint design and production of a large commercial aircraft (QSF, 1971).

Following these contacts, the three partners decided to study a 'Quiet Take-off and Landing Aircraft', with a capacity of 200 passengers. This aircraft was to be an answer to the A300 under development at the recently started consortium Airbus from which British Aircraft Corporation had withdrawn in April 1969 due to disputes concerning the engine of the A300.[8] In 1972, the Spanish firm CASA joined the project and the consortium Europlane Limited was created (Annual Report, 1972, p. 14; Flight International, 1973). However, by the end of 1973, the project was dropped. Reasons for this include the emerging oil crisis (Annual Report, 1973, p. 16), and competition from the Airbus consortium (Edlund, int., 1996).

1.2.2. Other attempts – the Mula
The end of the Europlane did not imply the end of the road for civil aircraft in Sweden. As a matter of fact, several civil aircraft were still being studied, even if it was on a smaller scale. These included, among others, the 1071, a four engine aircraft for 50 passengers, the 1072, a jet aircraft for 40 to 50 passengers and the 1073, a twin engine aircraft for 70 passengers (Rodling, int., 1998).

Following market studies about the needs of the industry, only a few engineers were assigned to work on these small projects. These engineers were given carte blanche, from the higher management of the firm, to investigate new civil aircraft. The projects were allocated a specific budget but were called 'dustbin' projects since they usually took up about six months and were then dropped for new studies. During these six months, an aircraft was sketched, and the first calculations about the weight and performance were effected. A basic knowledge and experience in aircraft design was enough for these calculations. However, none of these projects went beyond the stage of full-scale wooden mock-ups. This was due to the fact that the market was seen as too narrow by the management of the firm, and therefore no financing was granted for such aircraft (Bratt, int., 1998; Rodling, int., 1998).

In 1968, Saab bought a small Swedish firm, Malmö Flygindustri, whose main activity was the development of small and light aircraft for training, as well as the maintenance and repair of other aircraft (Annual Report, 1968, p. 16). In addition to the production of two small aircraft, the Safari and the Supporter, the firm was working on an aircraft for rough conditions (Annual Report, 1975, p. 17). Called the Mula, and later on the Transporter, the aircraft had a simple design and a robust structure, with a high wing and two piston engines.[9] A small team of 20 people was working on the project, but lack of interest from the management of the firm and difficulties in financing the project limited the scope of the studies (Edlund, int., 1996).

The 1977 Annual Report points out the fact that the firm needed capital to continue the development of the aircraft and that all the European firms entering the market were receiving some financial help from their respective states, while the Swedish state did not provide any support (Annual Report, 1977, p. 39).

1.3.   Attempting to Diversify During the 1970s

Since its early days, Saab had been living almost continuously in symbiosis with the Swedish government. The worries caused by the end of the Second World War had been of short duration. With a national defence policy strictly orientated towards a strong air force, Saab had good reasons to believe in a strong future and therefore had almost no incentives to enter the civil aircraft industry.

This does not mean that nothing was attempted, but the size of the investments in new ventures was always underestimated, as if the desire of the management of the firm was to avoid entering the new market. In fact, only two projects were reasonably successful, the Saab 90 Scandia which was eventually sold out to Holland, and the Saab 91 Safir, whose success was due to its simple design and its military orientation.

In actual fact, it appears that until the late 1960s, the Swedish state acted as a barrier to diversification in the direction of civil aircraft. Not only did it provide a market for the firm, but it almost forbade the firm to diversify into the civil aircraft industry. This may also explain why the investments of Saab were so limited in the various attempts. The situation had already existed where the state had stopped a civil programme. The management of the firm was aware of this and therefore may have been reluctant to invest heavily in civil aircraft.

2. POLITICAL AND MANAGERIAL TURMOIL DURING THE 1970s

Saab launched the military aircraft Viggen in 1963. This technologically very advanced military aircraft could easily stand comparison with international competition. However, because the aircraft had not been contracted on a fixed-cost basis, the total price of the aircraft continually rose (Krönmark, int., 1998). As a result, at the beginning of the 1970s, while the first batches of aircraft were being delivered to the Swedish Air Force, there prevailed a great amount of uncertainties in the Swedish parliament and at government level as to whether or not the programme should continue and also on the issue of the Swedish aircraft industry in general.

Saab had already started to study various types of aircraft to replace the Viggen in 1972 (Annual Report, 1973, p. 13; 1974, p. 13). These aircraft could either be built from the structure of the Viggen or be completely new machines. In 1975, Saab was able to present a new version of the Viggen, the A20 and in 1976, a completely new aircraft was on the drawing board, the B3LA (Annual Report, 1975, p. 15; 1976, p. 36). The B3LA was considered a new generation of military aircraft as it was smaller and cheaper than the Viggen and offered improved performance (Annual Report, 1977, p. 39).

The first part of this section describes the political situation around the development of the Swedish Air Force during the 1970s. It focuses on the parliamentary debate around the needs of the Swedish Air Force. The second part presents the management's answer to the political uncertainties. The third part discusses the decision-making process at Saab and at government level, leading to the diversification.

2.1. Political Background

The question of military aircraft was extremely sensitive during the 1970s. Not only did conflicts exist between political parties, but also within political parties. On the one hand, the aircraft industry represented prestige, competences and employment, but on the other hand, the military aspect of the industry was criticised.

This 'employment vs. military' dilemma created internal divisions within the Social-Democratic Party in power during the first half of the 1970s. As a result, at the party conference in 1972, it was decided that no new advanced military aircraft was to be developed in Sweden (Köhler, 1984, p. 7; Krönmark, int., 1998).[10] Since by political tradition, decisions concerning the procurement of defence equipment were to be agreed by all political parties, this decision was to block the question of the future of the Swedish aircraft industry until the end of the 1970s, as no additional funds were to be earmarked for the industry (Krönmark, int., 1998).

The problem raised by this political decision was the cost of procuring aircraft for an efficient air force. The experience of the Viggen had shown that it was very difficult to control the development cost of a military aircraft. In 1977, the budget allocated by the newly elected central/liberal coalition government to procure a new attack aircraft was too limited to allow the development of both the attack version of the Viggen, or A20, and of the B3LA (Köhler, 1984, p. 7). As a result, the A20 was dropped while the performances of the B3LA were regularly reduced to keep it within its allocated budget (Gustafsson, int., 1998).

In 1978, the new minority government, with Ola Ullsten as liberal prime minister and Lars De Geer as defence minister, was not able to obtain a majority vote at the parliament for the development of the B3LA, now called sk38/A38. The project was therefore cancelled on 23 February 1979 (Köhler, 1984, p. 3; Gustafsson, int., 1998; Edlund, int., 1996.).

During the ongoing parliamentary debate on the needs of the Swedish Air Force, there was a growing concern about the future of the Swedish aircraft industry in general. This was reflected in two parliamentary investigations. The first investigation was done by the Aircraft Industry Committee (Flygindustri Kommittén or FLIK) and started in January 1978. Its aim was to describe the structure of the industry and to identify the possibilities of conversion to civil aircraft, stressing the existing experience of Saab. Among other conclusions, it was recognised that the firm was too dominated by the Swedish state and had to find ways of becoming more independent (FLIK, 1978). The second investigation, published in 1980, was more specific on the possibilities of conversion of the aircraft industry (FLIK, 1980).

According to Krönmark, then Minister of Defence in Sweden, the Swedish government had a moral responsibility to help Saab out of that dependency (Krönmark, int., 1998). As was said in the previous section, Saab had already attempted to diversify in the civil aircraft industry in the 1950s and had been on the way to succeeding with the Scandia. However, the state had imposed that the firm should stay in the defence industry as the international situation was tense. As a result, negotiations started as early as Spring 1977 between

Nils G. Åsling, Minister of Industry, and Marcus Wallenberg, chairman of the board of Saab, on the issue of the development of a civil aircraft by the firm and its financial support (Åsling, int., 1998). According to Åsling, it is at that time that the Swedish government started to express worries about the future of Saab in the military aircraft sector (Åsling, p.c., 1999).

2.2. A New Military Aircraft

In the introduction letter to the 1978 Annual Report, Sten Gustafsson, the new CEO of Saab-Scania and Marcus Wallenberg, chairman of the Board, described the critical situation in which the firm found itself. They indicated the desire of the management to keep the position of Saab in the international aerospace industry (Annual Report, 1978, p. 3). In order to save the industry, new projects had to take off at Saab.

On the military side, a new programme could follow the general trend of designing multirole airplanes. Since the mid-1970s, a new concept for military aircraft had been taking form both in the aircraft industry in general and in air forces around the world. Combining the three main missions required for a military aircraft, i.e., reconnaissance, attack and fighter, into one single aircraft would eliminate the development cost of each separate version of the aircraft (Köhler, 1984, p. 5; Gustafsson, int., 1998). For Saab, this implied that a new project of military aircraft could still be viable provided it was accepted by the government.

This, however, was not enough. In order to avoid a repetition of the difficulties encountered during the 1970s, the firm had to invest heavily in civil aircraft activities. On 24 February 1978, one day after the decision by the state to cancel the B3LA, the CEO of Saab launched two ambitious programmes, a military and a civil one (Köhler, 1984, p. 3; Gustafsson, int., 1998; Edlund, int., 1996). The military programme was to become the JAS 39 Gripen, while the civil programme was to become the Saab 340.

During the latter part of 1979, the government had indicated that it was ready to support the development of the JAS 39 Gripen, a new military aircraft, following the proposal of the Swedish Supreme Commander to skip one generation of aircraft and to develop a multirole aircraft. In February 1980, a pre-study of the new fighter was decided upon and the government earmarked a budget of SEK200 million for the study until the end of 1981 (Flygbladet, 2689 extra bilaga 2).

On 6 March 1980 the government proposed to the parliament the following alternatives to replace the Viggen by the end of the 1980s:

- buying a foreign aircraft of the type F-16 from the US manufacturer General Dynamics;
- buying a foreign aircraft and producing it under licence in Sweden;
- developing and producing a new aircraft in a joint venture with another manufacturer; and
- developing and producing a multirole aircraft including more foreign equipment than was the case in previous aircraft (Flygbladet, 2696).

As the latter solution was adopted, an industrial consortium to design the new aircraft was set up between Saab, for the airframe and the systems integration, Ericsson, for the electronics and radar systems, and Volvo Flygmotor, for the engine. The industry was asked to invest as much as the state for the definition and the project studies of the aircraft until 1982. This budget was accepted by the parliament in June 1980 (Flygbladet, 2707).

The second condition for the new military project was that Saab would develop a civil aircraft. This was, as will be seen in the next section, effectively underway. The philosophy of the agreement between the Swedish state and Saab was new. The government wanted the aerospace industry to take its responsibilities in terms of technological development and finances.

2.3.   Shifting from Military to Civil

Efforts in the direction of a civil aircraft industry had intensified as early as 1977. In two years, Saab had succeeded in becoming a subcontractor to two large aircraft manufacturers, McDonnell Douglas and British Aerospace.

2.3.1. The first commercial contracts

In 1977, the American aircraft manufacturer McDonnell Douglas wanted to modernise its existing DC9 and called for bids from aerospace firms for the construction of a number of components of the aircraft. Saab made an offer for some components in April 1977. As such, the project was not seen by Saab as a means to increase its number of employees or to save the firm from its ongoing problems with the Swedish state. The idea was to enter the civil aircraft industry through the 'backdoor' and to learn from the experience of McDonnell Douglas. To ensure the success of the project, a financial support of SEK35 million was granted by the state to cover the risks (Flygbladet, 2521). In November 1977, McDonnell Douglas subcontracted Saab the production of the flaps for the new DC9-super 80. The contract was to give employment to 20 technicians and 75 workers, and some engineers of Saab went to the McDonnell Douglas Long Beach factory in April 1978 to study the development of the aircraft and to prepare the production of the flaps in Sweden (Flygbladet, 2551 and 2575).

Similarly, in 1978, Saab succeeded in getting involved in the development of the British Aerospace 146. This participation was to create about 200 employment positions, subject to the participation of Saab being accepted by British Aerospace (Flygbladet, 2567). To cover the risks of the project, Saab asked the government for financial support of SEK115 million as well as another SEK50 million to finance the credits to potential customers. The contract concerned the production of the horizontal stabiliser of 350 aircraft, for a total cost of SEK600 million (Flygbladet, 2576).

However, nobody really liked the idea of Saab becoming merely a subcontractor to other firms. The firm had had great autonomy in designing its products and was used to dealing with the Swedish state. The thought of another firm conducting Saab's development activities was considered unacceptable (Gustafsson, int., 1998; Edlund, int., 1996). This entailed the production of larger projects along the lines established on a small scale through the 1970s. However, the problem of finding the right niche on the civil market for the firm, both in terms of aircraft size and investments remained to be solved.

2.3.2. The deregulation of the American market

In 1978, the American airline market was deregulated by virtue of the 'Airline Deregulation Act'. Since 1938, the Civil Aeronautics Board had controlled airliners' routes and fares in the United States. The deregulation allowed airlines to start new routes and to compete freely on the market. It also offered new firms an opportunity to start on the market. This was to create a need for new small commuter aircraft with an approximate capacity of 30 passengers. This niche was not occupied at the time. Market studies carried out in the United States had clearly indicated the need for this type of aircraft. For Saab, the size of the aircraft was reasonable and since the market was large, the idea of developing an aircraft for that market began to be considered. There were at the time not so many manufacturers on the market for regional aircraft. Market studies showed that only three to five manufacturers would probably even try to enter. In particular the Franco-Italian firm ATR, the Brazilian firm Embraer, and the Canadian firm de Havilland had projects (Klofsten and Pettersson, 1984, 3).

Deregulation was coming at the right time for the firm. A new market was opening at the very moment when the Swedish government was pushing the firm in the same direction. Ulf Edlund, a former project director for the B3LA, was given the leadership for the development of a new civil aircraft on the basis of the previous study of the Transporter. His team was given six months to prove the feasibility of a small regional aircraft (Gustafsson, int., 1998; Edlund, int., 1996).

2.4.   A Forced Shift

All through the 1970s, the uncertainties and the debates in the Swedish parliament created a situation where it became impossible to clearly determine the needs of the Swedish Air Force. Ideological debates were mixed with technological issues, and the signals the firm received from its institutional environment were often contradictory. The development of an aircraft is a highly risky and expensive process which, moreover, extends over a very long period of time (more than 10 years). In other words, the constant changes of opinion at the parliamentary level did not provide the firm with the information needed to develop a clear strategy.

Nevertheless, this situation, fraught with uncertainty, was to trigger the diversification of the firm. In the foregoing section, it was seen that the firm was to some extent blocked in its attempts to diversify on account of the needs of the Swedish Air Force. Now that the state was reluctant to decide how the Swedish Air Force should be equipped, the firm had to take care of its own destiny.

The choice to diversify can, on the one hand, be seen as triggered by the institutional environment of the firm as it did not provide the stable situation that the firm needed to develop its product. On the other hand, this choice was also the result of a managerial decision, weighing the pros and cons of a new market and knowing about the possibilities of getting support from the state.

3.   SETTING UP A NEW CIVIL AIRCRAFT

In February 1979, right after the decision of the management to diversify, a team was set up under the leadership of Ulf Edlund. The firm had been through a ten-year period of uncertainties and now had the opportunity to find a way out of its difficulties. Time was however counted, as the race for the regional aircraft market had just started and several competing firms had similar projects. In order to succeed in the project, Saab had to develop a new aircraft, secure a market share and produce the aircraft in due time.

After recalling the existing competences of Saab in civil aircraft development, this section describes the search for a partner and the financing of the project. Finally, the organisation of the partnership is presented.

3.1.   Existing Competences at Saab

Since the late 1940s, Saab had had several civil aircraft on the drawing board, but only the Saab 90 Scandia had reached the production stage. However, the development of the aircraft had started more than 33 years before. Not only had all engineers and other personnel who had worked on the project retired, but the blueprints of the aircraft were outdated. This implied that the competences had to be found somewhere else (Edlund, int., 1996; Mobärg, int., 1998).

During the early 1970s, Saab had had a small team of engineers working on a civil aircraft, called the Mula. This aircraft originally had four piston engines and was of a relatively simple design, with a non-pressurised cabin. It first evolved into a two-engine aircraft and then into a pressurised aircraft, the Saab 1084. By the end of 1978, the aircraft was fairly well defined. About 20 people had been working on the project, under Björn Andreasson's leadership. A further development of the Mula resulted in the Transporter, which was also aimed at the market of military freighters (Sehlberg, 1988, pp. 20 and 21).

Since the end of the Scandia project, Saab had been producing high performance military aircraft. The Viggen, whose development had started in 1963, was a delta-wing aircraft with canards on its nose increasing its manoeuvrability. Its jet engine allowed supersonic cruise and a top speed of Mach 2 at high altitude.[11] This aircraft was meant for very specialised types of missions, such as attacking specific targets. It was a technologically very advanced aircraft.

The new aircraft was to be a regional aircraft with a capacity of about 30 passengers in a pressurised cabin. It had to be powered by two turboprop engines and would have a maximum cruise speed of around 500 km/h. The technological competences and the scientific expertise necessary for the development of the new aircraft already existed in the firm, in particular regarding the integration of the various parts of the system or the questions of quality and safety. The design of the aircraft would necessarily be different from that of previous aircraft at Saab, but the experience of the firm in developing military aircraft turned out to be useful for the development of the civil aircraft (Edlund, int., 1996).

The aircraft testing procedures were also well understood at Saab even though questions of time schedule now had to be taken into account. If testing military aircraft can take many years, testing of a civil aircraft has to be short because the aircraft must come out on the market in time, otherwise the competition will take larger shares of the market.

Finally, in its previous development programmes, Saab had mainly dealt with FMV (Försvarets Materielverk, the Swedish state's procurement agency for military material) and the partnership now worked smoothly. FMV was shouldering a large share of the responsibility for the project as they were buying aircraft on behalf of the state. What was now missing for Saab was the knowledge of how to handle a commercial programme, as well as how to handle Luftfartsverket, the Swedish civil aviation administration. Moreover, Saab did not know how airlines used their aircraft, what the requirements of the pilots were and how they worked (Esping, int., 1998). In order to be able to develop the aircraft and launch it in the market in time, Saab had to find a partner.

3.2. Looking for a Partner

The need of a partner was realised early at Saab. This need, however, was not due to a lack of technological competences necessary for the development of that type of aircraft. The marketing of civil products represented a more difficult issue for the management. As a defence firm, Saab had no experience of the civil aircraft industry. The partner the firm was looking for, therefore, had to have strong commercial and marketing capabilities. As the main market for the new aircraft was to be focused in the United States, the obvious choice for Saab was to look for a partner there.

Before the project started, some contacts had been made with a few American firms for the development of the Transporter. Among others, Beech, Cessna and Fairchild-Swearingen had expressed interest in collaborating with Saab (Sehlberg, 1988, p. 21). As a matter of fact, as early as 1977, discussions were underway concerning the possibility of producing the Transporter (Flygbladet, 2541).

From March to June 1979 contacts resumed with aircraft manufacturers who were already established in the production of smaller civil aircraft. Fairchild-Swearingen was the most interested firm regarding cooperation with Saab (Sehlberg, 1988, p. 21).

Fairchild was a well-established diversified aircraft producer involved both in military and civil aircraft programmes (Flygbladet, 2690). The Swearingen firm, in San Antonio, Texas, had been bought by Fairchild in 1970, and was producing various versions of the civil aircraft Metro. In 1964, Fairchild had acquired the military aircraft manufacturer Republic, in New York State. Finally, since 1953, Fairchild had been producing the Fokker F27 under licence (Faherty, int., 1999). Consequently, Fairchild was well-established on the civil aircraft market.

Fairchild wanted to develop a stretched version of its existing aircraft at their Swearingen plant in San Antonio, Texas. The aircraft Metro was then developed from the Merlin into a 19 passenger aircraft, and even though the fuselage was too narrow, the Metro became a very popular regional aircraft with several hundred aircraft in service by 1979 (Faherty, p.c., 1999). Fairchild was now interested in the corporate aircraft market and wanted to increase its share on the regional aircraft market (Sebold, int., 1998).

The first official contacts at higher management level were taken at the Paris Air Show in June 1979. That meeting led to a letter of intent between the two partners and just after midsummer 1979, four Saab engineers, including Ulf Edlund, were sent to the Swearingen plant, in San Antonio, to define the specifications of the aircraft with their American counterparts (Edlund, int., 1996).

The negotiations between Saab and Fairchild went on during the Summer and Winter 1979. During this period, the two partners defined the specifications of the aircraft. Saab's engineers had in mind a developed version of the Transporter, while the Americans wanted something more modern and more suited to the American market. For example, as the Transporter was designed as a bush aircraft, it had a high wing. This was considered by Fairchild as something outdated and too bulky for the corporate and regional airline markets, which wanted 'an aircraft that looked like the big ones' (Sebold, int., 1998). This meant that the wing had to be low and that the shape of the aircraft had to be streamlined. Other technical issues were discussed during that negotiation phase, such as the pressure inside the cabin.

Saab's steering committee was clearly in favour of the venture, considering that the future of the Swedish aircraft industry was at stake. On 25 January 1980, the agreement between Fairchild and Saab was finally signed at the Grand Hotel in Stockholm, after a week of negotiations (Åsling, int., 1998, Krönmark, int., 1998; Gustafsson, int., 1998).

3.3.   Financing of the Project

Discussion about the support of the Swedish state to the civil aircraft project had started during 1978. According to Nils G. Åsling, then Minister of Industry, both the CEO of Saab-Scania, Sten Gustafsson, and the chairman of the board, Marcus Wallenberg, were arguing that such a venture represented a high risk for the firm, hence trying to get the involvement of the state into the project (Åsling, int., 1998).

During the Autumn of 1979, the project of the military aircraft JAS 39 Grippen was presented to the Swedish state. Using the concept of a multirole aircraft, the new aircraft would be half the size of the Saab 37 Viggen for half the price. New negotiations were then started on the procurement of a new military aircraft, but this time under the condition that Saab would develop a civil aircraft. A second condition for the development of this military aircraft was that the industry be asked to take more responsibility in the financing of the project (Flygbladet, 2689 extra bilaga; Åsling, int., 1998; Krönmark, int., 1998).

During 1979, a successful project at Saab might have influenced politicians in their decision. The missile Robot 15 was the first project procured on fixed cost that Saab was to develop. This means that the price of the missile and its development had been fixed from the beginning and had not drifted. Usually in military projects, the cost tended to drift and increase dramatically. The American manufacturer Douglas had almost won the bid for the missile to the Swedish Navy, but the same day the contract was to be signed between the navy and Douglas, the government changed hands, from a right-wing coalition to a liberal government, and thereby a new decision had to be taken for the missile, leaving room for new bids from other firms. The Robot 15 programme had worked smoothly. The initial cost of the missile, SEK535 million, was respected. On the basis of the success of the project, Sten Gustafsson was in a good position to deal with the government for the procurement of the JAS military aircraft and to introduce the question of the development of a civil aircraft (Gustafsson, int., 1998).

In January 1980, the firm received a loan of SEK350 million from the Swedish State to cover the risks of the development of the new civil aircraft, from a newly started industry fund.[12] The firm was under the obligation to pay royalties to the state in order to pay the loan back. The loan amounted to about a quarter of the planned total development cost of the aircraft (ASS, 1980).[13]

3.4. Organisation of the Work With Fairchild

Saab lacked a number of competences to develop a civil aircraft, especially in terms of marketing of civil products. The joint venture with Fairchild aimed at acquiring these competences within a short time in order for the firm to be among the first to propose a regional aircraft on the market, as other competitors had similar projects. Another reason for the partnership was the fact that the project needed the support of a well-established aircraft manufacturer such as Fairchild (ASF, 1980).

Fairchild had two organisations manufacturing aircraft: a civil one, Swearingen in San Antonio, Texas, and a military one, Republic Aviation with plants in Long Island, New York State and Hagerstown, Maryland. Despite being the military division of Fairchild, Republic Aviation in Long Island started the work with Saab. Both Republic and Saab had a fairly similar technological background (Esping, int., 1998; Sebold, int., 1998).

The ongoing military programme at Republic, the A10 Thunderbolt, was coming to an end, and the plant at Hagerstown, Maryland, had a bonding facility which was to be an asset for the production of the Saab 340. Moreover, since Swearingen had only been producing smaller civil aircraft, it did not have the large production facilities or the in-depth technical expertise of Republic. Republic was consequently the logical choice for Fairchild (Sebold, int., 1998).

The division of work was carefully prepared so that Saab could learn as much as possible from the joint venture. As a result, Saab took a larger share than Fairchild in the project as a whole. The division of labour and of cost was as follows (ASF, 1980):

- Phase A: Definition of the project, 50% Saab and 50% Fairchild;
- Phase B: Development, 75% Saab and 25% Fairchild;
- Phase C: Production, 50% Saab and 50% Fairchild;
- Phase D: Marketing, 50% Saab and 50% Fairchild.

The division of labour for the ground testing of the aircraft was 80% Saab and 20% Fairchild and the flight-testing was 95% Saab and 5% Fairchild.

A management team was created including managers from both firms. Here again, the division of labour was equal between Saab and Fairchild and supervised by a neutral person, Knut Hagrup, the retired president of Scandinavian Airline Systems, SAS. The group was made up of the highest deputies of both firms, with both CEOs and vice-CEOs, as well as technical directors. According to Olof Esping, project manager of the Saab 340, such a high level of management was unusual for the development of an aircraft. It resulted in the fact that all design and development decisions had to be accepted by the management team (Esping, int., 1998).

This form of management became rapidly problematic, however, as decisions were taken for too many details, both technical and financial. As a result, the vice-CEOs of the two firms became responsible for the preparation of the meetings of the management board during meetings held in London (Sebold, int., 1998; Faherty, int., 1999).

3.5.   The Birth of a New Aircraft

As the decision to diversify was taken by the management of Saab, the implementation required some specific actions. The first of these entailed the firm having to find a partner for the venture as it was recognised early on that Saab lacked commercial competences. This partner was found in the United States due to the fact that this was where the potential market for regional aircraft was the largest. A joint venture was set up with Fairchild, and the work was divided between the two firms in a way that would allow Saab to learn how to develop and market a civil aircraft.

Financing the development of a new civil aircraft was achieved with the support of the Swedish state, which lent a quarter of the total development cost of the aircraft. This was part of an agreement between the state and Saab concerning the development of a new military aircraft. Saab was given the opportunity to develop a new military aircraft on condition that a civil aircraft was also developed. Even though it can be argued that the management of the firm had already decided to diversify, it would not have done it without the financial support of the state.

The agreement between the Swedish state and Saab for financing the development of the aircraft was signed in January 1980. Since the start of the project in 1979, a great deal of work had been done at Saab and at Fairchild and a new aircraft was now taking shape.

4.   DEVELOPMENT AND CERTIFICATION OF THE SAAB 340

Saab had succeeded in finding a partner for a new civil aircraft programme and had negotiated financial support with the Swedish state in the form of a loan covering parts of the development risks. The agreement between Saab and Fairchild provided a clear definition of the responsibilities of the two firms. Saab was to develop the fuselage and assemble the aircraft in Linköping, while Fairchild had to take care of the wing and of both the fin and the horizontal stabiliser. Some common work was needed in order to arrive at a successful integration of the elements of the aircraft.

This section presents the main steps of the development process of the aircraft, especially in terms of technology management and in terms of management of an international joint venture. The whole process of the testing and the certification of the aircraft is described with regard to the interaction of the firm with the civil aviation authority.

4.1. Technologies and Management

4.1.1. Developing new technologies

Early in 1980 about 50 employees from Saab left Sweden for a one-year stay at the Fairchild plant in Long Island. As a matter of fact, the personnel of Fairchild in Long Island did not have much more experience than Saab's engineers in matters of civil aircraft. Republic had been bought by Fairchild in 1964 and was manufacturing almost only military aircraft, although they also manufactured some parts for Boeing (Rodling, int., 1998). As mentioned earlier, Swearingen, the civil division of Fairchild, did not have the production facility for the production of a new civil aircraft while Republic did.

Most of the technologies could be developed either at Saab or at Fairchild. The two major exceptions were the wing and the bonding technology. The National Aeronautic and Space Administration (NASA) in the United States had influenced the design of the wing. While the research carried out by NASA is publicly available to American firms, it takes a year to have the technology available to the rest of the industry. Accordingly, thanks to the joint venture, Saab was able to gain rapid access to a technology which otherwise would not have been directly available. Moreover, Saab profited from the bonding technology developed by Boeing and used by Fairchild in its contracts with Boeing and Lockheed (Mowery, 1987, p. 88).

This latter argument is contested by Sebold, business manager of Fairchild, according to whom Fairchild had already started developing bonding technologies in the 1960s. At that time, Fairchild was a subcontractor to the US aircraft manufacturer Grumman. The bonding technology was used for the Grumman F-14 Tomcat. Some subcontracts also existed with Boeing for the production of all movable surfaces for the Boeing 747. Fairchild had acquired a lot of experience in bonding technology. However, this experience was mainly on metal to honeycomb or metal to composite bonding technology.

In the Saab 340 project, the firm had to deal with a metal to metal bonding technology. If mastering the process was not problematic, the question of testing and hence certifying was more tricky. As a matter of fact, the first batches of wings could not be properly tested as no method had been developed to test bonded parts. Ultrasonic testing methods that were to ensure the structural integrity of the bonded skins were still in development and were not consistently reliable (Sebold, p.c., 1999). The quality of the bonds of the wing skins could not be demonstrated to the satisfaction of the certifying authorities. As a result, Fairchild manufactured more than one hundred wings with supporting riveting because quality control of the bonding procedure could not be fully established until then (Sebold, int., 1998; Hedblom, int., 1998; Hedblom, p. 7; Hedblom, p.c., 1999).[14]

Saab received support from Boeing. Engineers were hired on a consulting basis for troubleshooting. Regular 'design reviews' were organised where Boeing engineers could criticise the design of the Saab 340. Some consultants from SAS were also hired. Both Boeing and SAS engineers were in the firm only for a few months, since no formal agreement existed between Saab and Boeing or SAS (Esping, int., 1998).

4.1.2. The choice of the engine

From the very beginning of the programme, the aircraft was designed with propellers driven by turboprop. This was the natural choice of the time, shared by competitors in France, Canada and Brazil. The oil crisis of 1978 had been followed by a dramatic increase of the price of aircraft fuel. As a result, operating a regional aircraft powered by jet engines would not have been economical. Moreover, the polluting emissions of jet engines were higher than those of turboprops. In order to be competitive on the market of regional aircraft, the Saab 340 had to be equipped with turboprops (Gustafsson, int., 1999).

Choosing an appropriate engine has always been one of the major problems of the aircraft industry in general. Developing simultaneously a new aircraft and a new engine was regarded by many as a very risky strategy. Saab had already experienced the difficulty of finding a proper engine during the first phase in the development of the Mula (Eliasson, 1995, p. 76).

Volvo Flygmotor had been working with Saab and was now involved in the JAS industrial group. Volvo was undergoing similar changes to Saab and was trying to diversify from military engines to civil engines. With a loan of SEK140 million, the firm took a 6% share in the development of the American engine General Electric CF6-32. Additionally, the firm started the development of a turbofan engine for both civil and military applications with the American manufacturer Garrett. This joint development resulted in a memorandum of understanding on civil engine collaboration between the two firms (Flight International, 1980a). At the beginning of February 1980, Volvo and Garrett announced that they were going to cooperate on the development and the production of the engine of the Saab 340 (Flight International, 1980b).

In April 1980, three firms, Garrett, General Electric and Pratt and Wittney were invited to present the types of engine they thought would be appropriate for the Saab 340 (MMB, 1980b). Due to some lack of communication between Volvo Flygmotor and Saab, the Garrett-Volvo engine proposed turned out to be not powerful enough for the 340. The engine proposed by Pratt and Wittney was a completely new engine that had not been tested, and consequently would have been too risky for the firm. General Electric's engine, the CT-7, which was a more mature engine, even if it was a derivative of the T-700 engine originally developed for helicopters, was finally selected for the Saab 340 (Sehlberg, 1988, p. 25).

4.1.3. Tensions and weight problems

At Saab, the emergence of civil activity had created a new situation for the personnel. Opinions diverge as to whether tensions between the two divisions existed or not. According to Sten Gustafsson, then CEO of Saab, there was no particular difficulty as the core competence of the firm lay in assembling large systems. Whether these systems were civil or military did not matter (Gustafsson, int., 1999). However, other engineers remember some difficulties.

In 1979–80, the situation at Saab was the following: the Saab 37 Viggen was at the end of its production phase and a new military aircraft was on the drawing board. In the meantime, a civil aircraft had to be developed in a limited period of time. The project director, Ulf Edlund, had the theoretical opportunity of choosing engineers in the military division in order to accelerate the work (Gustafsson, int., 1998; Mobärg, int., 1998). Olof Esping, who had been the project director of the Saab 37 Viggen for 19 years, had a perfect knowledge of the competences of his staff and was jealously keeping the most competent staff for himself. Ulf Edlund did not have this global overview of the competences at Saab (Mobärg int., 1998).

In April 1981, the steering committee of the programme decided to replace Ulf Edlund with Olof Esping as project director of the Saab 340. As a matter of fact, complaints had come from Fairchild concerning the fact that the time schedule was delayed, and the weight of the aircraft had increased excessively. Something had to be done and quickly. The fact that the weight of the aircraft had increased can hardly be attributed to Ulf Edlund's management. Throughout the project, the weight of the aircraft was the most contentious problem discussed at almost every steering management committee meetings (MMB, 1981b; MMB, 1981i).[15] In March 1981, it was reported that the initial low weight of the aircraft was due to the fact that the design team had been over-optimistic, and that many problems had emerged. For example, the joint between the wing and the fuselage had to be redesigned, new items had to be installed and the weight of the supplier equipment kept growing (MMB, 1981b).

Whether this drift can be ascribed to an underinvestment in personnel at Saab is unclear. In August 1981, the steering committee held an extra-ordinary meeting to discuss the issue. Ed Uhl, CEO of Fairchild, expressed his concern over the ability of Saab to complete the work on the Saab 340 since the firm was also involved in a very large military programme. Sten Gustafsson, who considered that the nature of the two programmes was largely different, both in terms of financing and in terms of timing, rejected this concern. Sten Gustafsson also reassured the management of Fairchild about the fact that adequate people as well as financial and physical resources were being given to the project (MMB, 1981e). Olof Esping, however, considers that at the beginning the project might have suffered from a too modest financing. He recalls that when he took over Ulf Edlund's position, he also took with him both his planning engineer and weight engineer. In May 1981, a new evaluation of the time schedule and of the weight was presented by Olof Esping to the board of management and accepted (MMB, 1981c).

Another reason for the shift of project director might be found in the management style. In Ulf Edlund's words: 'I am not a slave-driver and this might be why I was put on the side when it was time to start the detailed design of the aircraft (Quoted from Sehlberg, 1988, p. 27, author's translation).' It seems that Olof Esping's style and drive was better adapted to the American management style, especially that of Ed Uhl, CEO of Fairchild (Mobärg, int., 1998; Gustafsson, int., 1998).

However, weight problems are by no means unusual in the development of a new aircraft. Fairchild encountered similar difficulties in the design of the nacelle of the engines and received similar criticism from Saab in Autumn 1981 (MMB, 1981h; MMB, 1981i).

4.1.4. Management differences between Saab and Fairchild

Though no major problems emerged during the development phase and the initial production phase, the relations were often tense. Two radically different management styles were confronting each other, especially during the steering committee meetings, i.e., the hierarchical American type of management and the decentralised Swedish one.

Two levels of relationships could be observed in the joint venture. One at the top level of management and the other at the engineer's level. At the top level, Ed Uhl, the CEO of Fairchild was a very domineering man and was trying to take over control of the joint venture (Esping, int., 1998; Sebold, int., 1998). Robert Sebold, from Fairchild, recalls that if the three top managers from Fairchild had had their whole career in the aircraft industry, only one of the three Saab's top managers had experience of it. Neither Saab's CEO, Sten Gustafsson, nor the vice-CEO, George Karnsund, had a background in the aerospace industry, only Tore Gullstrand, technical director, had the technical competences required for the discussions. As the discussions during the steering committees tended to be very technical, the Americans felt this to be a problem (Sebold, int., 1998).

This form of management was troublesome, and a new form of management was adopted in 1981, with the creation of the London group. Under the leadership of George Attridge from Fairchild and Georg Karnsund from Saab, the London group met every month in London to prepare the meetings of the management board (Sebold, int., 1998; Faherty, int., 1999).

The management style of Fairchild's CEO, Ed Uhl, was considered by many as authoritarian. According to Robert Sebold (p.c., 1999), from Fairchild, Ed Uhl was an unforgiving manager whose philosophy to subordinates was 'if you can't do the job, I'll get someone who can.' If things were not going at a proper pace, then whoever he felt was responsible for the problem had to be sacked. Swedish engineers and managers also mentioned this authoritative behaviour and its effect on the way American engineers worked.

Eric Sjöberg, flight test-pilot at Saab, felt that although the relations between the engineers were very good, American engineers were not used to arguing with their superiors. This, he recalled, was creating some difficulties as both the American and Swedish engineers could agree about a problem but when reporting to the committee, the American engineers would withdraw and let the Swedish engineers take the whole responsibility or ignore the problem (Sjöberg, int., 1998). This issue is, however, contradicted by Robert Sebold, Fairchild's business manager for the Saab 340 and secretary of the managing committee. According to Sebold, American engineers also reported problems, accepting criticism for the problems and taking the responsibility for their solutions (Sebold, p.c., 1999).

Both companies had their own pride and did not really want to share problems. At the engineering level, the relations were much easier. However, again, each firm wanted to solve these problems affecting its part of the joint venture without having to discuss with the other part (Sebold, int., 1998).

What Swedish managers saw as decentralisation was seen by the Americans as loose management. This tendency to let subordinates take too many decisions without the agreement of higher managers, was seen as problematic for the American managers as they felt that nobody was really in control of the development of the aircraft in Sweden, and, as a result, important milestones would be missed (Faherty, int., 1999; Faherty, p.c., 1999).

A surprise for the Americans was the fact that the Swedes had six weeks of holidays. That the whole plant closed down during July was even more of a shock! Basically, the Swedes worked eleven months per year. Ed Uhl is reported have said once in late June: 'We could deliver an aircraft now, but the Swedes are away! They are out on their boats in the archipelago, somewhere. All of them!' (quoted from Sehlberg, 1988, p. 36, author's translation). To solve this issue, at least during the production phase, Saab was accelerating its schedules to have an inventory for July so that Fairchild could continue to work as if nothing had happened (Sebold, int., 1998).

Because of the management structure, equally divided between the two firms, nobody was taking control over the development of the aircraft. Both firms were trying to conduct their own development without clearly indicating it to the other (Mobärg, int., 1998). Attridge argues that a contractual relationship at fixed cost would have simplified the project (Sehlberg, 1988, p. 36). This argument is also developed by Mowery who argues that delays in the development of the aircraft emerged because no partner had authority over the other and technical decisions were not decentralised at lower management levels (Mowery, 1987, p. 90). However, for Sten Gustafsson, CEO of Saab, this form of management was the only one that was acceptable for both firms, as none of the firms wanted to become the subcontractor of the other (Gustafsson, int., 1998).

Even though there were some tensions, the joint venture had two main advantages. The first was that through the competition spirit it brought, it fostered the technological creativity of the engineers who had to show that they had done their part. Secondly, it convinced the engineers at Saab that they were talented and this gave them renewed confidence after the worries of the 1970s (Gustafsson, int., 1998).

4.2. Testing and Certification

At an early stage of the programme, Saab started developing a strategy for the testing and certification of the aircraft. The regulations imposed by the civil aviation authorities for the certification of an aircraft were to prove a radically new aspect in the development of an aircraft at Saab. This section describes the testing and the certification of the Saab 340 and the types of knowledge that had to be developed during these two stages of the development.

4.2.1. Preparation of the testing

In 1979, Per Pelleberg was chief test pilot at Saab and became responsible for the flight testing of the Saab 340. A total of eight test pilots were assigned to the programme. Two of the test pilots were from Fairchild, though they only came in at a later stage in the test programme. The contract between Saab and Fairchild specified that Saab had 95% of the testing, and Fairchild was not willing to come back on this point (ASS, 1980; MMB, 1982d). As there was no particular distinction between the military and civil division for testing, the two divisions sharing the same offices, pilots could share their experience about the flights. Moreover all the test pilots had experience in the testing of military aircraft (Sjöberg, int., 1998).

Testing a military aircraft or a civil aircraft was considered as being very similar: the methods were the same, only the nature of the aircraft differed. The Saab 340 was a twin-turboprop, and had to be tested as such. The preparation of the testing went on in parallel with the development of the Saab 340.

A major worry among the testing team was that they all had their background as military test pilots. They knew what a military pilot expected from his aircraft, but now they had to learn about how to fly a civil aircraft and about the needs of the airlines. Per Pelleberg organised a programme for all test pilots, which included a civil aircraft pilot certificate and training on most of the routes of the domestic airline Swedair, a potential customer for the Saab 340. As test pilots needed to gain an experience of flying in twin-turboprop civil aircraft, Saab consequently acquired a Convair Metropolitan 580 as a complement to Fairchild's Merlin already used for training. Both aircraft acquainted the pilots with the behaviour of passenger aircraft.

Specific knowledge was also needed in testing methods for civil aircraft. Courses were given by an English university in Cranfield, which sent some teachers to Linköping. Finally, a simple simulator was built to train the pilots in the reactions of the Saab 340. It was a simple cockpit in wood, with the instrument panel, some adjustment systems, pedals and yokes. Computer software, developed alongside the aircraft, drove it (Sehlberg, 1988, p. 49). This was a good training tool, but it could not really follow the development of the aircraft. Each time new elements were developed on the aircraft, large parts of the programme had to be changed, which was time consuming. However, it gave a good approximation of the flight behaviour of the aircraft. Whenever a change was planned for the flight control system of the aircraft, the first test was done on the simulator.

During that preparation phase, the test pilots were interacting a great deal with the development engineers, especially for the design of the cockpit. It was an intimate contact between the development team and the test pilots (Sjöberg, int., 1998).

Particular attention was given to the cockpit because the Saab 340 was the first civil aircraft to be equipped with a so-called glass-cockpit instead of separate instruments. Thus there would not be separate instruments but a couple of displays selecting information for the pilots. The advantage of such a system was that it would be more flexible for the pilots and also more reliable. The avionics manufacturer Collins provided the screens and helped in the installation of the system.

4.2.2. Testing a new aircraft

The preparation of the testing programme had started as early as the beginning of 1980. About five months before the first flight, testing as such could start. These tests essentially began after the roll-out of the aircraft, on 27 October 1982. They consisted of testing the engines, the various systems, such as the hydraulics or the electric systems, the taxiing, the brakes and the nose-wheel steering.

The first flight took place on 25 January 1983. The flight had been practised on the aircraft Merlin and consisted in taking off from Saab's airfield in Linköping, gently feeling the aircraft's behaviour and landing (MMB, 1983a). The whole test was done with the landing gear lowered, following the advice of Jack Waddell, the former programme manager of the Boeing 747 and chief flight test pilot of Boeing. The first flight showed some problems with the aircraft. It could not follow a straight path but drifted, forcing the pilot to correct it. Moreover, the rudder was over-dimensioned and the warning system kept warning about problems that did not exist. A total of four aircraft were used for the tests:

1. stability and control, as well as engines;
2. performance and engines;
3. systems and avionics;
4. testing of the extreme conditions in which the aircraft can fly, i.e., minimum landing and take-off distance with maximal load, maximal speed for landing, minimal speed for take-off.

During the tests, the aircraft was packed with measuring instruments, providing engineers with measurements from sensors installed in the aircraft. Telemetry enabled them to measure the behaviour of the aircraft in real time and to continuously inform the test engineers about the condition of the aircraft (Sjöberg, int., 1998).

Four people were on board the aircraft, i.e., two test pilots and two engineers to control the measuring instruments. When the aircraft landed, the test pilots wrote a report and the data from the measuring instruments were analysed. Some special equipment was installed in the aircraft in case of emergency. In order to complete the testing of the Saab 340 in time, some engineers from other firms, with some experience in these areas, were brought in Saab. For example, engineers from Boeing or Sikorsky, another American firm, came for some time for consulting missions. They were asked to look at the certification programme in 1980–1981, and investigated the so-called flight readiness. This kind of exchange was common and both parts benefited from the deal. When these engineers came in, Saab profited from their specialities. In the meantime, these engineers learned about what Saab was developing (Mobärg, int., 1998).

4.2.3. The type certification
The certification of an aircraft is a compulsory step in its development, since it specifies the details of the technical, safety and handling characteristics to which an aircraft must comply. However, it does not specify how the aircraft

should be built to reach the requirements of the specifications. The only consideration of the civil aviation authority is to ensure that the aircraft meets the safety requirements (Hedblom, int., 1998). The authority should basically have no commercial concern but has of course to apply realistic requirements and accept deviations or exceptions when they are acceptable on technical grounds from a safety point of view (Hedblom, p.c., 1999). The production facilities, in which aircraft are manufactured, have also to be certified.

Without being certified, a new aircraft does not have the authorisation to carry passengers and hence cannot be sold. At the beginning of the 1980s, an aircraft had to undergo a type certification in the country where the aircraft was designed and manufactured. Other countries, in which the aircraft would then be purchased, would either carry out their own type certification according to their national rules, or would in some cases perform a limited validation or even straightforwardly accept the basic certification. This process was time-consuming and expensive to manufacturers. Since the beginning of the 1970s the civil aviation authorities of a number of European countries together with AECMA (Association Européenne des Constructeurs de Matériaux Aérospaciaux – European Aerospace Industry Association) had worked together to overcome this problem through the development of Joint Airworthiness Requirements, JAR. The first priority was certification requirements for large aircraft, JAR-25, in order to facilitate future joint ventures in European aircraft development. The JAR-25 was based on the American certification requirement FAR 25, but there were in the beginning many deviations.

Reaching an agreement between the various European authorities and the industry had been a painful affair. Eventually, in 1979, the first complete issue of the JAR-25 was ready. A number of points, the so-called national variants, were still required by some national authorities, but the core of the type certification requirements were common (Kennedy, 1979; Nordström, int., 1998; Hedblom int., 1998; Nordström, p.c., 1999).

By the end of 1979, Lars-Erik Nordström, then flight-safety director at Luftfartsverket, the Swedish Civil Aviation Authority, was asked by Saab to find a way to certify the Saab 340. The challenge for the authority was that Saab wanted to have a type certification of the aircraft for both the European and the American market. Since the certification of the Scandia in the late 1940s, Luftfartsverket had been mainly concerned with the validation of aircraft for Swedish airlines and the certification of a few smaller aircraft. The knowledge of the authority was thus basically limited to the import evaluation of foreign aircraft (Hedblom, p.c., 1999). Saab in the meantime had no experience at all regarding type-certification processes (Nordström, int., 1998; Hedblom, int., 1998).

In essence, the Swedish Civil Aviation Authority had to carry out basic type certifications for both JAR-25 (including national variants) and FAR 25 and to arrange simultaneous processes through which national validations by the other authorities concerned would take place in parallel with, and not in sequence with, the basic certification. This had not been done before and no established procedure existed on the European side. However, the JAA (Joint Aviation Authorities having established the JAR-25) accepted the Saab 340 as being a project of reasonable size for which a joint validation procedure could be developed. Lars-Erik Nordström, who had the management responsibility for the basic Swedish certifications for JAR-25 and FAR 25, was asked by the JAA to develop and manage the joint validation procedure in parallel with the basic certifications (Nordström, p.c., 1999).

This was solved by establishing a Joint Validation Committee (JVC), to which the national authorities of the JAA appointed senior certification specialists. This involved Belgium, Denmark, Finland, France, Germany, The Netherlands, Norway, Sweden, Switzerland and The United Kingdom. JVC members were continually being informed about all aspects and findings of the basic certification process carried out under Ingmar Hedblom, certification director. The JVC met regularly under the chairmanship of Nordström to discuss and resolve critical issues and to ensure that the specific views of all authorities were taken into account in the basic certification (Nordström, p.c., 1999).

The basic certifications were carried out by a number of expert teams under Ingmar Hedblom. To strengthen the Swedish CAA staff with additional competence and capacity, a number of specialists were provided on a consultancy basis by the authorities of France, Germany, the Netherlands and the United Kingdom. Apart from giving valuable contribution to the basic certification, this also provided the authorities concerned with deeper insight in the process and therefore with additional confidence. This, in turn, facilitated their later validation or national certification.

Concerning the US certification, there was a bilateral airworthiness agreement in force between Sweden and the United States to the effect that a certification in one of the two states was to be recognised by the other state, provided it was certified that all the requirements of the other state had been complied with. In this case the Swedish certification had to show compliance with FAR 25 and the associated advisory, guiding and policy documents provided by the FAA. As with the European authorities the certification team worked in close contact with FAA staff, who also made some additional evaluations to confirm certain findings. The basic engine certification was a separate issue for which the FAA was responsible, as was the British CAA responsible for propeller certification.

Through these sets of arrangements it was possible for the Swedish CAA to issue its type certificate for the Saab 340 on 31 May 1984. Four weeks later, after a final meeting with the Joint Validation Committee, the validation documents of all JVC participants were handed over to Saab. At the same ceremony the US type certificate was handed over by the FAA (Mobärg, int., 1998; Nordström, int., 1998; Nordström, p.c., 1999).

As certification specifies in detail how an aircraft must be built and how it must fly, it implies a great deal of cooperation between the development team and the civil aviation authority. Every detail of the construction as well as the behaviour of the aircraft as a whole has to be approved by the authority. This approach implied a new way of working at Saab. The regulations had first to be learnt, analysed and interpreted by the development team. Moreover, the test pilots did not know about the rules of the JAR-25 and therefore had also to study them (Sjöberg, int., 1998).

4.3.   A New Aircraft Takes Off

The process of developing a new civil aircraft involved two complementary kinds of activity. First, Saab developed the product in cooperation with Fairchild. In parallel with this cooperation, intense work had to be done with civil aviation authorities in order to certify the aircraft.

Despite some difficulties during the cooperation between Saab and Fairchild, the two firms succeeded in developing the aircraft. In order to certify the aircraft, Saab had to undergo a completely new way of working with a new kind of partner. It is worth mentioning that fortunately for Saab, the cooperation between the European civil aviation authorities had finally led to the JAR-25. Saab came at the right time with the Saab 340. If the development of the aircraft had started a couple of years earlier, the certification process would have been very long and costly as the aircraft would have had to be certified in each of the respective countries. This parameter was to a large extent unknown to Saab and Fairchild before the project started. The competence and the entrepreneurship of the civil authority was very important for the success of the project.

5. CONCLUSIONS

The history of diversification from military to civil aircraft at Saab is complex. Because of the intensity of the relations between Saab and the Swedish state, it turned out to be very difficult for the firm to diversify successfully in areas not in line with Swedish industrial and defence policies. The influence of the Swedish state appears to have been of great importance in the strategic choices of the company. When the Swedish Air Force needed military aircraft, it was problematic for Saab to diversify. However, when the government realised the need to keep the Swedish aircraft industry alive, the diversification of the firm could go ahead. It can be seen that the institutional environment in which the firm is embedded was blocking every attempt to diversify in the first place, because on the one hand it did not provide any incentive for diversification, and on the other hand it simply forbade diversification. Later on, institutions provided incentives for the firm to diversify.

From the managerial point of view, the incentives for diversification did not exist, as the state was a stable customer. Orders were coming in regularly and payments were being made in advance. As long as these relations continued, the firm did not have to diversify. Moreover, the main attempt to diversify at the end of the 1940s had been stopped by the state. However, when instability made itself felt at the beginning of the 1970s, the management had to try to define new orientations for the firm and analyse what the competences of the firm were and how they could be reused.

The move towards diversification was then triggered by both the state and the reaction of the management to changes in their environments. As a matter of fact, diversification followed the institutional changes in Sweden, stemming from the uncertainties of the military budget during the 1970s.

The development of a new aircraft at Saab could be achieved by using government support and by setting up a joint venture with Fairchild. The government provided financial support in the form of a loan covering parts of the development risks. Fairchild provided a marketing organisation and the knowledge of how Saab had to work in order to be competitive on the civil aircraft market. The specific time pressure that civil activities implied was a new variable for Saab, used to negotiating with the Swedish military procurement agency FMV.

Eventually, the certification agency Luftfartsverket turned out to be decisive for the success of the project. Even though it is an obligation for Luftfartsverket to certify aircraft, the application of the JAR-25 was by no means a compulsory point. The entrepreneurship of the authority at this point was also decisive for the success of the project.

In the implementation of the diversification, the management of the firm had to define what type of competences were lacking and to find ways and means to acquire them within a relatively short period of time. The state provided financial support following the request from the firm. Again, the relations between the firm and the civil aviation authority were very important factors in the success of the project.

When Saab started working on the Saab 340, the ambition was to obtain 35% of the market for small regional aircraft. This goal was reached, and aircraft were sold in Europe, Asia and the United States. However, this success was short-lived. In the 1980s, when the aircraft was first produced, the market was just emerging and planes were being sold. In 1991, the firm launched a stretched version of the Saab 340, the Saab 2000. However, the Saab 2000 did not succeed in asserting itself on the regional aircraft market. The competition from regional jets increased while the Swedish government did not subsidise the civil activity of Saab, as other governments do to support their aerospace industry. As a result, in 1998, the management of the firm finally decided to stop the production of both the Saab 340 and the Saab 2000. The production of these two aircraft stopped in May 1999.

Table 5.1: Chronology of the Main Events Before and After the Diversification of Saab

Year	Events
1945	Start of the production of the Safir
1946	Start of the production the Scandia
1961	Draft of a civil version of the 105
1963	Start of the Viggen programme
1968	Draft of the Mula (Transporter)
1971	Saab enters the consortium Europlane Limited
1972	No new advanced military aircraft will be procured by the government.
1973	The project Europlane is abandoned
1975	Development of the A20
1976	Development of the B3LA
1977	The A20 is dropped as there is no budget for two military aircraft; Saab gets its first contracts with civil manufacturers
1978	Aircraft Industry Committee (Flygindustri Kommittén); First discussions between Saab and the government for the financing of a civil aircraft; Deregulation of the American airline market
1979	The B3LA is dropped as the parliament does not vote on its budget; Beginning of the Saab 340 programme; Beginning of the JAS programme; First negotiations between Saab and Fairchild
1980	JAS consortium accepted by parliament; Loan to Saab for the Saab 340; Agreement between Saab and Fairchild signed; Exchange of engineers between Saab and Fairchild
1982	Roll-out of the Saab 340
1983	Maiden flight of the Saab 340
1984	Certification of the Saab 340

NOTES

1. Glenn Curtiss was a pioneer in designing airplanes and engines at the turn of the nineteenth century.
2. In this chapter, Saab refers to the aircraft division of the larger industrial group Saab-Scania.
3. The aircraft was originaly referred to as the Saab-Fairchild 340 or SF 340 until Fairchild withdrew from the venture in 1985.
4. Twelve aircraft were sold under licence to Finland and produced by the Finish firm Valmet; 52 were exported to Denmark and the last 24 went to Austria as second-hand aircraft. Other exported aircraft are the Saab 105XT (40 aircraft exported to Austria) and the Saab 91 Safir.
5. This chapter deals with diversification at Saab from military to civil aircraft. For a description of the ventures of Saab in other industries during the 1970s and 1980s, read Feldman (1999a).
6. A very important diversification of the firm was in automotive production. This diversification followed studies done by the firm about the kind of civil product that could be developed from Saab's existing competences. The first car was on the roads in 1947 (Andersson, 1989, p. 35).
7. See Saabs Annual Reports (1970, p. 13; 1974, p. 13; 1975, p. 15; 1976, p. 36; 1977, p. 39 and 1978, p. 16).
8. The British aircraft industry came back into Airbus in September 1978. The firm British Aircraft Corporation was merged with Hawker Siddeley resulting in a new firm called British Aerospace.
9. High wing refers to the position of the wing relative to the fuselage. Aircraft with a high wing are more suitable for landing and taking-off from rudimentary airfields.
10. According to Köhler (1984, p. 7), the reason for this decision was the release of international tensions. But according to Krönmark (interview, 1998), the reason was instead to be found in the internal tensions of the Social Democratic Party, stemming from ideological conflicts following the Vietnam war. For some party members, the aircraft industry was a symbol that had to be suppressed.
11. Twice the speed of sound, or about 2,300 km/h at sea level.
12. The industry fund was started by the Swedish government in 1980. The aim of the fund was to finance the development of advanced technological projects and thereby support the high-tech industries.
13. In 2000, it had not been completely repaid and will not be repaid as the production of civil aircraft stopped in May 1999.
14. The reason why bonding two parts is better than riveting is that each rivet is in a hole in the structure of the aircraft inducing stress concentrations in the material adjacent to the centre of the hole. Cracks may occur as a result of metal fatigue over extended periods of usage. Moreover there is a weight advantage in using bonding.
15. Weight is a problem in almost every aircraft programme.

6. The First Indigenous Korean Aircraft: The Case of the Daewoo KTX-1 'Woong-Bee'

> *You'll be bothered from time to time by storms, fog, snow. When you are, think of these who went through it before you, and say to yourself, 'What they could do, I can do.'*
>
> Antoine de Saint Exupéry, 'Wind, Sand, and Stars', 1939.

In the many-faceted aerospace industry, one of the most striking features is that all the established airframe manufacturers, be they large like Boeing or small like Saab, started their history during the few decades following the turn of the century. Late-comers in the industry have had to face enormous difficulties in establishing themselves, especially in catching-up economies such as that of the Republic of South Korea.[1] This chapter will describe the development of the first indigenous Korean aircraft at Daewoo Heavy Industries. In order to give a clearer understanding of the chain of events that led Daewoo Heavy Industries to embark upon the KTX-1 programme, the present chapter will start by showing how the Korean aerospace industry as a whole developed. The interactions between the firms must be highlighted, especially with regard to the particular spirit of competition among the large Korean industrial conglomerates, i.e., the chaebols. These interactions must also be set against the context of the Korean political system.

This chapter distinguishes three phases in the development of the Korean aerospace industry, as identified during the research. One must bear in mind this development in order to understand why Daewoo Heavy Industries chose to diversify.

The phases identified here are to some extent characteristic of catching-up economies striving to enter the aerospace industry. In successive order, they are as follows:

1. a phase of licence manufacturing of airframes;
2. a phase of commercial contracting of aerospace parts for established firms; and
3. a final phase in which an indigenous product is developed.

Although it has been argued that the second phase in the newly industrialised countries is one of co-development with established aerospace firms (Kim, 1998, p. 340), evidence from the present study shows that a phase of commercial contracting occurs before co-development. Leaving one particular phase to enter the following one depends on the previous accumulation of knowledge but also on the level of trust achieved with the rest of the established aerospace industry worldwide. These phases, as will be seen in this chapter, can overlap.

The firms are described here as diversifying in their systems of innovation. This implies that understanding why Daewoo Heavy Industries diversified into the aerospace industry as well as the development of an aircraft requires looking at the relations the firm has developed with the other firms in Korea. It also requires looking at the nature of the relations between the Korean government and the firms. Hence, the reasons for diversification can be both internal and external to the firm, resulting at the same time from the firm management's decision and the government's will to create an aerospace industry.

The same reasoning applies regarding the implementation of the strategy. As the firm diversifies, knowledge, in terms of technologies, but also in terms of financing, management, market and institutions, has to be acquired. While diversifying, Daewoo Heavy Industries had to invest in its own internal development, and at the same time had to seek instructive cooperation with other firms and organisations. In actual fact, one central government organisation, the Agency for Defence Development, initiated the KTX-1 programme and answered for the basic design of the aircraft.

Before taking a deeper look into this case, a general outline of the political and industrial context of Korea is in order. Section 1 of this chapter will hence be devoted to some considerations on the Korean political history and expound the relations between the industry and the government in that country. In Section 2, the political context is examined as well as the early development of the aerospace industry in Korea and the ensuing incentives or constraints for the firms. This section will focus on the role of the Korean state in the decision to set up the Korean aerospace industry. Section 3 will examine the entry of Daewoo Heavy Industries into the aerospace industry in parallel with the emergence of the second phase of the industry. Section 4 will consider the development of the first indigenous Korean aircraft at Daewoo Heavy Industries.

1. HISTORICAL AND INDUSTRIAL BACKGROUND

If the development of the Korean aerospace industry and the building of a first aircraft in Korea is to be understood, a few important facts have to be borne in mind. Asian countries have only in recent years emerged as strong economic actors in the world economy. Furthermore, there is relatively little known in the western world about their political history. The first part of this section will, therefore, present the political events that have some bearing on our subject. The relations between the Korean state and the firms will later be discussed as much as they are relevant to the development of the aerospace industry.[2]

1.1. Korean Political History in a Nutshell

The armistice of Panmunjom in July 1953 put an end to the Korea War; three years of devastating war between North and South Korea. The armistice led to the creation of a demilitarised zone at the 38th parallel. A formal peace treaty was never signed between the two countries, however.[3] Following the war, President Rhee Seungman, in spite of the financial and organisational support of the United States, did not succeed in reconstructing South Korea and was deposed in 1960 by student demonstrations supported by the population in general. General Park Chung Hee grasped power by a military coup in 1961. No institutions had really been set up to spur economic growth and the Korean industry was still in the process of recovering from the war. With an iron hand, Park Chung Hee created institutions aiming at the development of heavy industries and promoted the development of large family businesses, the chaebols (Kim, 1997, p. 27). Banks were nationalised, giving the state control over allocation of resources, and export industries were backed up through state-subsidised loans.

Park Chung Hee was undoubtedly successful in fostering Korean economic growth. With an average growth rate of 9% per year after 1962, Korea rapidly left its position as one of the poorest countries in the world as early as 1961 (Lee, 1989, p. 187). In October 1972, he placed Korea under martial law, strengthening the power of his military regime, with the intention of reinforcing the internal security of the country, accelerating the reunification process between the two Koreas and taking the so-called Nixon doctrine into account (Keon, 1977, p. 149). The latter, enforced by the Nixon administration at the beginning of the 1970s, aimed at reducing the American presence overseas. This created fresh national security problems in Korea (Keon, 1977, p. 152).

Two major consequences of the martial law were the new focus of Park's industrial policy regarding the localisation of the defence industry as well as human rights violations. In 1972, after evaluation of the capacities of Korean private firms, the government required the participation of 24 firms in the building up of the defence industry. This number rose to 52 in 1976, when the US president, Carter, threatened to withdraw the American forces from Korea completely (Hwang, 1998, p. 14).[4]

The human rights issue gave rise to tensions between the United States and the Korean government. As a result, the US government decided to reduce its industrial support to Korea, giving the country a new incentive to accelerate its industrial catching-up. However, the defence industry was considered too large by the United States, which attempted to force the country to reduce its military expenditure during the 1980s (Kim, 1997, p. 52).

Park Chung Hee was assassinated in 1979. The relations between the United States and Korea were still conflictual but more due to the Korean economic policy than to human rights preoccupations. In terms of defence policy, however, the two countries had similar views. The United States had a strong military presence in Korea and were buttressing the Korean defence both financially and materially. This military presence created a dependency of the Korean forces upon American equipment. These two-way relations between the Americans and the Koreans ought to be kept in mind when analysing the development of the Korean aerospace industry, the reasons being twofold. On the one hand, for economic reasons, the United States were taking action against the successive Korean governments, and on the other hand, on account of the Korean 'cold war', the United States had to provide the Korean forces with equipment, or give access to military technologies.

1.2. The Chaebols and Their Relations to the Government

Chaebols can be defined as large diversified conglomerates usually controlled by the founder or his family. The relationships between chaebols and the state used to be very close, the state backing the firm financially and protecting its market. According to Whitley (1992), the chaebols were the main driving force behind the successful Korean economic growth through continuous diversification (Whitley, 1992, p. 42).

There are several explanations for the diversification dynamism of the chaebols. As the control of the chaebol was in the hands of the founder of the firm, creating subsidiaries was a means of giving positions to members of the family (Whitley, 1992, p. 45). In the meantime, diversifying was a way to avoid being dependent upon subcontractors that might be in competition with chaebols. This pattern of competition and striving to become larger than the competitor is also a distinctive feature of the chaebols. Instead of focusing on improving the quality of their production and on increasing their profits, chaebols tended to concentrate on internal growth and increasing their market share on the Korean market (Amsden, 1989, pp. 118 and 126; Whitley, 1992, p. 45).[5]

Amsden (1989) argues that another reason for diversification in Korea is to be found in the great diversity of managerial capabilities in chaebols. The management of the firm is seen as being particularly skilful at creating task forces to evaluate new fields, purchasing foreign assistance or designing new plants (Amsden, 1989, p. 128). As a matter of fact, the propensity to take risks was always high in chaebols. Diversification was also a way to internalise risks through vertical integration, although always with state support (Amsden, 1989, p. 67).

The role of the state in the diversification process is constant, be it through selecting the industries where diversification was desirable or through financing of the diversification itself. For example, one of the most striking 'methods' used by the Park government to induce diversification in firms was to arrest thirteen conglomerate managers for illegal accumulation of wealth and then to release them on the condition that they diversify their firms in compliance with the government's industrial programme (Kim, 1997, p. 25).

Through bank control, the state was in a position to enable firms to enter specific industries, targeted for their growth prospects, such as the heavy industries, the car industry or the electronic industry. According to Amsden (1989, p. 104), the average debt to equity ratio in manufacturing during the 1970s and the 1980s was greater than 300%. Thus, chaebols were highly dependent upon bank loans for financing their growth, and the state was in full control of investments, hence controlling the firm's development. Besides the credit rationing and control of the banking system, the government could use its control over licences and use of the tax system as tools to implement its industrial policy (Amsden, 1989, pp. 79 to 93).

The role of the government did not limit itself, however, to the bullying of the chaebols. Certain firms were selected to enter specific activities. When attempting to establish themselves, these firms received governmental support. In the process, the tools used for support were very similar to those used for coercion. Firms entering the industry benefited from low interest rate loans, market protection and tax reduction.

With regard to the aerospace industry in particular, the tensions during the 1970s resulted in the issuing of the Aircraft Industry Promotion Act by the government, which aimed at supporting the development of the aerospace industry for military purposes. Later, during the 1980s, the government shifted its objectives in terms of defence needs, under pressure of the United States. Nevertheless, the aerospace industry remained in the government's good books, this time on account of its economic and technological prospects. In 1987, the government issued the Aircraft Industry Development Promotion Act, thus completing the previous act dating back to the late 1970s. It aimed at promoting new programmes for the industry, such as multi-purpose satellites and commercial aircraft (E, int., 1999).

2.   THE DAWN OF THE KOREAN AEROSPACE INDUSTRY

The events of the 1960s and the sharpening of tensions between the US government and the Korean government, led by General Park Chung Hee, had triggered the Korean decision to develop a defence industry. The recently developed heavy industries were to take part in the production of military equipment and a new defence agency was created in 1969, the Agency for Defence Development (ADD).[6] The mandate of the Agency for Defence Development was to do research for the various forces of the Korean defence.[7] Although developing and producing new military equipment was often more expensive than purchasing it from other countries, the government was cornered as the United States were reducing their support. Moreover, acquiring competences in military technologies was seen as of paramount importance to the independence of the country (X, int., 1999). Research divisions were created within the Agency for Defence Development with specific orientations towards the Army, the Navy and the Republic of Korea Air Force (ROKAF). The Agency for Defence Development also became the procuring agency for the military forces in Korea.

The choice of a first project for the aerospace industry was severely limited by four inescapable facts. Firstly, because of the mountainous nature of the terrain in Korea, a helicopter was seen, at the outset, as the most suitable project. Secondly, a helicopter was cheaper to produce under licence than an airplane. Thirdly, the American export policy toward Korea entailed limitations as to the type of material that could be bought. The American firm Hughes was permitted to export the Hughes 500 (later MD-500) because it was a simple light helicopter. The government wanted to import F-4 military aircraft but was not allowed to (Q, int., 1999). Finally, a helicopter was easier to build than an aircraft. Besides, the most urgent need was for helicopters for the Korean Army (Ann, p.c., 1999). What the government now needed was a firm to produce the machine.

2.1. From Aircraft Overhaul to Licensed Production – Korean Airlines

The firm Korean Airlines was established by the Korean government in 1962 but was never a successful company.[8] Lack of capital and proper investments rapidly led the firm to a situation that could not be sustained very long. The government required the Hanjin chaebol, whose main activity was in the transportation business, to take over Korean Airlines in 1969. As a matter of fact, the losses of Korean Airlines and the amount of capital needed to rescue the firm were strong disincentives for such a takeover (Hwang, 1998, p. 4). However, Cho Choong Hoon, chairman of the Hanjin group, did not have much of a choice. The transportation empire he had built during the 1960s was mainly based on logistics operations for both US and Korean forces during the Vietnam War (Q, int. 1999). In other words, some of the previous operations of the chaebol could be condemned by the government and used as a means of pressure to convince the firm to take over Korean Airlines.

During the first half of the 1970s, Korean Airlines developed in terms of fleet and operating efficiency but also in terms of maintenance capability. The ability of the firm to maintain its own fleet was viewed by the government as a sign that Korean Airlines would be able to manufacture other types of airplanes. The reasoning of the government was that an overhaul, consisting of completely disassembling and reassembling a whole aircraft after inspection and repair, was very close to assembling a new aircraft under licence (Hwang, 1998, p. 6). The conclusion was that the only candidate for the assembly of aircraft or helicopters was Korean Airlines. No other firm would have been able or even wanted to compete, even if some, such as Samsung and Daewoo, had started to develop some competences in the field of precision machinery, which could later on be used in the industry (G, int., 1999; M, int., 1999; A, int., 1999).

In 1976, the government bought 220 Hughes 500 helicopters from the American manufacturer Hughes, 20 of which were designed for civil purposes. The helicopters were to be assembled by Korean Airlines (Q, int., 1999). In the same way as the acquisition of Korean Airlines in 1969, the firm was requested to comply with the government policy (Hwang, 1998, p. 9). As an incentive to work on the MD-500, the government was ready to purchase the helicopters at a higher price than their market value (H, int., 1999).

Because of its defence nature, the programme was entirely financed by the government. This involved all expenses in terms of personnel training, building of new facilities, and tooling. On this basis, Korean Airlines could make a reasonable profit, amounting to around 6 – 13% for each helicopter (Q, int., 1999). The first helicopter was produced in 1977, and production continued until 1985.

Despite the existing in-house competences, Korean Airlines did not have the capability to carry out the whole programme. As the helicopter was sold under licensed assembly, Hughes corporation was very active. During the first phase of the programme, assembly consisted mainly of the putting together of pre-assembled elements produced by Hughes. Later on, a small number of components were to be manufactured in Korea, and the level of complexity of the assembly gradually increased. Some mechanics and engineers of Korean Airlines were sent to the US to be trained by Hughes, subsequently bringing complementary knowledge to the 200 persons involved with the assembly and testing of the helicopters.[9] Other specific production technologies, such as sheet metal technology with tight tolerances and machining technologies, already existed in other Korean firms. Samsung Precision Industry did the overhaul of the engines, under the control of the US manufacturer Pratt and Whitney (Q, int., 1999; R, int., 1999).

The second programme was initiated in 1980, when the Republic of Korea Air Force[10] decided to replace some of its ageing military aircraft. The government bought 68 F-5 Freedom Fighters, under licence from the American firm Northrop. The aircraft was to be assembled by Korean Airlines. Up to 68% of the airframe was built locally, although this accounted for only 20% of the total production cost of the aircraft (Q, int., 1999; Ann, p.c., 1999). This imbalance would later prove to be detrimental to Korean Airlines when the allocation of another military aircraft programme was decided by the Korean government, that of the KFP, Korean Fighter Programme. The firm was then accused of not having profited enough by the technological spillovers of the programmes (B, int., 1999; X, int., 1999; I, int., 1999).

The MD-500 programme had not brought about any changes in the management of Korean Airlines. In 1980, however, the maintenance and the assembly divisions were separated. The reason for the separation was that the F-5 programme was much bigger and far more complex than that of the helicopter. The cost per unit of the MD-500 amounted to around US$350,000 while it reached around US$10,000,000 for the F-5. Similar to the MD500 programme, mechanics and engineers were trained in the United States, and the experience from the maintenance division of Korean Airlines was very useful. Finally, Samsung was required to produce the engines under licence (Q, int., 1999; X, int., 1999; I, int., 1999).

2.2. Licence Production of Engines at Samsung

An aero-engine manufacturer was needed for the licence production of both the MD-500 helicopter and the F-5 aircraft. The government selected the precision industry division of Samsung, on account of its experience in precision machinery, for the overhaul of the MD-500 engines in 1978. Subsequently, in 1980, the firm was entrusted with the production under licence of the F-5 engine. The precision industry division had been created in 1977 by the firm in order to comply with the requirements of the government for the development of a defence industry in Korea (Hwang, 1998, p. 14). The move into aero-engine manufacturing was strongly encouraged by the government, although the management team was reluctant to enter the defence industry. With the objective of convincing the firm to enter the aerospace industry, the defence division was authorised to diversify into commercial activities (Hwang, 1998, p. 16).

This was not the only incentive. For a Korean firm, government programmes also involved a number of special advantages: the government covered all expenses and guaranteed a market, tax benefits followed and the firms had the opportunity to negotiate low or zero interest rates on loans. In other words, if the project succeeded, then the firm had to pay back the loan, but if the project failed, the firm did not have to pay anything. Despite some reluctance on the part of Samsung management to diversify into aero-engines, the initial investments were to open up a new field for the firm. When the programme ended, however, the firm did not have the technological capabilities to produce engines for the market, let alone to build a new engine. As a result, after this first experience in the aero-engine business, the firm went through a period of sluggish activity, at least in this particular field (X, int., 1999).

2.3.   The Take-Off of the Industry?

Since the mid-1970s and the Park government's decision to acquire an aerospace industry, a first step had been taken by successfully inducing firms to enter the field. Government pressure combined with strong incentives to diversify had convinced both Korean Airlines and Samsung of the benefits to be reaped from entering the aerospace industry. Building on existing in-house competences and a protected market, the firms managed to learn about the less problematic aspect of the industry, namely, the assembly of an aircraft under licence from foreign manufacturers.

During this phase of industrial development, the firms involved had the opportunity to become acquainted with the sectoral environment of the aerospace industry and its institutions. Korean firms had also begun learning about the specific requirements of aerospace firms. In addition, they were able to learn about the technologies that would enable them to go a step further and obtain manufacturing contracts with foreign firms. That was to be the second phase in the development of the industry. Whereas the first phase had involved heavy state intervention, the second phase, now to be described in further detail, turned out to be instead based on fierce competition between the chaebols.

3.   COMMERCIAL CONTRACTS, THE EXPANSION OF THE INDUSTRY

The Northrop F-5 programme ended in 1986. By then, it had given Korean Airlines considerable time to enhance its competences in assembling military aircraft. At Samsung, however, the workload in engine manufacturing was not very heavy, leaving the firm the opportunity to return, for a time, to its original activities in precision machinery. The emerging Korean aircraft industry was now trying to assert itself as a subcontracting partner for large established aerospace companies.

As this chapter will show, despite the existing capabilities in both Korean Airlines and Samsung Aerospace, the first firm to obtain a manufacturing contract from a foreign aerospace firm was to be Daewoo Heavy Industries. With the emergence of a third organisation in the industry, together with new political orientations within the state, an era of competition between the firms began. The reluctance of the firms to enter the industry during the 1970s had disappeared; now the time was ripe for intense rivalry between the chaebols. This was to lead to the assignment of the Korean Fighter Programme to Samsung Aerospace against all odds.

This section describes the second phase in the development of the Korean aerospace industry. The first large offset programme is outlined as well as the development of the Korean fighter.[11] Finally, the first commercial contracts between Korean firms and established aerospace companies are given due attention.

3.1. The First Large Offset Programme of Daewoo Heavy Industries

During the 1970s, the Korean Air Force had informed the Ministry of National Defence as to its future needs, and evaluations of potential aircraft started. All the chaebols were aware of the long-term plan, which involved the purchase of military aircraft during the mid 1980s, as well as an ambitious programme leading eventually to the production of a Korean fighter with foreign technologies. The procurement procedure of defence equipment was opened to firms through the Ministry of Commerce and Industry (MOCI),[12] evaluating their industrial competences on behalf of the Ministry of National Defence (O, int., 1999).

In 1982, negotiations started between the American firm, General Dynamics, and the Ministry of National Defence. These negotiations led to a proposal from General Dynamics to sell F-16 military aircraft to the Korean Air Force through an offset programme involving Korean industry. The condition to be met was that a Korean firm possess the competences necessary to carry it out (O, int., 1999.).

Following the general procurement routine, MOCI selected four firms in heavy industry. These firms were Daewoo Heavy Industries, Korea Heavy Industries, Daedong Heavy Industries and Korean Airline. General Dynamics presented the content of the offset programme to the firms, but none of them had the know-how necessary for manufacturing aircraft components on a large scale. Besides, as for all aerospace programmes, the risks involved were high and the returns on investments uncertain. The outcome was that none of the firms except Daewoo submitted a bid to MOCI.

The decision by Daewoo Heavy Industries was motivated by some considerations the management had made as early as the beginning of the 1980s. The management was then looking for new areas of diversification for the firm. The firm had the financial means for diversification towards the aerospace industry, but no project existed. Nevertheless, that decision gave rise to controversies within the firm. High risks and low return on investments were not agreeable to the managers of the established divisions of Daewoo Heavy Industries, as profits from these divisions were to be used as guarantees to cover potential losses. Less than a third of the higher management in the firm favoured entering the aerospace industry, but orders had been given by the chairman, Kim Woo Choong, and they could not be disobeyed (O, int., 1999; D, int., 1999). The hierarchical structure of command in the Korean industry usually implied that the chairman of the firm always had the final word in strategic decisions. Generally speaking, the role of the chairman, founder of the chaebol, was decisive in all strategic decisions.[13]

Daewoo Heavy Industries was involved in the production of fork-lift trucks, machine tools, diesel engines, rolling stock and various military armoured vehicles. In other words, the firm had a strong background in mechanical production and assembly of precise machinery. In addition, the firm produced and used machine tools and lathes that could be used in the manufacturing of aircraft parts. The new materials to be used in the F-16 were mainly aluminium alloys and honeycomb panels. This implied that the firm had to learn how to manufacture these materials (O, int., 1999; Q, int., 1999).

On the basis of the competences of the firm and the decision of the chairman, a small task force of roughly 20 senior engineers was designated within Daewoo Heavy Industries to investigate the possibilities of the firm entering the aerospace industry. They inquired abroad, contacting existing firms in the aerospace industry. Following these inquiries and under the recommendation of the government, closer contacts were established with General Dynamics. In 1983, the survey team visited the US manufacturer three times in order to draft a proposal for the offset. When in 1984 the Korean Air Force bought a batch of F-16s, the offset programme was granted to Daewoo Heavy Industries. The offset programme included the production of the cockpit area of the F-16, the centre section of the fuselage and the ventral fins (O, int., 1999; Q, int., 1999).

In late 1984, a new manufacturing facility was built in Changwon. The plant was aimed at the production of the offsets and was over-dimensioned in order to allow the firm to expand in the production of parts for the aerospace industry. Moreover, the management of the firm also had plans to get the contract of the Korean Fighter Programme which should logically be granted to the most capable firm in the 'infant' industry. The pre-production of the parts was carried out in other facilities of Daewoo Heavy Industries while the new facility was being built. In mid-1985, the first parts were produced and the offset programme for General Dynamics ended two years later (O, int., 1999).

3.2. The Korean Fighter Programme – KFP

The long-term plan formulated by the Korean Air Force during the late 1970s contemplated the purchase of new military aircraft in the late 1980s. These aircraft, which were to be produced and assembled by Korean firms, were to replace the ageing F-4s and F-5s of the Korean Air Force. The programme was known as the Korean Fighter Programme (KFP). Several aircraft had been selected as possible candidates for the programme: the General Dynamics F-16, the McDonnell Douglas F-18 and the Northrop F-20. All the competing aircraft were American as the US military command in Korea required compatibility between the weapon systems of the Korean and US forces. The prime contractor of the programme was to be chosen by the government by late 1986.

After the crash of an F-20 during a demonstration for the Korean Air Force only the F-16 and F-18 remained in competition. The Korean Air Force wanted the F-18 for reasons concerning the performance of the aircraft and the fact that it was a twin-engine aircraft. The aircraft was finally selected as the prime candidate of the Korean Air Force in 1989. However, due to some political and financial considerations,[14] the F-16 was eventually chosen, despite the fact that it was a simpler aircraft (X, int., 1999; I, int., 1999).

Competition between the firms during the whole of the 1980s was fierce. In order to get the contract for the KFP, the chaebols started informal negotiations with the US manufacturers. This reduced the negotiation power of the Korean government to selecting the aircraft. The problem was that the US manufacturers could argue for their products on the basis of their existing relations with the Korean firms. It was, therefore, decided that the selection procedure would be reversed, with the selection of the prime contractor being effected before the selection of the aircraft (B, int., 1999).

Before an aircraft had been chosen, the firms were again asked by MOCI to bid for the programme and to demonstrate that their technological capabilities as well as financial status enabled them to produce the aircraft. The importance of this programme in economic terms and in terms of technology acquisition was much greater than for any previous programme. The total cost of the programme was estimated at US$5.2 billion (Flight International, 1998c). Another important point to bear in mind was the competitive character of the relations between the largest chaebols. As a tacit rule of conduct, competing chaebols systematically entered the industries in which other chaebols had started an activity (D, int., 1999).

This competitive spirit resulted in bids from Daewoo Heavy Industries, Korean Airlines and Samsung Aerospace.

3.2.1. The bidding firms

Daewoo Heavy Industries
Thanks to the experience acquired through the manufacturing of F-16 parts for the Korean Air Force, Daewoo Heavy Industries was in a good position to bid for the KFP. The offset programme was a success, as the firm had received new orders from General Dynamics. This time the orders were on a commercial basis and not dependent on any form of agreement between the Korean state and General Dynamics. The quality level of the manufactured parts was high and fully satisfactory for General Dynamics. In the event that the F-16 would be chosen as the KFP, the firm already knew the management methods of General Dynamics. Finally, the firm had a facility in Changwon that could be used for the KFP (O, int., 1999).

It has been argued that Daewoo Heavy Industries could not demonstrate superiority in terms of technological capability since their interest in the aerospace industry started at about the same time as the evaluation process. As a matter of fact, the investigation for the selection of the prime contractor of the KFP started in 1981, while the first products from the offset programme of the F-16 started being manufactured in 1984 and were ready only in 1985, a year only before the government decision (B, int., 1999).

Korean Airlines
The firm had a broad knowledge of the aerospace industry in general through its airline activity. The assembly of the MD-500 and later of the Northrop F-5, had given Korean Airlines a wide experience in the integration of military aircraft, even if its manufacturing capability was still minor and dependent on other firms. The position of the chairman of the firm was, however, unclear

as to Korean Airlines' desire to continue its activities as a producer, given the costs involved in such programmes and a certain reluctance to work for the defence industry. Despite this ambiguous position, the firm was confident that it would be granted the contract. According to some sources, the reason for this confidence was that there were rumours concerning a tacit agreement in the industry about the respective roles of the firms. Thus, Korean Airlines was to be the integrator of the aircraft while Samsung Aerospace was to be producer of the engines and Daewoo Heavy Industries the components, as was the case regarding the assembly of the helicopter MD-500 and the military aircraft F-5 (Q, int., 1999).

However, owing to the over-confidence of its chairman, Korean Airlines neglected to lobby the government while the two other firms did not. Korean Airlines' chairman had expressed the view that the firm did not want to make profits on military business but was willing to do its best for the government. This was seized upon by the competitors, who said that the management did not really want to carry out the programme (Q, int., 1999). In the battle to obtain the contract, the other firms presented two main arguments against Korean Airlines:

- the management was unwilling to continue in the aircraft manufacturing business because it was not their core business, which consisted in being an airline;
- the firm had not profited enough from the technology transfers in the previous programmes, as no new technologies had been developed (X, int., 1999; I, int., 1999; O, int., 1999; A, int., 1999).

Samsung Aerospace
Thanks to its previous involvement in the production of aero-engines for the F-5 and later for the F-16 with the Pratt and Whitney 400, Samsung Aerospace had accumulated a certain competence for the production of precision machinery. This implied competences in metal forming and precise foundry techniques for advanced materials. Moreover, the firm enjoyed a strong financial situation that would enable it to make the necessary investments in the programme, provided it became prime contractor of the KFP.

3.2.2. The selection process
MOCI started the evaluation process of the three competitors in early 1981, under the direction of the new president of Korea, Jun Doo Hwan. An

evaluation committee made up of researchers and civil servants was created. The committee had to take stock not only of competences existing within the firms, but also of the financial situation and the prospective technological diffusion of the new technologies (H, int., 1999; B, int., 1999). The latter aspect turned out to be most important, as a shift in policies regarding the aerospace industry was to occur in the 1980s. Whereas the 1970s were marked by a development of the aerospace industry for defence purposes, the 1980s and the 1990s testify to the interest in developing the industry for the sake of its technological spillovers, in the direction of the rest of the industry, as well as to enhance the technological capability of the nation (S, int. 1999; X, int. 1999). It follows that the evaluation committee examined the prospects for in-house technology development by the firms.

On the basis of the evaluations, one firm was to be selected as prime contractor for the KFP. The decision was to come late in 1986, in order not to interfere with impending presidential elections in 1987. Daewoo Heavy Industries was the firm that presented most assurances for a successful production of the KFP, closely followed by Samsung and Korean Airlines (O, int., 1999; Q, int., 1999; H, int., 1999). In other words, Daewoo Heavy Industries was in a position to demonstrate that, in terms of competences, technology, means of production, and financial situation, it had the edge over its competitors, as far as manufacturing the aircraft was concerned.

3.2.3. The decision

However, to the dismay of both Daewoo Heavy Industries and Korean Airlines, Samsung Aerospace was selected to become the prime contractor for the KFP. Yet, the evaluation committee had found Daewoo Heavy Industries better suited to carry out the job. What happened in October and November 1986 is something that is always mentioned with some embarrassment. It reveals another facet of Korean industry, namely the relations between top-level managers and politicians.

As it was rumoured that Daewoo Heavy Industries was to become prime contractor, a week before the decision was formally taken, new negotiations took place between the chairman of Samsung and the President of the Republic of Korea. These negotiations led to the decision to grant the contract to Samsung Aerospace (O, int., 1999; Q, int., 1999). The previous reluctance of the firm to enter the aerospace industry had vanished. Samsung's chairman, Lee Byung Chull, who kept an eye on the diversification path followed by Japanese firms and their entry into the aerospace industry, was now convinced that Samsung was called upon to be a strong organisation in the industry.[15] Somehow, he succeeded in convincing President Jun Doo Hwan to entrust Samsung Aerospace with the production of KFP (Q, int., 1999).

It is unclear to what extent the final negotiations between the President of Korea and the chairman of Samsung really biased the selection process. Although Daewoo Heavy Industries was found 'first' by the selection committee, it was by a very narrow margin. The committee only evaluated the firms and did not grant the contracts; that was the President's prerogative (B, int., 1999; H, int., 1999).

3.2.4. Implementation of the programme

In order to produce the KFP, Samsung Aerospace had to increase its production capacity and also to train engineers and managers for the integration of the aircraft. Some engineers were sent to the American firm Lockheed-Martin, for training purposes. In the United States, the trainees were taught how to manage a programme, how to assemble and integrate the system and to flight-test it. More specific training programmes, such as painting, systems engineering and weapon systems integration were also organised. The duration of the training depended on the skill level required of the workers (O, int., 1999).

Though Samsung Aerospace was the prime contractor of the KFP, partners were needed as subcontractors. A natural subcontractor was Daewoo Heavy Industries because of its experience in the production of parts for the F-16. However, after the announcement that Samsung Aerospace was to be the prime contractor for the KFP, Daewoo Heavy Industries decided not to have any involvement at all with that programme.

In the face of the refusal from Daewoo Heavy Industries to participate in the KFP, the MOCI had to step in and convince Daewoo to cooperate in the project. As seen before, the government had means to persuade the firm to enter into a programme. These included the possible reduction of market shares in specific sectors, tax increases on specific products or even the suppression of bank loans. However, none of these means were actually employed. The management of Daewoo Heavy Industries was nevertheless aware of the threats and complied only to avoid retaliation.

In reality, the help of Daewoo Heavy Industries was a necessary ingredient for the success of the programme. In 1989, Daewoo Heavy Industries decided to get involved as a subcontractor to Samsung Aerospace. This involvement began with special training programmes for Samsung Aerospace engineers at Daewoo Heavy Industries. The second aspect of Daewoo's involvement consisted in the production of parts for the KFP, using competences the firm had previously acquired during the offset programme for the F-16 (O, int., 1999).

3.3.   Commercial Contracts in the Civil Aircraft Industry

The ongoing discussions regarding the KFP revealed the unreliability of the military programmes. Since defence markets tend to fluctuate, the firms had to find some commercial contracts. This was a way to secure employment for mechanics and engineers in times of low activity in the military division (Q, int., 1999).

Using its existing networks with airframe manufacturers, Korean Airline was able, in April 1986, to sign an initial contract with Boeing for the production of the flap track fairing for the Boeing 747. This contract was different from an offset programme. The firm was now in a position to give evidence of its competences in commercial activities, demonstrating that it was competitive in price, quality and delivery time (Q, int., 1999).

A second large contract concerned the extended wing tips of the Boeing 737-200 in 1987. This was the first time that Boeing outsourced parts of wings. During 1986, six Boeing engineers had stayed at Korean Airlines to evaluate the capabilities of the firm. Their conclusions were that the firm had the competences to manufacture these parts (Q, int., 1999).

In late 1985, Daewoo Heavy Industries had already been contracted by the American firm Northrop to manufacture 48 stretched upper decks for the Boeing 747. At all events, this contract, together with the previous commercial contract with General Dynamics did not suffice to sustain the aerospace division of Daewoo Heavy Industries. Other programmes had to be found: one in the helicopter business and another in the development of a small trainer aircraft (O, int., 1999).

3.4.   Competition and Politics in the Korean Aerospace Industry

The second phase in the development of the Korean aerospace industry turned out to be more turbulent than the first phase. Three firms were now competing for contracts and market shares. Firms were now eager to be part of the industry. Whereas the first phase in the development of the industry entirely bore the mark of massive intervention of the government, the second phase was definitely coloured by the competitive spirit of the firms and of the state's new science and technology policy of the late 1980s.

For Daewoo Heavy Industries, this phase was marked by the disappointment of not being chosen as prime contractor for the KFP. Given the size of the Korean market, the contract for the KFP was particularly important. Even though Daewoo Heavy Industries could get contracts with international aerospace firms, these were bound to be limited. Getting a national contract entailed more prestige and greater economic advantages. On the credit side however, it must be said the period in question gave the firm the opportunity to extend its competences regarding manufacturing parts, both for the civil and the military aerospace industry. On the other hand, it also left the firm with unused production capacities for which substitutes had to be found.

During the initial development phase of the Korean aerospace industry, Daewoo Heavy Industries had not been involved in any project, except on a very small and almost insignificant scale, with the production of a few components for Korean Airlines during the licensed production of the MD-500 and of the F-5. The second development phase of the industry was more intense and dynamic for Daewoo Heavy Industries. The management's desire to be active in the industry had led the firm to bid for some first commercial contracts with established aerospace firms. At Daewoo Heavy Industries, the management's awareness concerning the forthcoming military programmes for the 1980s and the fact that the government was now planning to develop the industry, induced the expansion of the firm in the sector. Failing to obtain the contract for the KFP was a severe blow, but the management remained eager to continue the diversification. It was only in need of a project.

4. THE FIRST DEVELOPMENT PROGRAMME – THE KTX-1

The government's desire to spur the development of the aerospace industry was strengthened in 1987 with the issuing of the Aircraft Industry Development Promotion Act. This act supplemented the previous act dating back to the late 1970s. It aimed at promoting new programmes for the industry, such as multi-purpose satellites and a commercial aircraft. The act also implied enforcing the development of the industry (E, int., 1999). In the wake of the act, the Korean Aerospace Research Institute (KARI) was created in 1989 for the promotion of research for the civil aerospace industry. As such, it was to be a complement to the Agency for Defence Development.

Now that newcomers in the industry had shown to established firms worldwide that they had acquired considerable know-how, at least in terms of manufacturing technologies, fresh programmes were initiated, on government initiative, both for helicopters and aircraft. Smaller development programmes sprang up. For example, Daewoo started a programme for a light trainer on behalf of the Korean Air Force in 1988 and for a light Korean helicopter in 1989.

This section describes in detail the development of the light trainer KTX-1. It goes through the struggles of the Agency for Defence Development to produce the aircraft and through the efforts of Korean Airlines to support the agency. It then discusses the involvement of Daewoo Heavy Industries and shows how the firm managed to acquire competences for development purposes.

4.1. The Initiation of the Programme by the Agency for Defence Development and Korean Airlines

In the mid-1980s, a programme for a basic trainer was initiated by the Agency for Defence Development, after the Korean Air Force had expressed its need for a small two-seater training aircraft powered by a turboprop engine to the Ministry of National Defence. The Agency for Defence Development was allowed to start the conceptual design of the trainer on its allocated budget. Nobody at the agency had the basic competences in aeronautical engineering to complete the conceptual design. This implied that from the earliest stage of the design some support had to be found in the Korean aerospace industry.

The problem the Agency for Defence Development was dealing with was in fact a common problem in the industry. So far, work had been carried out in manufacturing technologies, but nothing had been done in development and design. Moreover, the Agency for Defence Development had a tight budget for the project as the Ministry of National Defence was not willing to invest in a project that was seen as too risky. Despite this, the agency had carte blanche to carry out its own programme. It would take several years to convince the government of the feasibility of the aircraft.

Since its first licence agreements with Northrop and Hughes, Korean Airline had built a R&D facility in Taejon and in Pusan. A total of 90 researchers were working mainly on developing the manufacturing capacity of the firm. The management of Korean Airlines had allocated a total budget of US$4 million to a team of engineers to develop a prototype of a simple single-engine aircraft. The basic aim of the project was to demonstrate the capabilities of the engineers of the firm and to improve the confidence of the engineers about their own competences. Only two prototypes of the aircraft, the Changong 91, were built, but no plans existed for manufacturing (Q, int., 1999).

Aware of the Changong 91 project, the Agency for Defence Development informed Korean Airlines about the KTX-1 project and asked the firm to participate in the conceptual design in 1986. The engineers of the research department of Korean Airlines worked on the basic design of the aircraft, which consisted essentially in defining the preliminary dimensions of the aircraft as well as making the first calculations of the loads (Q, int., 1999; O, int., 1999).

In 1988, President Ro Tae Woo's government alluded to a possible decision to develop a basic trainer. This would answer the dual needs of the government: on the one hand, to have a fully independent industry for all military products and, on the other hand, to develop new technologies in the country. Despite these intentions, the funding earmarked for aircraft development was minimal. The manufacturing of a prototype and the detailed designing of the aircraft, consisting in dimensioning its structure, could not be carried out at Korean Airlines in the absence of proper financing from the Agency for Defence Development. The refusal of Korean Airlines to finance the continuation of the programme and its withdrawal led the Agency for Defence Development to look for a new partner willing to fund the project (Q, int., 1999; O, int., 1999).

4.2. Daewoo Heavy Industries as a Development Partner

Since the loss of the contract for the KFP, Daewoo Heavy Industries had been looking for other projects to confirm its position in the industry. The ongoing helicopter project and the commercial programmes were too small. As a result, Daewoo Heavy Industries was quick to react when the Agency for Defence Development expressed their need of a partner for the development of the Korean Trainer (Q, int., 1999).

The Agency for Defence Development indicated to the state which firm was to be involved in the project, and Daewoo was selected for its recognised experience in the manufacturing of airframe parts, as Samsung Aerospace was now occupied with the KFP and Korean Airlines had pulled out of the programme (Q, int., 1999).

During 1988, the Agency for Defence Development and Daewoo Heavy Industries reached an agreement to start the first development stage of the trainer as a follow-up to the work previously done by Korean Airline and the Agency for Defence Development. The objective of these preliminary studies was to try to determine whether or not the project was feasible and what technologies were lacking in the firm and at the Agency for Defence Development. The ADD was to pursue the dimensioning of the aircraft, while Daewoo's task concentrated on the development of the structure and the manufacturing. Thus, there arose a division of labour and management between the two organisations. Lee Jae-Myung, from the Agency for Defence Development, became project manager for the development of the aircraft, while Ra Duck Joo, from Daewoo Heavy Industries, became project manager for the engineering of the aircraft (O, int., 1999; P, int., 1999; T, int., 1999).

The entry of Daewoo Heavy Industries in the KTX-1 project was again the source of controversies at Daewoo's higher management level. The reasons for the involvement of the firm in the project were not clear to most of the managers. It seems here that the higher management of the firm was desperate to achieve a stronger position in the industry. It is not clear whether the firm was aware of the emerging plans of the Ministry of National Defence concerning more advanced projects for military aircraft, such as the KTX-2 advanced jet trainer. The reluctance of the Ministry of National Defence to accept the KTX-1 is also surprising. It was not until late 1991 that the government started to finance the programme. This took place during the second stage in the development of the aircraft. The ambiguity of the Korean state with regard to the industry is disconcerting. On the one hand, the Act of 1987 clearly targeted the aerospace industry as an industry for the future of the nation, but on the other hand, the investments were never in step with this ambition.

4.3.   The Development of the KTX-1

In 1990, the government announced six localisation programmes in order to sort out the roles of the firms in the ongoing projects.[16] Korean Airlines was selected as prime contractor for the UH-60 helicopter and the F-5 avionics upgrade programmes. Samsung Aerospace was granted the prime contract for the KTX-2, as well as the F-4 upgrade programme. Daewoo Heavy Industries was designated prime contractor for the KTX-1 and for a light-helicopter programme (O, int., 1999; B, int. 1999).

During the first feasibility period of the KTX-1, from 1988 to 1990, the Agency for Defence Development and Daewoo Heavy Industries had extensively surveyed the technology capabilities of the firm and the Agency for Defence Development. Besides, the initial studies regarding the design of the aircraft had been carried out and some preliminary contacts had been made with consulting firms specialised in aerospace engineering. During the pre-study stage, about forty people, from both Daewoo Heavy Industries and the Agency for Defence Development, were involved (P, int., 1999; O, int., 1999).

The above-mentioned organisations understood early that they lacked a number of competences to carry out the programme. The conceptual design done by Korean Airlines had shown the technological and scientific limitations of the industry and led to a search for some external support. This was to lead to a short-lasting relationship with the Swiss firm Pilatus. In order to succeed in the development of the programme, it was decided that the firm needed to learn quickly about the design of a trainer. Three stages of development were sketched out from 1990 to 1992, from 1993 to 1996 and from 1997 to 1998. For each of these three development stages, the organisations would first design an aircraft, then manufacture and test it. In the following stage, the same development procedure would then be repeated, but be improved on by incorporating what had been learnt from the ealier process (P, int., 1999; O, int., 1999 and T, int., 1999).

The first stage of the development was to be explorative, building on what had been learnt from the first basic design of Korean Airlines. The Agency for Defence Development could now leave the specifications of the KTX-1 to Daewoo Heavy Industries, for the development of the structure of the aircraft and the manufacturing of a prototype.

4.3.1. The explorative stage of the development in cooperation with Pilatus

Since the mid-1980s, the Korean Air Force had informed the Ministry of National Defence about its needs for a first batch of 20 turboprop trainers. Only two aircraft manufacturers could be serious candidates for that market, namely the Swiss firm Pilatus and the Irish firm Short. Both firms had representatives in Korea. According to Korean sources, Pilatus was trying to sell the PC9 as a trainer for the Korean Air Force, and in 1988 proposed the production under licence of the aircraft by a Korean firm, guaranteeing a technology transfer (O, int., 1999; D, int., 1999; T, int., 1999). However, Pilatus argues that the firm was asked only in 1991 by the Ministry of National Defence to make an offer to the Korean Air Force (Pilatus, int., 1999). There was, however, no acute need for the Ministry of National Defence to procure the new aircraft, and negotiations started instead between Pilatus, the Agency for Defence Development and Daewoo to develop a Korean trainer (Q, int., 1999; O, int., 1999).

These initial negotiations led to exchanges of engineers between the firms, and some preliminary information was handed over by Pilatus to the Agency for Defence Development. However, the level of information of the documents was not very high, so nothing new could really be learned from them.[17] From 1989 to the end of 1991, Pilatus worked on a consulting basis for the Agency for Defence Development and Daewoo Heavy Industries. The preliminary designs that had been made by the organisations were handed over to Pilatus engineers, who reviewed and corrected them accordingly. Pilatus was fairly critical of the solutions proposed by the Agency for Defence Development and Daewoo Heavy Industries. A number of changes had to be made in order to have a proper aircraft. Pilatus was leader in the market of small trainers, a highly specialised niche. The Agency for Defence Development and Daewoo Heavy Industries were complete newcomers. However, the solutions proposed by Pilatus were very often rejected by the Korean organisations and, if not, they were usually transformed into something completely different.

Pilatus was accused by Korean sources of systematically proposing its own existing systems to the Agency for Defence Development and Daewoo. As a matter of fact, the Swiss firm already had satisfactory technological solutions to the problems encountered and did not see the necessity to develop the whole aircraft again (O, int., 1999; P, int., 1999; Y, int., 1999). For example, Pilatus wanted to use the wings of the PC9 on the KTX-1. This being accepted, would mean that the fuel system of the PC9 would have to be used also, as well as the control systems, and so forth. In other words, the Koreans felt that Pilatus was intent on selling its own technology and did not want to provide real technical support (P, int., 1999).

Despite the tensions between the organisations, the development of the aircraft continued. After the testing of a model in a wind tunnel in the United States, an aircraft with a concept similar in terms of dimensions but not in terms of internal structure to that of the Pilatus PC7 was manufactured. During the year of development, the jigs had also been designed, using previously acquired competences in manufacturing aircraft parts. The first stage of the development was then to be completed by testing the aircraft to ensure that further development would be realistic (P, int., 1999; O, int., 1999; Ra, p.c., 2000).

A whole testing procedure of the aircraft had to be designed, as nobody in Korea really knew how to test an aircraft fully. The various systems of the aircraft had first to be tested separately, then the aircraft as a whole would be ground tested, and finally flight tests would be conducted. Again, this was explorative work; the second stage of the development would finalise the method. In December 1991 the first aircraft flew. While this aircraft was being tested, another aircraft was being manufactured, encorporating the corrections from the first one (P, int., 1999; O, int., 1999).

One of the solutions proposed by Pilatus was accepted after the first tests. The preliminary concept of the KTX-1 was similar to that of the Pilatus PC7, and the aircraft had accordingly been equipped with a similar 550 SHP engine.[18] However, the KTX-1 turned out to be largely overweight, and in 1991, Pilatus proposed to equip it with the engine of the PC9. This was a major problem, as it would necessitate a number of structural changes on the aircraft. During the following stage of development, the PT6A-62 from Pratt and Whitney, that was developing 950 SHP, was therefore installed on the KTX-1 (Pilatus, int., 1999).

Pilatus had been providing information on the basis of its long experience. However, the Korean organisations were determined to develop an indigenous aircraft in Korea. In other words, the projects aimed at learning the technology and not at buying it. Thus, there was a clear divergence of interest between the organisations. The Koreans saw Pilatus as bent on selling its aircraft and technologies off the shelf, which was actually one of the goals of Pilatus. However, the Korean organisations wanted to learn about the development of an aircraft. Conversely, the desire of the Agency for Defence Development and Daewoo Heavy Industries to acquire the technologies was not understood by Pilatus, which considered their quest as useless and costly.

Continuing to work with Pilatus did not produce the indigenous technology envisioned by the Agency for Defence Development but, on the contrary, led to a Korean PC9. The contacts between the two firms ended in late 1991. According to Pilatus, when in December 1991 the Ministry of National Defence asked the Swiss company to make a proposal, the Agency for Defence Development and Daewoo Heavy Industries understood that they were no match and broke off relations (Pilatus, int., 1999).

The negotiations between Pilatus and the Ministry of National Defence lasted from early 1992 until May 1993, when Pilatus was granted a contract involving the purchase of 20 aircraft and the offset of all the PC9 technology. However, the Korean government broke the contract shortly after (Pilatus, int., 1999).

The disagreement with Pilatus did not signify the end of the programme. Now that the aircraft had flown, the firm felt more confident regarding its potential. Besides, the government could now see that the programme was realistic. This was important for Daewoo Heavy Industries and the Agency for Defence Development, as it meant that the programme could, henceforth, be financed by the state. The latter agreed to finance the continuation of the programme in late 1992. The last four years had been almost entirely supported by Daewoo in terms of costs which, at this stage, amounted to around US$10 million (Won13 billion).

Despite the crash of the first prototype during the flight-tests, the explorative stage in the development of the aircraft had shown that the Agency for Defence Development and Daewoo had the potential to develop the aircraft further.[19] The programme could now go on to the next phase.

4.3.2. Confirmation of the concept

Now that the government was financially backing the programme for the KTX-1, the second development stage of the aircraft could start. The government financed the whole of the next two stages with US$45 million, and US$28 million, respectively. The first stage had shown that the concept of the aircraft was good, and also indicated defects that had to be corrected by the design team. The change of engine, for example, implied a number of corrections to the structure of the aircraft.

The tests carried out on the aircraft had shown the feasibility of the programme but also its limitations. The fact that a new engine had to be installed simply complicated the whole process. Carrying out the second stage within a reasonable time span required the firm to seek additional expertise. A French consulting firm, GECI, was then asked to provide competences in the various areas where the in-house capabilities of Daewoo Heavy Industries and the Agency for Defence Development were not up to standard. Expertise was then provided in specific areas such as structural engineering, aerodynamics, flight mechanics and flight-testing.[20]

Two more prototypes were manufactured during that phase, and in November 1995, the KTX-1 took the name 'Woong-Bee' or 'great flight.' New flight tests took place with these new prototypes. A critical part of the flight tests lay in the ability to monitor the evolution of the flight parameters of the aircraft in real time. A telemetric system was developed accordingly by Daewoo Heavy Industries. This system enabled the test team on the ground to monitor the behaviour of the aircraft in real time (O, int., 1999).

Other firms began being involved in the production of components for the KTX-1. In November 1992, Daewoo Heavy Industries signed a contract with Kia Heavy Industries for the development of the landing gear with technologies from the British manufacturer Fairay (Lorne, 1996a, Chapter on

Kia). Samsung Aerospace was contracted to design the engine mount and the fuel system, and Korean Airlines was contracted to design the fuselage and the canopy (ITC, 1998, pp. 5 to 17; Lorne, 1996a, Chapter on Korean Air).

After four years of development and the manufacturing of two prototypes, the aircraft was ready to enter the third development stage in 1997.

4.3.3. Finalising the concept

The aim in the third development stage was to finalise the aircraft and define the configuration of the series production. So far, the first and the second stage had been concerned with the development of the aircraft. Now that the design was ready, a last prototype, more or less the model that was to enter production, was manufactured (O, int., 1999).

It is only at this stage that the Korean Air Force informed Daewoo about an existing procedure before flight-testing a new aircraft. Known as the FFRRT, or the First Flight Readiness Review Team, this procedure was meant to correct a number of defects and thus reduce the firm's risks before flying the first prototype. The FFRRT consisted of 15 people from the US Air Force with different areas of specialisation. They went through the whole aircraft and controlled all the systems. During the three weeks of the evaluation, everything was carefully checked. A report was then issued giving recommendations as to what had to be changed later on, as well as recommendations as to what had to be changed before the first flight. It is to be noted that the FFRRT is not a compulsory review of an aircraft. Using the competences of the FFRRT in the programme permitted the reduction of risks in order to ease the marketing of the aircraft to the Korean Air Force (O, int., 1999).

4.4. Marketing the Aircraft

Despite the fact that the government supported the programme financially, it was not clear before the end of 1998 whether the Korean Air Force would actually purchase the KTX-1. The idea of buying trainers from Pilatus was not abandoned by the Korean Air Force so easily. This created an uncertainty for the project managers of the KTX-1, as to whether the aircraft could be sold. From 1993 onwards, Lee Jaem Young and Ra Duck Joo, project managers for the KTX-1 at the Agency for Defence Development and at Daewoo Heavy Industries respectively, regularly visited the Ministry of National Defence in order to get the aircraft accepted. They had to convince the ministry that the aircraft was of a high standard and would answer to the needs of the Korean Air Force perfectly (O, int., 1999).

Convincing the ministry to buy the aircraft was one thing, but convincing the Korean Air Force, namely the user, was quite another matter. Constant negotiations took place and the programme managers tried to integrate the air force into it by using test pilots from the Korean Air Force to flight-test the KTX-1. In 1998, the Korean Air Force announced its decision to order 105 aircraft (an initial batch of 20, followed by 85), under the name KT-1, to replace its ageing Cessna T37 and T41 (O, int., 1999; Flight International, 1998a; Ra, p.c., 2000). With production starting in August 1999, this would keep Daewoo Heavy Industries busy until 2005 (Flight International, 1998b).

As the aircraft was a military aircraft it did not have to go through a certification process. Avoiding the difficulties of such a procedure was a relief for the firm. However, the consulting firm GECI suggested that Daewoo certify the aircraft according to the FAR 23 in Italy. The certification would imply the compliance of the aircraft with the US specifications for trainers and for aerobatics. The reason why the Italian authority was chosen for certification was due to the terms offered. Besides, the Italian certification authority (RAI) had a bilateral agreement with the US Federal Aviation Authority (FAA), allowing for a certification in the two countries.

4.5. The Will but Not the Means?

The KTX-1 was the first aircraft fully developed in Korea. Developing an aircraft, even a simpler model, proved far more difficult than anybody at the Agency for Defence Development or at Daewoo Heavy Industries would have ever thought. Owing to the fact that various in-house competences were lacking, an effort to acquire them through external support was indispensable. This could be achieved first through cooperation with Pilatus and, subsequently, with the help of the consulting firm GECI.

The development process of the aircraft shows the difficulties encountered by the two organisations carrying out the programme. Here the relative lack of interest from the government in supporting the programme must be stressed. At the same time, it is difficult to see why, right from the outset, the Agency for Defence Development and Daewoo Heavy Industries were allowed to start a programme without full government backing. This apparent contradiction in the Korean aerospace policy seemed to occur frequently: the will was there but not the means.

5. CONCLUSIONS

Ten years after the start of the programme, the Korean government finally purchased the KTX-1 for the Korean Air Force. Despite it being of a relatively simple construction, compared to the productions of the aerospace industry in general, the KTX-1 is a major achievement for Daewoo Heavy Industries and the Agency for Defence Development. Following a test done by the aerospace magazine 'Flight International', the aircraft was evaluated as a good trainer with a satisfactory manoeuvrability (Flight International, 1998b).

It remains that carrying the project through was a long and painful process. The reason for the diversification of Daewoo Heavy Industries springs on the one hand from the government's policy and on the other hand from the competitive spirit among the chaebols.

All through the 1970s, President Park's desire to develop an indigenous defence industry, combined with the necessity to defend the country against North Korea, had spurred the start of the aerospace industry. However, firms were reluctant to enter the industry because of the risks involved and because of their almost complete lack of competences. The dominant role of the state, using a 'stick and carrot' policy to carry out its decisions, must be underlined.

The second phase in the development of the industry was marked by a clear change of attitude on the part of the firms, with regard to the industry. This shift of interest can be accounted for by the fact that the programmes increased in volume (the KFP, for example, cost US$5.2 billion), all the while benefiting from powerful government incentives. The second main reason for that shift can be found in the competitive spirit between the firms. Whether it was the government's intention to exacerbate this spirit in order to get the utmost from the firms remains unproven. Be it as it may, this competitive spirit was an important factor in the expansion of the industry and in Daewoo's decision to enter it.

Korea's democratisation in the course of the 1980s did not radically alter the government's agenda. The aerospace industry was still a target industry but it was now because of its socio-economic prospects, and not anymore for its defence prospects. The industry would provide the country with new technologies and wealth creation.

During the three phases of the development of the Korean aerospace industry, i.e., licence assembly, commercial contracting and development of an indigenous aircraft, technologies gradually developed in firms. The first programmes of licence assembly gave the firms an opportunity to enter the industry through the 'back door' and show what they might be able to achieve. The effort to become commercial contractors was to increase the competences of the firm as well as finally prove to the rest of the world aerospace industry that Korean firms were reliable partners. The development of trust relations between firms in the aerospace industry is particularly important since in the end-product passenger lives are at stake.

Had it been designated as prime contractor for the KFP, Daewoo Heavy Industries would probably not have entered the KTX-1 programme at all. Although reasons for entry can always be found in the need for the firm to acquire new technologies to sustain its growth, a more trivial reason was that the firm had to be active in the aerospace industry, due to Samsung's existing involvement. As a matter of fact, Hyundai, one of the five largest chaebols of Korea, entered the industry in 1994 for precisely that reason (D, int., 1999).

The development of the aircraft was a painful experience for the Agency for Defence Development and Daewoo Heavy Industries. The laborious cooperation with Pilatus showed not only the difficulties of entry into the industry but also the enormous cultural gap between the Swiss and the Koreans. The cooperation with the French firm GECI was successful, because it was based on a purely contractual relationship in which GECI's interest was restricted to seeing to that the aircraft flew.

Although the KTX-1 was bought by the Korean Air Force, it is doubtful whether it is a success for Daewoo Heavy Industries. According to Pilatus, designing, developing and building a military trainer in this category is a very small niche. The technologies developed for such an aircraft cannot easily be applied to any other type of aircraft. This means that Daewoo Heavy Industries may have locked itself into a niche from which it will be difficult to escape. Transferring the technologies developed to another project will hardly be possible. The Korean Air Force has bought the aircraft, but will the KTX-1 sell in other countries? That is a different question.

During its 25 years of existence, the Korean aerospace industry has succeeded in surviving a number of difficulties. Firms involved and the government have both had to learn the rules of the aerospace industry world-wide. It appears, though, that the government, despite a strong and persevering commitment in favour of the industry, has never accepted shouldering the full responsibility for its financial support, contrary to what has been happening in other countries with a strong aerospace industry.

*Table 6.1: Chronology of the Main Events Before and After the
Diversification of Daewoo Heavy Industries*

Year	Events
1972	Building up of the Korean defence industry
1976	Contract of the MD500 to Korean Air
1977	Samsung Precision Industries Co. Ltd.
1980	Programme of the F-5 to Korean Air and Samsung
1981	Airframe part manufacturing by Samsung
1984	Daewoo launches its aerospace division and gets contract to supply parts of F-16 fuselage
1986	Pre-studies of the KTX-1 by Korean Air and Agency for Defence Development; Samsung is designed prime contractor of the KFP
1987	Aircraft Development Promotion Act
1988	Korean Air ends its participation in KTX-1; Daewoo enters the programme; Cooperation with Pilatus initiated
1989	Creation of the KARI by the state
1990	Daewoo is designated prime contractor of the KTX-1 by the state
1991	Maiden flight of KTX-1; Pilatus leaves the programme after tensions between organisations; GECI consulting
1992	End of the first development stage of the KTX-1; The state starts to support the programme financially
1993	Second stage of development of the KTX-1
1995	The KTX-1 takes the name 'Woong Bee'
1997	Pre-production stage and finalisation of the concept
1998	First contract to buy the KTX-1

NOTES

1. In this chapter, the Republic of South Korea is referred to as Korea.
2. This chapter deals with the development of the Korean aerospace industry and of an aircraft, the KTX-1. Readers interested by the Korean history or the firm–state relationships in Korea

can read: Keon (1977), Jones and Sakong (1980), Jacobs (1985), Amsden (1989), Whitley (1992), Hobday (1995) and Kim (1997).

3. Note that the situation has not changed since then. The two Koreas, have not reached any peace agreement and are officially still at war.
4. This decision was never carried out, however.
5. Note that this focus on the market share instead of on the profits of the firm has then changed. The Korean government insisted in its new industrial policy in 1998/99 that for the recovery of the Korean industry, chaebols should change their objectives and increase their profits.
6. The equivalent of the Agency for Defence Development in Sweden would be FOA, Försvaretsforsknings Anstalt.
7. Because the ADD is a defence agency, it was very difficult to get detailed information on its structure and activities.
8. The name of the firm Korean Airlines became Korean Air in 1984.
9. This strategy is usual in the industry to acquire competences.
10. The ROKAF is later referred to in the text as the Korean Air Force.
11. Offset programmes are current practice in the aerospace industry. As the term 'offset' implies, in compensation for the purchase of aircraft the local industry becomes subcontractor to the contracting firm.
12. The name of this ministry has been constantly changing during the past decades. Until the early 1990s the name was Ministry of Commerce and Industry (MOCI). In 1993 it was changed to the Ministry of Trade, Industry and Energy (MOTIE). In 1999 it changed again to the Ministry of Commerce, Industry and Energy (MOCIE). In this chapter I will use the name MOCI.
13. More details on the role of the founder of the chaebols in decision-making can be read in Kim and Kim (1989).
14. McDonnell Douglas, who wanted to sell the F-18, kept increasing the price of the aircraft, adding new avionics and new systems so that the procurement cost of the F-18 soared by 46% (Hwang, p.c., 1999).
15. It should be noticed that Lee Byung Chull was among the thirteen industry leaders arrested for illegal wealth accumulation by the Park regime (Amsden, 1989, p. 236).
16. By localisation is meant the production of military equipment by the local industry in Korea.
17. It is unclear how much Korean engineers were able to learn from this first cooperation.
18. Shaft Horse Power, a unity of measure of the power developed by the engine.
19. Note that the fact that the aircraft crashed is by no means problematic *per se*. Almost all development of a new aircraft involves crashes, even in the most advanced firms.
20. Because GECI is a consulting firm and their relations to the ADD were on a contractual basis, it was only possible to receive very limited information from the firm.

Part III

Analysis and Conclusions

7. Why Did the Firms Diversify?

> *What kind of man would live where there is no daring? I don't believe in taking foolish chances, but nothing can be accomplished without taking any chance at all.*
>
> Charles A. Lindbergh, at a news conference after his transatlantic flight.

The empirical chapters described in detail the process by which each of the firms initiated a diversification strategy and implemented it. In this chapter, the reasons for diversification in the firms are analysed in relation to the corresponding sections in the theoretical framework of Chapter 2. These analyses are done first for each case separately in order to provide the reader with an overview of the cases before comparing them along specific dimensions. The comparison aims at showing the similarities and discrepancies in the decision process within the firms as well as which institutions influenced this process and how. Finally, a last subsection takes up the elements of the theoretical framework which could not be validated by the empirical research.

1. ANALYTIC SUMMARY OF THE CASES

1.1. Dassault

The institutional context of the post-war period in France had a number of particularities, especially with regard to the industrial policy supporting the aircraft industry. Following the Second World War, the restructuring of the aircraft industry by the government aimed at first helping the state-owned firms out of their disastrous situations.

The production of aircraft was a role dedicated to state-owned firms, while private firms were allowed to develop and manufacture prototypes of both civil and military aircraft. However, because of the difficulties of the state-owned aircraft industry, private firms engaged rapidly in the production of their own aircraft.

Large civil airliners' programmes were granted to the state-owned firms, leaving no room for other large civil programmes. Private firms became in effect banned from the development of large civil aircraft since French state-owned firms dominated the French civil aircraft market, while the international market was dominated by US and British firms. Private firms could develop civil aircraft but since the market was utterly limited they mostly abstained from doing so. National institutions, in the form of laws and industrial policies, thus locked private firms out of the civil market as all opportunities were blocked (Chapter 4, Section 1).[1]

In a context where the state would not financially support the development of a civil aircraft by private firms, the strategy of Dassault was to maintain its competences in the transport aircraft industry – whether military or civil – through prototyping. Although the prototyping policy was oriented towards liaison military aircraft, the prototypes very closely resembled smaller civil transport aircraft. The main differences concerned the market and not the technologies. Despite the fact that there was no clear policy to invest in the civil aircraft industry, the constant attempts of the firm to design transport aircraft, as well as the vision of Marcel Dassault to return to the civil industry, show an attempt by the management of the firm to get around the institutional constraints of the time (Chapter 4, Section 2).[2]

At the beginning of the 1960s, Dassault started the development of a twinjet liaison aircraft, the Mystère 20 (Chapter 4, Section 4.1). Being constantly in contact with ministers and air-force officers, Marcel Dassault was able to understand the needs of the military market in France. Meanwhile, the relations between Marcel Dassault and the various CEOs of the state-owned firms also allowed him to evaluate the critical financial and social situation of these firms and hence understand the concerns of the state regarding their future (Chapter 4, Section 1).[3]

Because of his ability to understand the institutional environment of his firm, in terms of firm-government interactions, and his patience to wait for an opportunity, Marcel Dassault was able to turn the institutional obstacles to his advantage. This created a window of opportunity for a diversification into an industry in which the firm had been locked out.

In terms of market, the emergence of the business jet market was clearly advantageous for the firm. It was the opportunity that had been awaited so long (Chapter 4, Section 3.3). At the very beginning, the Mystère 20 was developed without the intention of producing a business jet. It was developed as a transport aircraft for military liaison. However, it rapidly became obvious that the aircraft would fit perfectly in the emerging business jet market.

The marketing division of the firm reinforced the possibilities for the aircraft to find a position in the new market, as it enabled the management of the firm to understand the emergence of this market more clearly. This division also promoted the firm in the United States, while the French civil aviation authority (SGAC) also supported the development of the Mystère 20 as a civil aircraft at the French government level. The opportunity of entering the business jet industry was made even more promising by the deal with Pan Am. The fact that this airline was looking for an aircraft and bought the Mystère 20, 40 aircraft and 120 options, allowed Dassault to make its commercial breakthrough (Chapter 4, Section 4.2).

Besides the numerous attempts of Dassault to design a transport aircraft, the state was committed to supporting the state-owned firms. Allowing the private firm, Dassault, to continue its development work on the Mystère 20 was thought of as a possibility to provide the state-owned firm Sud-Aviation with a manufacturing role for some components for the aircraft. The national aero-engine manufacturer, SNECMA, was also thought of as a partner in the production of engines for the new aircraft. There were therefore political and industrial reasons to support the entrance of Dassault into the new civil venture anyway and put an end to the informal division of labour that had emerged between state-owned and private firms (Chapter 4, Section 4.3).

As summarised in Table 7.1, the reasons for the diversification of Dassault are to be found at several levels. At the level of firms and organisations, the management of the firm did not plan a diversification, but the owner of the firm wanted one. Several prototypes of transport aircraft were designed and Marcel Dassault tried to sell them to the French government, waiting for the right opportunity to succeed in selling them. The civil aviation authority, SGAC, was early to see the possibilities Dassault had with regard to developing a civil aircraft and was therefore pushing the firm to do so. The SGAC was also supporting the firm at the state level.

At the state and market levels, the firm was hindered to diversify by the fact that the market for military transport aircraft was limited and the national institutional environment created by the state did not provide incentives for private firms to develop civil aircraft for the French market.

As the business market emerged in the United States and as the firm Pan Am decided to buy the Mystère 20, the situation changed dramatically. Dassault was able to take advantage of the new opportunity provided that the state agreed to support the venture. As state-owned firms could take advantage of the venture, this support was granted. The division of labour, as an institution which had emerged informally between state-owned and private firms was then changed.

Table 7.1: Factors Affecting the Diversification of Dassault

	Time period[4] 1950s and early 1960s	1963 (diversification)
Dassault	• No plans to diversify • Marcel Dassault wants to design a civil aircraft • Follow the needs of the state and lobbying • Wait for an opportunity	• Take advantage of the market opportunity
Other organisations	• SGAC pushes for diversification	• Pan Am needs a business jet
Market	• No market for military transport aircraft	• The emergence of the business jet industry
State	• Private firms cannot compete with the state-owned firms on same premises	• Need for the state to find activities for the state-owned firms

1.2.   Saab

The neutrality of Sweden led the country to develop its own military equipment. This created very close relations between the Swedish state and Swedish defence firms. The state was the main customer for military aircraft and was regularly procuring new military aircraft. As a result, except for the

Scandia, a civil passenger aircraft developed and produced at the end of the 1940s, most of the production at Saab had always been military aircraft, procured and bought by the Swedish procurement agency FMV. Therefore, the national institutional environment, in the form of the established relations between the state and Saab, did not provide the firm with any incentives to diversify since its one main public customer was willing to absorb practically all of its production (Chapter 5, Introduction).

During the 1970s, however, the situation at Saab became critical. The state was not willing to finance expensive new military aircraft, while Saab's export market was traditionally limited. Thus, the uncertainties and instabilities of the political and institutional environment of the firm were leading to a dramatic dead end. (Chapter 5, Section 2). As a matter of fact, export figures of Saab had always been very low, as the firm never managed to compete against other larger international firms.[5] Besides making new prototypes of fighter aircraft, the prototyping policy of the firm became more and more orientated towards military transport aircraft. Although these aircraft were planned for the military market, civil versions were thought of at an early stage (Chapter 5, Section 1).

In the meantime, the political confusion in Sweden about the defence industry led to uncertainties concerning the procurement by the state of new military aircraft. Hence, the state came to the conclusion that Saab had to diversify its activities and that this had to be done with government support. The state required the diversification of Saab in 1979 as a condition for the procurement of the new military aircraft JAS 39 Gripen. (Chapter 5, Section 2.2). A similar conclusion had emerged for the management of Saab. The firm had to relax the links it had with the Swedish state, and find new markets, thereby becoming independent (Chapter 5, Section 2.3).

Saab had long had a policy of prototyping transport aircraft and complemented it with a policy of subcontracting for larger aircraft manufacturers during the 1970s. This combined strategy aimed at establishing the firm as a serious partner in the international civil industry. As Saab was aware, successfully entering this new market would end the traditional relations with the state because the firm would have new commercial partners (Chapter 5, Section 2.3).

The emergence of the regional aircraft industry was the opportunity the firm needed to start the diversification. The impact of the US Airline Deregulation Act of 1978 on the American market was the main reason for the emergence of the new industry, since it enabled existing airlines to open new routes and new airlines to enter the market. This implied a need for small, high-performance aircraft in the United States. This opportunity was ideal for Saab, as the firm needed a reachable goal. Regional aircraft were in the reach of the capabilities of the firm, in terms both of technologies and investment (Chapter 5, Section 2.3.2).

Table 7.2 summarises why Saab diversified. At the firm level, Saab had reached a dead end at the end of the 1970s. The relations between the state and the firm implied that the firm had to take its destiny into its own hands. The same reasoning existed in the Swedish government. A new form of relations between the firm and the state had to develop. There would still be a need for military aircraft, but there were too many uncertainties about the future of the firm on the national Swedish market. The emergence of the regional aircraft industry was the opportunity that triggered the final decision to diversify and to identify the market into which the firm could enter. The fact that Fairchild was willing to enter the venture reduced the risks involved. The diversification of Saab was therefore a managerial decision constrained by the changing environment of the firm.

Table 7.2: Factors Affecting the Diversification of Saab

	Time period 1960s and 1970s	1978 (diversification)
Saab	• Wait for an opportunity • Constraints from the environment • Uncertainties about the future of the firm	• Take advantage of the market opportunity
Other organisations		• Fairchild
Market	• No market for military transport aircraft	• The emergence of the regional aircraft industry
State	• No new military aircraft procured	• Save the industry in Sweden

1.3. Daewoo

At the beginning of the 1970s, the development of the aerospace industry in Korea was triggered by the aspirations to military independence promoted by General Park Chung Hee, president of the country. At the beginning, firms were reluctant to enter this new industry. The government provided Korean Airlines, the national airline, and Samsung with incentives to become assemblers of aircraft and of aero-engines, respectively, for the Korean Air Force (Chapter 5, Section 1.2). During the 1980s, the Korean government targeted the aerospace industry as important because of its prospects in terms of technological spillovers to other sectors and for reasons of national prestige. The reluctance of the chaebols to enter the aerospace industry diminished, and the competitive spirit between the chaebols took over (Chapter 6, Section 2.3).[6]

Daewoo became interested in the aerospace industry at the beginning of the 1980s mainly because Samsung was acquiring market shares in a now prestigious industry (Chapter 6, Section 3). The good relations between the chairman of Samsung and the Korean President were to impede Daewoo's entrance into the industry. Officially, the government did not want too many organisations in the infant Korean aerospace industry. However, the friendship between top decision-makers is now considered a more important reason for keeping Daewoo out of the industry. Therefore, the state did not provide the firm with any particular incentive.

The national institutional environment of Daewoo, in term of traditional rules of conduct between decision-makers, did not provide opportunities for the firm to diversify, although the will existed within the ownership and top management of the firm during the 1980s. The industry was prestigious, and Samsung, the old rival, was strengthening its position with the support of the government. Daewoo had to either wait for an opportunity or try to create one of its own.

In the mid-1980s, Daewoo engaged in subcontracting for established American aerospace firms. The first manufacturing programme, producing parts for the fighter aircraft F-16, was to give the firm not only a foothold in the industry but also the right to claim a competence in the sector. This strategy was implemented in order to give the firm a chance to become the prime contractor of a much larger programme, the Korean Fighter Programme (KFP). The KFP was initiated by the Korean government to buy new fighter aircraft for the Korean Air Force. A Korean prime contractor was to be identified by the end of the 1980s. Against all odds, the programme was granted to Samsung. This setback disillusioned the management of Daewoo, but did not suppress the vision of the chairman, the founder of the firm, to develop aircraft. Therefore, during the late 1980s, the firm continued to build up its technological production capabilities, keeping an eye on any possible new state-supported aerospace projects (Chapter 6, Section 3.4).

The opportunity came in 1988 when Korean Airlines withdrew from a project that had been started by the Agency for Defence Development, the Korean Trainer eXperimental, KTX-1. As Samsung had its hands full with the Korean Fighter Programme, Daewoo became the prime contractor for this small mono turboprop trainer.

Table 7.3 summarises the findings. The Korean national institutional environment of the 1970s and 1980s and the small size of the Korean market did not provide possibilities for a diversification of Daewoo into aircraft development and production, despite the will of the top management of the firm. The fact that the major competitor had engaged in the industry at the beginning of the 1980s was a strong reason triggering the diversification. Moreover, the industry was identified as prestigious by the government and hence the chaebols had to participate. The traditional management style of Korean chaebols implied that besides dimensions as profit, the prestige of the conglomerate was also to be taken into account while formulating new strategies. During the late 1980s the Korean government had targeted the aerospace industry, and Samsung was involved as a manufacturer. Therefore, Daewoo felt compelled to diversify into the aerospace industry because of its prestige, despite the risks the venture would imply.

Table 7.3: Factors Affecting the Diversification of Daewoo

	Time period 1970s and 1980s	1988 (diversification)
Daewoo	• Enter a prestigious industry • Owner's will • Competitive spirit	• Take advantage of the market opportunity
Other organisations	• Samsung and the KFP	• ADD needs a partner
Market	• Narrow market in Korea	• Trainer for the ROKAF
State	• Targeted industry • Relations between the Korean President and a competitor	• Development of the first Korean aircraft

2. COMPARISON OF THE CASES – WHY DID THE FIRMS DIVERSIFY?

In this section, the three cases are compared to identify the reasons for the diversification. It is first observed that the firms were to varying degrees waiting for an opportunity to diversify, while they were impeded in doing so by an institutional lock-out shaped by their respective national institutional environments. The emergence of an opportunity loosened the institutional lock-out, allowing for diversification. It is then inferred that in all cases, the state could take advantage of the diversification. This section refers to the theoretical framework but does not attempt to appraise it. This will be done in Section 3 of this chapter.

2.1. Opportunities for Diversification in a Situation of Institutional Lock-out

The comparison of the three cases shows first that the predominant reason for the firms to diversify is to be found in how they assessed their respective national institutional environments. It is striking to see that in the three cases, some elements of the national institutional environment initially blocked any move of the firm in the direction of the new industry. In this situation of institutional lock-out, the firms were willing to diversify and expected an opportunity that would allow the strategy.

Dassault wanted to stamp its name on the civil aircraft industry but could not because of the industrial policy of the state, restricting the opportunities of private firms attempting to enter the civil aircraft industry.

At first, Saab had no incentives to diversify because the Swedish state absorbed most of the production. However, at the end of the 1970s, the firm needed to find a way out of the crisis in which it had ended up due to the cutbacks of military expenditures in Sweden.

Daewoo had to diversify in order to follow the competition between the chaebols but was stopped in its attempts during the early 1980s because of established relations between a competitor and the state.

Even if these basic reasons differ, they belong in every case to the national institutional environment of each firm. The three firms ended up in situations where their national institutional environments, or parts of them, did not allow for diversification, even though the possibility of selecting a diversification strategy had been envisioned at some point by the management of the firm.

174 *Industrial Diversification and Innovation*

Existing institutions, therefore, can constrain the strategy of the firm, while a transformation of the national institutional environment can trigger the strategy, as it opens up new opportunities for the firm. Institutions are seen here as either established patterns of behaviour governing the relations between firms, as in Korea, but also as rules created by industrial policies as in Sweden, France and Korea. These institutions were also part of the respective national systems of innovation, including the organisations of the industry, the organisation of the relations between the state and the firms and science and technology policies. Informal national institutions, as traditions, were also constraining the firms in their existing industrial activities.

2.2. Emergence of an Opportunity

The three firms were all waiting for an opportunity to diversify. In each case, the shift of activity and the investment of the firm in the new venture started soon after the emergence of the opportunity. As argued in Chapter 2, Section 2.1.3, the nature of the opportunity – whether technological or market related – can be a reason for diversification. In other words, the emergence of a new market is a reason for diversification *per se*.

In the French and the Swedish cases, the opportunity was the emergence of a new market, i.e., the business jet market and the regional aircraft market. Dassault would probably not have diversified if Pan Am had not shown an early interest in the Mystère 20, as the French state was not interested in this small aircraft. Dassault had some individuals actively working at the marketing division to try to understand the development of the new market. The top management of the firm also made efforts to convince the French state about the economic prospects of the Mystère 20, indicating the will of the firm to diversify. In order for the firm to diversify, however, some changes in the national institutional environment had to occur to allow the move into a civil industry.

A similar situation applied for Saab. However, the cuts in military expenditures of the 1970s added a new dimension. Although these cuts were by no means a surprise for the industry, they were so large that they threatened the very existence of the firm. As a result, it was clear from the mid 1970s onwards that the firm would have to diversify. Attempts to diversify into other industrial sectors, such as submarines or wind energy, had shown that despite the fact that the firm could find small niches for its competences, these would not sustain the firm as they were too small (Feldman, 1999a).

Therefore, a larger-scale diversification had to occur. The technical and financial capabilities of the firm allowed the development of a relatively small civil aircraft. A minor market existed for such an aircraft before the US Deregulation Act of 1978, but it would not have been sufficient for the firm to survive. The deregulation was the opportunity the firm had been waiting for. The main reason for the diversification can hence be found in the fact that the traditional market of Saab shrank due to the prevailing political turmoil in Sweden during the 1970s. This was a consequence of developments in the national institutional and political environments of the firm, as defined in the theoretical framework.

The Korean case differs as the opportunity was not the emergence of a new market but the withdrawal of Korean Airlines from the development of the KTX-1. Since Samsung was busy trying to start the production of the KFP, Daewoo finally gained the opportunity to develop an aircraft and became prime contractor of a military aircraft for the Korean government. A potential market existed with the Korean Air Force. For Daewoo, the political game between the state and the partners in the industry had previously not provided the firm with possibilities for diversification in the development of aircraft.

2.3. Advantages for the State

In the three cases, the state could take advantage of the diversification of the firms. In France, the state-owned firm Sud Aviation was running into difficulties as the airliner Caravelle was facing the severe competition from new US airliners. To avoid unemployment and social conflicts, new contracts had to be signed by French manufacturing firms. The contract between Dassault and Pan Am, as well as the fact that the state-owned aero-engine manufacturer SNECMA could produce the engines, was, therefore, fortunate for the state.[7]

In Sweden, the state was worried that the whole aerospace industry would disappear. This would mean new unemployment and social conflicts, as well as a loss of competences and of technological development potential for the nation. The diversification of Saab would instead save the industry and free the state from an uncomfortable situation.

It is less clear in the case of Daewoo that the state would benefit from the diversification of the firm. However, the state had made the development of the national aerospace industry a clear priority. By the end of the 1980s, the state was willing to let new firms enter the industry in order to increase the

competition between the firms. This competition could then trigger an
increase in the technological development of the country by way of the
technological spillovers of the aerospace industry into other industries.
Moreover, in terms of prestige, the KTX-1 was to be the first indigenously
developed Korean aircraft.

The industry chosen for this study has traditionally had close relations
with the state. The prestige of the industry and its spillovers to the rest of the
economy are reasons for these good relations. Another reason is the fact that
the cost of developing new aircraft is so high that there is a need for state
support to the industry. This last section confirms these relations.

Table 7.4: Comparison of the Reasons for Diversification in the Three Firms

	State	Market	The firm	Other organisations
Dassault	• Institutional lock-out • Advantage: employment	• Business jet industry	• Market opportunity	• Pan Am
Saab	• Institutional lock-out • Advantage: employment	• Regional aircraft industry	• Market opportunity	• Fairchild
Daewoo	• Institutional lock-out • Advantage: prestige of the nation	• Korean Air Force	• Opportunity with ADD	• ADD

Table 7.4 summarises the findings, showing why the firms diversified. The
firms were waiting for an opportunity in a situation of institutional lock-out,
while the emergence of an opportunity triggered the diversification. In two
cases the opportunity took the form of a new emerging market. In the Korean
case, the opportunity came with the withdrawal of Korean Airlines from a
programme and the need from the Agency for Defence Development (ADD)
to have an industrial partner.

3. APPRAISAL OF THE THEORETICAL FRAMEWORK

The previous sections have described the reasons for the diversification of the firms, relating these to the theoretical framework presented in Chapter 2, Section 2. New theoretical insights as to why firms diversify or do not diversify have been provided. A major reason for diversification in the three cases was the emergence of an opportunity, following a period of expectations during which the firms could not diversify because of a national institutional lock-out.

The following section discusses how the theoretical framework is reflected in the empirical work as well as the new findings of this research. These aspects of the discussion are then summarised in Tables 7.5 and 7.6. Section 3.1 considers the elements of theory which deal with the reasons for diversification internal to the firm and within the control of the management of the firm, while section 3.2 discusses the aspects of the diversification which are external to the firm, or beyond the control of the management. It should be noted that the reasons for diversification can be related.

3.1. Internal Reasons for the Diversification

The first argument as to why firms diversify was developed by Penrose (1959) in the *Theory of the Growth of the Firm*. According to the theory, the diversification of the firm is caused either by the need for expansion of a growing firm or as a strategy for growth. A growing firm has to find fields of expansion, either through increasing its existing activities or through diversification. Conversely, a firm can sustain or accelerate its growth by engaging in diversification in a sector which grows faster than the one in which the firm is already engaged (Chapter 2, Section 2.1.1).

These arguments will now be discussed in the light of the three cases. Although the growth of the firms has not been studied specifically, the diversification of the firms has a connection to their growth. Dassault was a successful firm in the business of military aircraft. It had established itself as the main supplier of military aircraft for the French Air Force and was successfully selling military aircraft to foreign countries (Carlier and Berger, 1996b, pp. 32 and 80). However, the limitations of the military market implied that the firm had to find ways to continue its growth in a new market. The diversification of Dassault can hence be seen as a consequence of its own success on the military market.

In the case of Saab, the firm saw its market declining and therefore had to enter a market with better growth potential. The very survival of the firm was at stake and the diversification can then be regarded as a way to sustain the growth of the firm or at least to avoid its demise.

In Korea, although ideas of prestige and competition were important, prospects of growth in the aerospace industry were also taken into account by the management of the firm to some limited extent. Diversification as a strategy for growth is hence found as reflected in the three cases.

The theory of economies of scope as developed by Teece (1982) infers that the firm might find it interesting to diversify into a new activity because the production cost of making the two products can be lower than the production cost of making each product separately (Teece, 1982; Chapter 2, Section 2.1.2). In none of the cases, however, was the manufacturing of the new product thought of as allowing economies of scope in production *per se*. The production of both military and civil aircraft could be reorganised in the long term to take advantage of the existing commonalities in the production of the products, but this was merely happening after the diversification.

The theory of economies of scope did not stop at the production level but was extended to other activities of the firm, in particular, the research and development activity as well as the know-how existing within the firm. The three cases, then, exhibit economies of scope as expected by the theory. The firms were able to use their existing research and development capabilities to start the programme, without stepping on the existing programmes.

In relation to the theory of economies of scope, it was argued that the diversification of the firm could be explained by the need for the firm to find a use for its unused resources. Unused resources could be found in the managerial or in the technological and production resources of the firm (Chapter 2, Section 2.1.3). Neither management nor technologies or production facilities could be found as being unused in the cases.

The last reason for diversification as discussed in the theoretical framework of Chapter 2, concerned the emergence of opportunities in terms of market or technologies (Chapter 2, Section 2.1.4). As Section 2 of this chapter has previously shown, the firms diversified in order to take advantage of opportunities. Besides, there existed a vision within the management of the firms that diversification had to take place in one very specific field. The opportunity would hence trigger the shift. Although the opportunities emerged outside the firms, it was the management perception of its environment, combined with its existing will of diversification, that allowed the strategy to begin.

Table 7.5: Relevance of the Theoretical Framework for the Analysis of the Cases (Internal Perspective)

Theory		Dassault	Saab	Daewoo
Growth of the firm		relevant	relevant	relevant
Economies of scope		relevant	relevant	relevant
Use of unused resources	Management	not relevant	not relevant	not relevant
	Technologies	not relevant	not relevant	not relevant
Taking advantage of new opportunities	Technologies	relevant	relevant	not relevant
	Market	very relevant	very relevant	relevant
Other reason found by the research: vision of the owner or the management		very relevant	relevant	very relevant

Table 7.5 summarises the findings and the relevance of each theoretical argument for the analysis of the cases. This work recognises that the theory of the growth of the firm, as well as the theory of economies of scope, can enlighten some aspects of the cases. The theory of the use of the unused resources of the firm, however, does not help to interpret the cases. The study acknowledges the role of opportunities in the choice of the strategy as a major reason for the diversification. Finally, in each of the three firms there existed an ambition by either the owner or the top management of the firms to diversify in the new industry.

3.2. External Constraints on, or Incentives for, the Management of the Firm

As argued in the introduction to this chapter and in the theoretical chapter, the reasons for diversification can be found both within the firm and outside the firm. This opens up two alternatives. In the first, the management of the firm could take the decision to diversify by analysing the market and the existing resources it controls. However, the previous section has shown that although managerial dimensions, as described in the theoretical framework, could be part of the explanation for the diversification, they were not enough to clearly establish why the firm had diversified.

A second alternative was that the diversification can be triggered by reasons that are beyond the control of the management of the firm. The transformation of the market and of the institutional environment of the firm constrain or incite the management of the firm to initiate a diversification. Diversification, it was argued, could be a strategy aiming at reducing the exposure of the firm to risks not necessarily related to the market or institutions (Chapter 2, Section 2.2.1). Secondly, the transformation of the institutional environment itself could trigger a diversification, as the firm, embedded in its system of innovation, passively embarked in the transformation (Chapter 2, Section 2.2.2). Conversely, the firm could take an active part in the transformation of its environment. Finally, it was argued that through technology procurement, either public or private, the firm could be prompted to diversify (Chapter 2, Section 2.2.3). These different alternatives do not exclude each other.

With regard to risk spreading, Saab was the only firm facing a threatening situation because of the absence of a market. This triggered the diversification of the firm. If risk-spreading was a reason for the diversification of Saab, it is more difficult to see that Dassault and Daewoo were exposed to risks. Neither the market nor the technologies of Dassault were threatened. Daewoo was already a very diversified firm and saw its diversification into the aerospace industry more as a question of prestige than a response to a threat.[8] Other explanatory factors to establish why the firms diversified must therefore be found in addition to the argument that firms diversify in order to reduce their exposure to risks.

A second reason for diversification was developed in the theoretical framework as a strategy whereby the firm passively participates in the transformation of the national system of innovation (Chapter 2, Section 2.2.2). The theoretical framework argued that because of the embeddedness of the firm in the system, the transformations of the system would constrain the firm to diversify. In both of the cases of Saab and Daewoo, this argument is proven to be relevant. In the case of Saab the institutions in question did not concern the national system of innovation but, rather, the political system. However, it can be argued that the two systems are interdependent, especially with regard to science and technology policy, and that transformation of one provokes transformations of the other.[9]

The transformation of the Swedish society during the 1970s led to reduced military expenditures and hence to Saab's diversification. Smaller-scale diversification in other industries was not enough to sustain the firm, and Saab, therefore, had to enter the manufacturing of civil aircraft. In the Korean case, the science and technology policy of the state, aiming at a rapid growth in the country, created incentives for Daewoo to move into new technologies and industries. In the case of Dassault it was the development of a new international market and the entrepreneurship of Pan Am which triggered the diversification.

The third dimension of the theoretical framework was concerned with an active perspective of the diversification (Chapter 2, Section 2.2.2). The firm was considered as proactive in trying to transform the institutional environment, taking advantage of the right institutions at the right time, participating in their transformation, and creating its own opportunities. Both Dassault and Daewoo attempted to create opportunities by addressing their respective national institutional environments. Dassault was not successful on the national market but scored on the international one. However, its success was due to the efforts carried out in France to allow the production of civil aircraft. Daewoo was also willing to diversify and struggled both at the government level and in the aerospace industry to get into a development programme.

The last element of the theoretical framework was concerned with the role of private and public technology procurement in the diversification of firms (Chapter 2, Section 2.2.3). In the case of Dassault, the contract with Pan Am was very similar to a private technology procurement in which a private firm asked another firm to develop and produce a product which did not exist on the market. This was however not the case for Saab and Daewoo. Saab had taken advantage of previous procurement contracts with the Swedish government, but these concerned military programmes.

Daewoo is a particular case because the firm developed a military aircraft without the support of the Korean government. This situation is very unusual in the military aerospace industry. The usual procedure for firms embarking on the development of military aircraft is always to bid for government programmes and to obtain a contract with the government before starting the production. The fact that Daewoo did not wait for the Korean government to procure the KTX-1 reflects the inexperience of the firm regarding the procurement procedures in the aerospace industry in general.

Table 7.6: Relevance to the Theoretical Framework for the Analysis of the Cases (External Perspective)

Theory		Dassault	Saab	Daewoo
Spreading risks	Leaving a declining industry for a growing one	not relevant	very relevant	not relevant
	Spreading activities in different growing businesses	very relevant	very relevant	not relevant
Passive perspective	Change in national science and technology policy	not relevant	not relevant	very relevant
	Change in public opinion	not relevant	relevant	not relevant
	New laws regulating or forbidding specific products	not relevant	not relevant	not relevant
Active perspective	Taking advantage of the institutional environment	relevant	not relevant	relevant
Technology procurement		relevant	not relevant	not relevant
Other reason found by the research (Section 2): Institutional lock-out and interest of the state		very relevant	very relevant	very relevant

Table 7.6 summarises the findings and shows that the decision to diversify is taken with regard to the assessment of the national institutional environment of the firm. The transformation of the national system of innovation of the firm can trigger the diversification of the firm, either passively, as in the case of Saab or Daewoo, or actively, as for Dassault. The fact that the institutional environment was locking the firms out of the industry is here emphasised as one of the major reasons to explain why the firms did not diversify. The institutional lock-out could be relaxed when an opportunity arose, provided that the state could find some advantages in the venture. Finally, it can be

noted that the state had an interest in allowing diversification through institutional changes.

NOTES

1. Private firms participated in the development of civil aicraft to a limited extent during the 1950s and 1960s. When Dassault developed and produced the airliner Mercure at the end of the 1960s, it never succeeded in selling it in large quantities to the state-owned airline Air-Inter because priority was given to civil airliners developed by state-owned firms.
2. Note that Marcel Dassault, although not being the CEO of the firm, had a considerable influence on the strategic decisions taken by the higher management of the firm. He was the founder of the firm and to some extent its soul.
3. It should also be remembered that one of these state-owned firms, Sud Aviation, was the result of the fusion of SNCASO and SNCASE, while SNCASO was the result of the fusion of one of the first firms created by Marcel Dassault and the firm Potez. During the late 1930s, Marcel Dassault had also been the CEO of SNCASO.
4. The years are just given as references to place the events in time. A full chronologial description of the events is given at the end of each empirical chapter.
5. There are several reasons for this situation. First, Saab did not really need to export its products because of its relations with the Swedish state. Secondly, Sweden is a small country, outside NATO, with limited political power as compared to other nations such as France or the United States. The competition on the military aircraft market is based not only on technologies but also on political strength.
6. Chaebols are large family owned conglomerates in Korea. See Chapter 6, Section 1.2.
7. Ultimately, SNECMA did not produce the engine as another type of engine was later selected.
8. However, it can be objected that Korean chaebols can not lose face in front of other chaebols. Staying outside the aerospace industry would have involved a loss of prestige for Daewoo. This, as such, was a risk for the firm.
9. The relationship between the political system and the system of innovation is unclear and not discussed in the literature on systems of innovation, leaving a field wide-open for further investigations.

8. How Did the Firms Diversify?

*The course of the flight up and down was
exceedingly erratic, partly due to the
irregularity of the air, and partly to lack of
experience in handling this machine.*

Orville Wright

Once firms have embarked upon the strategy of diversification, there are
numbers of ways to implement it. The three first parts of this section analyse
the way the firms diversified, how they accumulated competences and how
they were able to develop a new product. In Chapter 2, Section 3.2, the
theoretical framework identified five learning dimensions that had to be taken
into account by firms during the diversification. These dimensions were: the
technologies, the market, the financing of the venture, the management and
organisation and finally the institutions. It was also recognised that these
dimensions might overlap. Furthermore, they imply a degree of practice or
'learning by doing' in order to be integrated in the firm. The following
analysis focuses on how firms integrated these dimensions into their existing
activity. This is done first by looking at the firms separately with respect to
the five learning dimensions and secondly by comparing each learning
dimension in the three firms. The final section appraises the theoretical
framework and discusses the discrepancies and similarities that were
observed between the cases and the theory.

1.   ANALYTIC SUMMARY OF THE CASES

1.1.   Dassault

There was a direct connection between the Mystère 20 and the traditional military activity of the firm. The technologies used during the development of the aircraft had to a very large extent been developed for military programmes. The wings and the hydraulic actuators, for example, had been developed for supersonic and subsonic military aircraft, while the prototyping policy of the firm had led to improvements in the technological capability of the firm, especially with regard to the fuselage (Chapter 4, Sections 2.3 and 4.1.2). Nevertheless, much development work was needed to complete the development of the aircraft, and the requirements of Pan Am implied a large number of changes affecting the aircraft as a whole. Accordingly, it was only after the contract had been signed with Pan Am in 1963 that one may speak of a diversification. From that point, new technologies had to be developed in order to fulfil the conditions of Pan Am. Moreover, the role of the certifying authorities increased since the aircraft was to be civil.

Coming from the defence industry, the firm had to learn how to manage the new civil market in which it was engaging. This learning process was started by the marketing division, which was looking for potential customers. The division worked on understanding the market conditions in the United States and on advertising the brand name of Dassault. Despite these efforts, the main element of learning about the new market came from the direct relations with the airline Pan Am, which procured the aircraft and sold it on the North American market (Chapter 4, Section 5.4). This private technology procurement set the technological specifications of the aircraft and created an initial market for Dassault. The procurement implied the purchase of 160 aircraft, but also contributed to upgrade Dassault's civil market capability. Pan Am sent a team of engineers to follow the development of the aircraft. These engineers had extensive knowledge about the commercial market as they had been involved in the large commercial operations of Pan Am. This support allowed Dassault rapidly to assimilate the way the market functioned, preparing the firm for further civil sales. A major difference with the traditional market of the firm was the fact that the development of the new aircraft was at fixed costs and the buyer would not accept delays. Although Pan Am was the first major customer of the Mystère 20, a number of other buyers followed (Chapter 4, Section 5).

Dassault's first step in the civil aircraft industry was also supported by the state-financing of the start of the production of the aircraft. The loan represented 50% of the development cost of the aircraft and was to be shared between Dassault and the state-owned firm Sud Aviation during the production of the aircraft.[1] Even if the programme had started on private funding, completing it would not have been possible without the financial support of the state. In fact, the contract between Dassault and Pan Am would have been invalidated if the state had refused to support the Mystère 20 (Chapter 4, Section 4.3).

In the first stage of the development of the aircraft, the organisation and the management of the venture were completely integrated with the rest of the organisation. The management capability of the firm was found in-house and there was no organisational restructuring. The civil division was completely integrated with the military division of the firm. Although the firm was not reorganised on paper, the development team of the Mystère 20 was located in Bordeaux, about 600 kilometres from the central organisation of the firm in Saint-Cloud near Paris. This geographical division allowed for a certain autonomy of the design team. The owner of the firm, Marcel Dassault, was also supporting the independent development of the aircraft against the central management (Chapter 4, Section 4.4).

The main institution the firm had to learn about was not of a national nature but was connected to the sectoral system of innovation of the firm. The certification of the aircraft imposed a number of rules the firm had to follow in order to enter the market. The certification process had to be learned from scratch by the firm in order to succeed in the venture (Chapter 4, Section 5.2). Learning about the certification was done with the support of two types of organisation, i.e., the certification authorities in France and in the United States as well as the firm Boeing, which provided advice.[2]

Another institution that the firm had to take into account was the division of labour for the production of aircraft between the state-owned firms and the private firms. This institution was both national and sectoral, although it addressed more the industrial policy of the country than the aircraft industry *per se*. In this case, the firm was used to dealing with the state-owned firms through its previous experience in the military programmes. There was therefore no need for specific learning on this particular issue (Chapter 4, Section 5.3).

Table 8.1: Factors Affecting the Learning Process of Dassault

	Internal	External
Technologies	• Most of technologies in-house • Wings • Powered actuators	• Design of the podded engines • CAA • Pan Am
Market	• Learn from Pan Am	• Pan Am
Financing	• Private funding	• Loan from the state
Management	• Integrated but geographical independence	• Follow the technical requirement of Pan Am
Institutions	• Cooperation with Sud Aviation to get the financing	• Certification of the aircraft • Boeing

Table 8.1 summarises how the management of new knowledge was carried out in order to succeed in the diversification. Technologies, as well as management capabilities, were to a very large extent found in-house, while the requirements of Pan Am affected the choices of technology and the management of the venture. The financing of the project was divided between internal funding and external support, but without the external support the programme would not have been completed. Managing the new market and the new institutions was done mainly with the support of organisations within the sectoral environment of the firm. These took the form of the firm's customer for the market and of the CAA and Boeing for the certification of the aircraft.

1.2.   Saab

After the decision to diversify had been taken at the beginning of 1979, almost everything remained to be done within the firm. Although studies of passenger aircraft had been carried out during the whole decade preceding the diversification, nothing had led to more than a wooden mock-up of an aircraft. The management of the firm decided to find a partner in the United States in order to reduce the development cost for Saab and to secure a share of the American market. The technological learning needed by the firm in order to succeed in the development of the Saab 340 implied a joint venture with a partner knowledgeable in smaller civil aircraft. The knowledge required could then be gathered both in-house and in the joint venture with the American firm Fairchild (Chapter 5, Section 3.2).

Despite the joint venture with Fairchild, a number of technologies needed to be developed in-house, either on the basis of previous technological development or on the basis of new research and development. The division of labour between the firms aimed at allowing Saab to learn about the civil aircraft industry in terms of technologies, market and institutions. This explicit division of labour implied, for example, that Saab was responsible for the testing and the certification of the aircraft (Chapter 5, Section 4.1).

The deregulation of the American air traffic in 1978 was an opportunity for Saab to diversify into the civil market, as it provided a market. However, Saab was completely unknown in the United States and needed a partner with a brand name and experience. Fairchild had this experience and in the meantime wanted to broaden its own product catalogue. The joint venture between the firms allowed Saab to learn about the market on the basis of the competences of Fairchild. The role of the partner in the joint venture was hence both technological and commercial (Chapter 5, Section 2.3).

Financing the project was done with the support of the Swedish state. The firm could not have entered the venture without this financial support. The state was also responsible for the critical situation of the firm. Several military programmes had been cancelled during the 1970s and the firm did not know about the future of its relations with the state. The future of the aircraft industry as a whole was at stake. The social and economic consequences of the shutdown of the industry would have been dramatic for Sweden. The state therefore granted a loan to cover an extensive part of the development cost, the remaining part being shared by Saab and Fairchild. Thus, the diversification of Saab into civil aircraft depended on the co-financing of the project by two external organisations, the state and the American firm Fairchild (Chapter 5, Section 3.3).

In terms of management, the two partners shared responsibilities fully. A management board was created, including the top management of both firms. All technical and operational decisions were to be taken by the board. This co-management structure was problematic because it implied rigidities with regard to separate initiatives. Moreover, each of the firms had to learn about the management characteristics of the other. The management traditions of Saab and Fairchild differed, especially with regard to hierarchy. This led to inevitable cultural confrontations, but as the reputation of both firms was at stake, both American and Swedish engineers worked very hard to make the programme a success. However, since the management board was covering all issues of the programme, it was rapidly felt as being too rigid and an intermediate management board was created to solve direct technical issues (Chapter 5, Section 4.1.4).

During the first years of the diversification, the civil activity of Saab was integrated with the military operations, despite the worries of Fairchild that relevant resources were not given to the civil project. Fairchild withdrew from the venture in 1985 as it experienced some internal financial difficulties.[3] Saab then took over the whole operation. Later, Saab was reorganised with separate military and civil divisions.

Learning about the institutional environment of the aerospace industry was done with the support of the Swedish civil aviation authority.[4] The entrepreneurship of the Swedish CAA is significant here. The process of the certification of the aircraft would have been very difficult and expensive, were it not for the initiative taken by the Swedish CAA to certify the Saab 340 according to the newly established European certification JAR-25. The European CAAs had set-up the JAR-25 to facilitate the certification of European aircraft, but this certification procedure had never been fully applied to an aircraft. The Swedish CAA rapidly identified the Saab 340 as a perfect first attempt to apply the new certification (Chapter 5, Section 4.2).

The support from Boeing should also be mentioned. The certification of the aircraft was to be done according to both European and American standards. Understanding the American standard and interpreting the regulations was accomplished through cooperation with Fairchild and Boeing.

Table 8.2 summarises how the firm acquired the competences needed to diversify. The role of external organisations in the diversification of Saab is extensive. This table shows that an external organisation was needed for all aspects of learning. It also shows that once the diversification had begun, the learning processes in the five dimensions were addressed essentially in the sectoral system of innovation of the firm rather than in the national system of innovation. As a matter of fact, the Swedish state is only present in the financing of the project and no national research organisations or firms became involved. All other aspects of the diversification were carried out within the aerospace sector, including firms, organisations such as the Swedish CAA, and institutions.

Table 8.2: Factors Affecting the Diversification Process of Saab

	Internal	External
Technologies	• Based on the previous competences of the firm	• Wings from Fairchild • General design of the aircraft
Market	• Development of the firm's own marketing capacity	• Fairchild takes care of most of the marketing of the aircraft
Financing	• Financial resources of the firm	• Loan from the government • Financial resources of Fairchild
Management	• Integration of the civil and military divisions	• Co-management with Fairchild
Institutions		• Certification authorities • JAR-25 • Boeing

1.3.   Daewoo

The diversification of Daewoo into the aerospace industry and the development of the KTX-1 implied a great deal of technological learning for the firm. During the 1980s, the firm had started the production of parts for large established aerospace firms. Production facilities were then built and a workforce was educated for the production of aircraft parts. However, this did not provide the firm with any competences in aircraft development. The technological competences needed to develop an aircraft are not related to these of developing a forklift truck or rolling stock, although the production of specific parts for these products can be related. The firm therefore needed to find a way to rapidly acquire new and much more complicated technological competences (Chapter 6, Section 4.1).

The basic design of the aircraft had been carried out by the Agency for Defence Development and Korean Airlines. In other words, the external dimensions of the aircraft had been fixed and an engine had been chosen. However, the entire process of defining the aerodynamics of the aircraft, its structure and all its systems remained. The need for support by an external organisation was quickly identified by Daewoo and the Agency for Defence Development. The Swiss firm Pilatus guided the first steps of the development of the aircraft, advising Daewoo and the Agency for Defence Development in their technological choices. Despite the tensions that emerged between the firms, the role of Pilatus was very important in defining the first detailed characteristics of the aircraft, as Pilatus had an extensive expertise in the training aircraft business (Chapter 6, Section 4.3.1). The French consulting firm GECI, which replaced Pilatus in 1991, provided a similar type of service although on a different basis. Pilatus wanted to be part of a joint venture and GECI was a consulting firm, applying existing technologies and solutions to the problems identified by Daewoo and the Agency for Defence Development. Daewoo would never have been able to develop this aircraft without the external firms and other organisations participating in the programme (Chapter 6, Section 4.3.2).

Daewoo and the Agency for Defence Development identified the Korean Air Force as the main potential customer for the KTX-1. Thus, the market would be military. As a matter of fact, the firm already had some knowledge about the defence market in Korea since it was producing other kinds of defence equipment. However, this does not mean that the firm knew about the structure of the military aerospace market. The usual procedure in the industry worldwide, in developing a military aircraft, is to make a basic design, in response to a competition initiated by the government. It is only after the choice of an aircraft has been made that the second phase of the development can start. However, Daewoo entered the venture only with unclear signals from the air force. A need for small trainers existed but this was not a priority for the Korean Air Force, which was already involved in a number of other purchases (Chapter 6, Section 4.4). The time selected for the diversification was therefore not the most appropriate in terms of market. The management of Daewoo took the risk of developing an aircraft for which no real market existed, presuming that the air force would be *de facto* forced to buy it.[5]

Financing the development of the aircraft was mainly done by drawing on the resources of the firm. The strategy followed by the chaebol was common to all the large Korean conglomerates. The firm was able to finance the development of the aircraft out of the profits of the other divisions of the conglomerate. The state was reluctant to finance the programme during the first phase of the development because of the growing number of projects in the infant Korean aerospace industry and because it was already engaged in a number of very expensive programmes. Furthermore, the need for such an aircraft had not been clearly identified by the Korean Air Force (Chapter 6, Section 4.5).

Learning about how to manage the development of the KTX-1 was very problematic for Daewoo. The profound lack of technological competences meant that external organisations had to be heavily involved in the programme. The Agency for Defence Development and Daewoo did not have the competence to develop the aircraft in-house and therefore required and received the help of Pilatus. The divergence of management culture between the firms, as well as the cultural discrepancies leading to conflicts of interest, were never handled in a proper way. The firms did not make it clear enough to each other what their expectations were. Pilatus wanted to sell its existing technologies and Daewoo wanted to reinvent the technologies in order to have a Korean aircraft. The conflict that emerged shows that the objectives of the programme were not clear for the Swiss firm. It withdrew in 1991 and was replaced by the French firm GECI. The role of GECI was limited to troubleshooting and consulting on a contractual basis. They were not developing the aircraft, but solving the technological problems that emerged in the course of the development by Daewoo and the Agency for Defence Development (Chapter 6, Section 4.3).

Understanding the institutional environment of the aerospace sector internationally was not an easy task for Daewoo. Despite the fact that the aircraft did not have to be certified because it was a military aircraft, other institutions regulating the market had to be taken into account during the diversification. Within the firm, the management needed to be convinced about the validity of such a programme. Although Korean firms were very keen to take risks, the management of Daewoo was not clearly willing to enter into the new venture, even though the chairman of the firm had given orders concerning the diversification. Other managers were not willing to have their divisions used as 'cash cows' for a very risky venture with only long-term, if any, return on investments (Chapter 6, Section 3.4). Another dimension the firm had to learn, but failed to do so, was how to handle development work with a foreign partner.

Table 8.3 recapitulates the element of learning Daewoo had to achieve in order to succeed in its new venture. The role of external organisations is overwhelming, with one national research organisation providing the basic technological support and two private foreign firms providing the specialisation in the technologies needed to complete the actual development of the aircraft. The government, although not present during the first step of the development, turned out to be a strong organisation when the risk of the venture was decreased, financing the programme and ultimately buying the aircraft.

Table 8.3: Factors Affecting the Diversification Process of Daewoo

	Internal	External
Technologies	• Detailed design and development • Production facilities existing in Changwon	• Basic design by the Agency for Defence Development • Cooperation with Pilatus • Consulting from GECI
Market	• Trying to convince the Korean Air Force	• Korean Air Force (although hard to convince)
Financing	• Financial resources of the firm from other divisions • Relatively low cost of development	• Refusal of the state to finance the project during the first phase • Loan from the state during the last two phases
Management	• Dependence of the division on the rest of the firm	• Cooperation with Agency for Defence Development
Institutions	• Convincing the management of the feasibility of the programme • Characteristics of the industry • Understanding how to work with a foreign partner	• No certification needed, but took Italian aerobatics certification • Gain the confidence of the industry worldwide

2.   COMPARISON OF THE LEARNING DIMENSIONS IN THE CASE-STUDIES

The three case-studies have been described with their characteristics. This section compares the cases with regard to the five dimensions of learning identified in the theoretical framework and discussed in the preceding analysis. This section aims at identifying and understanding the similarities and the differences between the cases. Having already summarised the process of the diversification in the three cases, this section discusses the ways the firms have learnt. It addresses in turn the various dimensions of learning encountered during the process of diversification.

2.1. Technologies

The three firms learned about technologies using their internal resources and then completing them with external support. The ability to use internal resources depended on the nature of the previous capabilities of the firm and on the technological relatedness of the new product. Dassault was almost self-reliant as the new aircraft was to a great extent similar to what the firm had been developing before. Saab had been developing aircraft, but these were highly specialised military jet aircraft; the new aircraft was a regional turboprop airplane. The firm could use some of its existing technological competences, but it also had to find an external partner for the venture. In the case of Daewoo, the firm had no competences in the development of aircraft.[6] Everything had to be developed from scratch and the firm had to rely heavily on the support of other firms and organisations.

The technological relatedness between the previous product and the new product is here shown to be crucial in the success of the diversification. The reliance of the firm on its own technological competences and its attempt to use existing technologies saves time and financial resources. As a result, the more the firm can use its internal capabilities, the less it needs to look for other sources of knowledge, either in other firms or in other kinds of organisations.

It is also interesting to note that the firms did not find any significant support for their technological development in their national system of innovation. Before the diversification occurred, the European firms had developed their competence base in military programmes with the support of national R&D organisations and procurement policies of the state. While diversifying and developing a new product independently from the state, the European firms did not profit from the support of the national R&D organisations. Daewoo is an exception, as the Agency for Defence Development provided important support.

The firms found technological support in the aerospace sector, inside or outside their respective countries, to a larger extent than in the national system of innovation in which they operated. This means that the sectoral system of innovation was more important for the firms than the national one. Most of the technologies used by the firms to develop the product already existed within the sectoral system. Identifying the technologies and recombining them was as much part of the learning process as the creation of new technologies. In turn, the success of the venture depended on the degree of integration of the firms in the aerospace sectoral system of innovation, and on their capacity to identify proper organisations in the system.

Table 8.4: Comparison of the Technology Acquisitions by the Firms

	Technologies	
	Internal	External
Dassault	• Internal development	• Limited support from ONERA
Saab	• Internal development	• Cooperation with Fairchild
Daewoo	• Detailed design and development	• Basic design by the Agency for Defence Development • Pilatus • GECI

Table 8.4 summarises the findings, showing that each firm started the venture using its existing internal development capabilities. External support was needed, however, but varied according to the existing technological competences of the firms and of their ability to transfer these competences to the new venture.

2.2. Market

The attempt to access the market was planned differently in the three firms. Dassault had a marketing division scanning the American market, but the role of Pan Am, as the buyer, was overwhelming. The decision of the customer to buy a large quantity of aircraft simplified the learning process about the market. Dassault was then able to take advantage of the commercial experience of Pan Am because the airline was willing to invest heavily in the venture and had the financial capacity to sustain this investment.

In the case of Saab, the firm learned about the new market through the structure of the joint venture with Fairchild. Fairchild was an established aircraft manufacturer for the civil market and was selected for this very reason. The partner in the venture had been chosen more for its market competences than for its technological competences.

Daewoo found it difficult to understand its new potential market although the firm already had some information about other parts of the Korean military market. The firm had the support of the Agency for Defence Development, the procuring agency of defence equipment of the Ministry of National Defence. This should have simplified the process, but neither the Agency for Defence Development nor Daewoo clearly assessed the needs of the customer, the Korean Air Force. The marketing was directed towards the end users, the pilots, and not enough towards the real buyers, the Korean government.

Understanding the new market is seen here to depend on the quality of the relationship existing between the customer and the supplier. User–producer relations can provide valuable learning in the market dimension. The fact that both the French and the Swedish case involved international organisations in the aerospace industry confirms the argument developed in the previous section; the sectoral system as a whole was more important than the national one. Learning about the new market is faster when the customer is directly involved in the development of the product.

Table 8.5: Comparison of Access to the Market by the Firms

	Market	
	Internal	External
Dassault	• Market studies in the US	• Pan Am
Saab	• Development of the firm's own marketing capacity	• US market covered by Fairchild
Daewoo	• Trying to convince the Korean Air Force	• Korean Air Force • Korean government

Table 8.5 summarises the findings. The sectoral system of innovation of the firms is central to the firm's understanding of the market. Firms established in the market, such as Pan Am, Fairchild or Pilatus, were in each case providing the diversifying firms with information concerning the new market.

2.3. Financing the Ventures

The financing of the ventures was, in each case, done in two steps. First, all the firms used their internal financial resources to start the development and the pre-studies. However, these resources were not enough to finance the development of the programmes as a whole. The state was subsequently asked to finance the project in the form of loans covering part of the development or production costs. Dassault received proportionally the highest loan while Daewoo was granted the smallest one. The state is naturally less inclined to support a programme that is highly uncertain and risky than one which already has a market.

Succeeding in the diversification strategy required a proper financing of the venture. Each firm had to demonstrate the reliability of its venture to its potential creditors. For the management of the firm, it was a question not only of reducing the risks involved by the venture but also of showing that these were properly evaluated and understood.

Receiving financing from the state was made easier if the project could be fitted within the industrial science and technology policy of the country, so that the government could find some interests in the development of a new product, for example, in terms of employment. The aerospace industry is also an industry in which governments, whether European, American or Asian, have traditionally intervened and financially supported technological development. Hence, the national system of innovation is directly important for the financing of the programme, especially if the industry in question is targeted by the state's science and technology or industrial policies. The firms were aware of the needs of the government and succeeded in identifying how they could satisfy the expectancies of the state. Conversely, the sectoral system of innovation of the firm was less relevant in the matter of understanding the nature of the financing of the new venture.

As shown in Table 8.6, the state had an interest in financing part of the programme in all the three cases. In the two European cases, the state wanted to support the industry and to avoid increasing unemployment. In Korea, the state aimed at raising the technological capability of the country through the development of a new high-tech programme. Unemployment was not a worry for the Korean government, as such problems only emerged during the late 1990s.

Table 8.6: Comparison of the Financing of the Venture by the Firms

| | Financing | |
	Internal	External
Dassault	• Financial resources of the firm	• Large loan from the state to provide employment in the state-owned firm Sud Aviation
Saab	• Financial resources of the firm	• Medium-sized loan from the state to support the firm
Daewoo	• Financial resources of the firm	• Small loan from the state for the prestige of the industry

2.4. Management and Organisation

In each of the three cases, the respective firms did not immediately reorganise their activities between the existing product lines and the new one. The reason for this was that the risks involved in the new venture were too high to justify the separation of the division from the rest of the firm. Saab was reorganised at a later stage, with both a military and a civil division. This did not occur in Daewoo and in Dassault.

In France, although Dassault was not divided into two separate organisations, the geographical separation allowed for a great degree of autonomy. Moreover, the owner of the firm had given the team the freedom to develop the aircraft. The central organisation in Paris, however, constantly controlled the development of the Mystère 20. In Sweden, the firm was not reorganised, but the management team was largely independent from the military divisions. The higher management of the firms was, however, still making all major decisions regarding the operational development of the programmes. The Korean case is atypical because the new aerospace venture was kept inside an industrial division that had virtually nothing to do with the aerospace industry. The management of the venture was carried out by a team responsible for the aerospace division, but was given neither freedom nor independent finances to develop the aircraft.

Each of the three firms had to learn how to manage a venture involving new kinds of partners. The development of the new product was constrained by the expectations of the partner. Although Pan Am was a customer of the aircraft developed by Dassault, the size of the contract and the fact that the firm was the first customer forced the firm to find new ways of managing the programme, concentrating on cost, efficiency and customer satisfaction. Both in Sweden and in Korea, the presence of a foreign partner created troubles due to the cultural differences, either in terms of management or in terms of understanding the respective needs of the firms.

Table 8.7: Comparison of the Management and Organisation of the Venture by the Firms

	Management and Organisation	
	Internal	External
Dassault	• Geographical separation of the divisions	• No constraints from Sud Aviation • Pan Am
Saab	• No organisational separation of the divisions	• Joint management Saab Fairchild
Daewoo	• No organisational separation of the divisions • Dependence of the aerospace team on the higher management of the Chaebol	• No constraints from ADD • Pilatus and GECI

Table 8.7 summarises the findings and indicates that the main managerial difficulties did not come from the existing managerial tradition of the firm but from the new form of management required by the involvement of one or more external partners. The fact that the divisions were not separated from the beginning did not cause particular problems, while the interventions of external partners created tensions and doubts.

2.5.   Institutions

In the theoretical framework of Chapter 2, Section 3.2.5, it was argued that the firm needed to learn about the institutional environment that mattered for the new product. Learning about institutions was separated from learning about the market to emphasise that the institutional environment is not necessarily dependent on the market and its rules. However, the reverse is certainly true. The market and its rules is a sub-set of the institutional environment. In other words, the concept of institutions encompasses the regulation of the market but extends to other spheres.

The main institution identified in this work concerns the rules related to the certification process of the aircraft. The constraints imposed on the firm by the certification rules are mainly of a technological nature because they concern the safety of the aircraft. Certification regulations have evolved in parallel with commercial aircraft transportation, building on the identification of safety problems. When reasons for failures were identified after an aircraft accident, the regulation evolved in order to avoid similar accidents in the future. Certification as an institution does not directly depend on the market, but it affects the relationship of the firm to its market as civil aircraft that are not certified are simply not allowed to fly.

Although being about technologies, certification rules do not provide technological solutions. The firm must find the appropriate technology to achieve certification. Even though the certification *per se* does not provide solutions, the manager of the certification authority can support the firm with his or her experience from previous certifications. Certification rules as an institution must hence be separated from the certification authority, i.e., the organisation that certifies the aircraft.

For the two European firms, entering the civil market meant showing compliance of military technologies with the certification rules of a civil programme. In other words, the technologies and the technological solutions chosen by the firm had earlier often been applied to its military aircraft. The development teams did not question these choices since the reliability of the technologies had been established empirically on military aircraft. This reasoning was, however, not enough in terms of civil certification. This shows that learning about institutions took place inside the European firms. The change of institutional framework, from military to civil, required a learning process for the firms in order to be effective in the new institutional environment.

The first step in learning about the certification was therefore to understand exactly what was needed by the certification authority to show the compliance of a technology with the regulations. The entrepreneurship of the certification officials in smoothing the process for the firm simplified the certification. Based on their experience of the certification and on their existing networks, they provided support and advice. Another external organisation was the firm Boeing. Both Dassault and Saab had developed relations with Boeing and were able to benefit from its experience during their own certification processes.

In the case of Daewoo, the fact that the aircraft was military greatly simplified the task for the firm. The aircraft was certified according to the American regulation FAR 23, a certification for aerobatics aircraft with relatively low requirements, as the aircraft was not designed for carrying passengers. This certification, although not required, was seen as a quality stamp by Daewoo.

Certification rules were not the only institutions the firms had to learn about. The relations between the firms in the sectoral system of innovation are also institutionalised, although in the case of the aerospace industry these too are connected to the certification rules and authorities. Suppliers of parts, for example, must follow the stringent quality rules imposed to achieve safety. As a matter of fact, production facilities are also certified.

Dassault and Saab were already established in the aerospace industry. Previous programmes in the military aircraft industry in France had involved the participation of a number of aerospace organisations including Dassault. As a result, the firm did not need to learn about the institutional environment regulating the structure of the aerospace sector worldwide. Besides, the firm was well aware of the way the French aerospace sector was organised in particular with regard to the relations between state-owned and private firms. The same applies to Saab as the firm was a renowned military aircraft producer and had started to produce parts for the civil aircraft industry during the 1970s in order to learn about its characteristics and to show the capability of the firm. Daewoo followed a path similar to Saab in trying to become visible in the aerospace industry as a component producer and showing that it could comply with the regulations in terms of quality.

A final institution, which at least Dassault had to learn about, concerns the very strong relations between airlines and producers, as well as the procurement procedures of new aircraft. This institution is especially characteristic of the jetliner industry in which airlines usually procure aircraft fulfilling very specific needs (Carroll, 1975, p. 165). Although Saab did not have to learn about procurement while developing the Saab 340, it went, to some extent, through this institution while developing the stretched version of the Saab 340, the Saab 2000, which was developed in close cooperation with the Swiss airline Crossair.[7]

This indicates that firms diversifying in new industries must integrate the new institutions in their management structure. It is not only a question of understanding that these institutions exist but also learning how they can be managed.

Although not being the only institutions of the aerospace sector, certification requirements are shown as encompassing a large number of issues for the firms, in particular with regard to development of technologies, production and user–producer relations. As such, the certification rules are sectoral institutions greatly affecting the whole process of aircraft development and production. However, it can be argued that the certification regulations have some elements of a national nature. Certification rules are issued by the Federal Aviation Administration in the United States and by the Joint Aviation Authorities in Europe. Although these rules are very similar, they may differ on some points. As a result, certification rules can easily be used as trade-barriers between the United States and Europe (Hedblom, p.c., 1999).

Table 8.8: Comparison of How Firms Learnt About the Institutional Set-Up

	Institution	
	Internal	External
Dassault	• User–producer relations • Learning the rules of certification	• Role of the CAAs
Saab	• User–producer relations • Learning the rules of certification	• Role of the CAAs
Daewoo	• User–producer relations • No certification needed	• American certification for aerobatics (in Italy)

Table 8.8 summarises how the firms learnt about the new institutions. The role of external organisations in the process is again important. The experience that was missing within the firm could be rapidly gathered outside the firm, providing that the firm had a proper network in its sectoral system of innovation.

2.6. Management of New Knowledge

In the last five sections, the three cases have been compared with regard to the five learning dimensions of the theoretical framework. This section summarises and concludes the discussion while results are shown in Table 8.9. The cases have shown that all firms had to learn about each of these five dimensions. The theoretical framework described the learning process of these dimensions as internal to the firm. However, it appears that knowledge necessary for the diversification was, to a large extent, found in the national and the sectoral systems of innovation of the firm, i.e., through other firms, research organisations, certification authorities or government policies. The learning process involved the use of existing internal resources as well as the internalisation by the firm of external resources.

Learning processes occurred through the interactions of the firm with other organisations. This process of interactive learning, by which firms learn from their external environment is decisive for the success of the strategy. Diversifying firms usually lack some competences and do not always know where these competences can be found. In the three cases, it was not only the awareness of the nature of the learning dimensions that mattered but also an identification of where the resources could be found and internalised. Moreover, the firm could only learn in interaction with other firms and organisations. These interactions allowed for an identification of problems early in the development of the product and also indicated possible solutions.

The management of new knowledge required an understanding of two systems of innovation and their overlapping areas. Technologies were developed in-house or with the support of organisations from the aerospace sector, and also with the support of national research organisations. The financing of the programmes was mainly done with the support of the respective states, which could find advantages in supporting the venture. The certification of the aircraft mainly involved organisations belonging to the aerospace sectoral system, although the rules could be influenced by elements of the national system of innovation in which the firm operated. Market and management dimensions mainly involved the support of organisations from the sectoral system of innovation.

Table 8.9: Managing New Knowledge

	Dassault	Saab	Daewoo
Technologies	Existing	Existing	All new
Market	External	External	Internal
Investment	Known from previous programmes	Known from previous programmes	No experience
Management capability	Internal	Internal	Internal
Institutions	Certification	Certification	Industry

3. APPRAISAL OF THE THEORY

The previous section has described how the firms developed their competences during the implementation of the diversification strategy. However, the theoretical framework did not stop at the development of competences but extended to other elements explaining how the firm diversified. This section takes up the various elements of theory describing how firms diversify and discusses whether they are relevant for the analysis of the cases. Tables 8.10 and 9.11 summarise the findings.

3.1. Managerial Practices

The theoretical framework of Chapter 2, Section 3.1, pointed out that the implementation of the diversification strategy was based on three types of capabilities. These were:

1. the acquisition of new firms having an activity in the field of the diversification;
2. contractual relationships with other firms; and
3. internal development of the technologies.[8]

3.1.1. Acquisitions

The theoretical framework developed the option of acquisition as a means of rapidly implementing the diversification. This was also described as an economical way to acquire competences and physical resources (Chapter 2, Section 3.1.1). In none of the cases, however, was acquisition used as a strategy during diversification. It can be argued that an acquisition can only be made if there is something to acquire, such as a firm with its technologies or products, and if the buyer has the financial means to complete its takeover. These conditions were not present in these cases even though there are a number of known instances of aerospace firms diversifying through acquisition, such as Boeing or Bombardier (Feldman, 1997).[9]

At the time of the diversification of Dassault and Saab, the newness of the product and of the market niche implied that no firms could be bought in order to accelerate the pace of the diversification. In the case of Daewoo, the firm wanted to have a Korean aircraft, meaning an aircraft developed in Korea. Hence, a purchase of a foreign firm was never an option.[10] Since the aerospace industry in Korea was at an infant stage, no firm in the country could be bought. Furthermore, the competition between the chaebols did not allow competing conglomerates to sell their technologies to each other.

However, the three firms could have bought smaller firms in order to acquire technologies related to the development of the aircraft. None of the firms did so and, as will be seen later, they only relied on their own development capability and on external partners. The European firms were in situations where their technological competences were already at the forefront of the aerospace industry. Moreover, the process in which they had engaged and the difficulties of managing large ventures with external organisations under extreme time constraints might have reduced the incentives to acquire small firms. Acquisition is a process which can be time consuming, because of organisational difficulties, while its outcomes are not necessarily more promising than these of internal research and development.

3.1.2. Contractual relationships

Contractual relationships were crucial for the development of the aircraft. Three types of contractual relationships were observed in the research, i.e., customer contracts, joint ventures and consulting (Chapter 2, Section 3.1.2).

The nature of the contract between Dassault and Pan Am was a private technology procurement. The customer provided the exact specifications of the product it wanted and commissioned it from the developer. Moreover, the customer provided technical support during the development and facilitated the commercialisation of the aircraft by taking the responsibility for selling the aircraft in the United States. This type of user–producer interaction, where the user sets up the specifications of a product that does not exist on the market, was very important for the success of the venture. Procurement, whether private or public, has now become the most common type of contractual relationship during aircraft development, especially military aircraft. The development costs of new aircraft are now extremely great. Firms cannot afford to launch new aircraft before the customers have precisely defined their functional requirements.

In the case of Saab, the type of contractual relationship was a joint venture in which the firms shared the burden of the development of the aircraft. The firms had the same amount of responsibility and they developed their shares of the programme separately. The relations between Saab and Fairchild were hence horizontal. Two potential competitors decided to cooperate for the development of an aircraft in order to share their resources and develop a new product.

In the case of Daewoo, private consulting enabled the firm to compensate its lack of knowledge. The relations with Pilatus were not designed as a joint venture and were not clearly defined. Both firms were uncertain about the expectations of the other. The agreement between the firms was never contractual. The conflicts of interest that emerged were rooted in the misunderstandings between the firms. In the second phase of the programme, Daewoo learnt from its previous mistake with Pilatus. It contracted GECI to solve specific technological problems in the development work. This indicates the need for firms to define the terms of their relations by contract, in order to establish precisely the projected outcome of the venture.

The nature of the contractual relationship differed in the three cases. The French case was a vertical relationship with a knowledgeable customer defining the product and the market. In Sweden, the contract involved another producer interested in increasing its own range of products in a joint venture where responsibilities were shared. In Korea, the relationship with Pilatus, a direct competitor on the Korean market, was not clearly defined and the objectives of both firms were not clear. In a second stage, a contractual relationship was designed with a consulting firm as a way to increase the in-house competences of the firm with the help of an external organisation.

3.1.3. Internal development

The theoretical framework indicated that firms can use their existing resources in terms of research and development to carry out the diversification (Chapter 2, Section 3.1.3). It was also noted that the diversification could be a result of the research and development activity of the firm. As a matter of fact, internal research and development is often the basis for the firm's technological capabilities. This was the case for both Dassault and Saab, but not for Daewoo, which had never been involved in the development of an aircraft. In the three cases, the programmes did not involve specific basic research activity but only extensive development work.

In the cases of Dassault and Saab, the firms had extensive technological capabilities due to their previous programmes in military aircraft. Although they are two different types of products, military and civil aircraft rely on a number of similar technologies. Technological transfers between the divisions could then allow for a rapid development of the civil aircraft. The developing teams had all been previously involved in the development of military aircraft and could use their knowledge in the development of the new aircraft. Moreover, the structure of the firms allowed for exchanges of information between military and civil organisations. If the two organisations had been separated from the beginning, the development work might have suffered from delays. This indicates that the new venture should be given a certain autonomy, for example geographically, in order to have the necessary freedom to develop a new product. At the same time, the new organisation should stay close to the older one in order to be able to take advantage of the technological competences existing in-house.

In the Korean case, the firm did not have technological capabilities to develop an aircraft and therefore had to build a new team of Korean aerospace engineers for the development work. The Korean development team consisted of engineers with an aerospace background, usually from American universities, but lacked both the experience of developing a new aircraft and the support of an experienced management team. This problem did not occur at Dassault or Saab since the firms already had the necessary managerial competences to successfully carry out military programmes.[11]

Table 8.10: Practices for the Implementation of Diversification

	Dassault	Saab	Daewoo
Acquisitions	No	No	No
Contractual relationships	Yes, customer	Yes, joint-venture	Yes, consulting
Internal development and R&D	Yes	Yes	Yes

Table 8.10 summarises the findings of Section 3.1. The firms did not implement the diversification through the acquisition of other firms. Contractual relationships with other knowledgeable firms were an important source of support, although the nature of the contracts varied between the cases. Finally, the internal development capacity of the firm is shown to be a very important element for the success of the diversification.

3.2. National Support for Diversification

The theoretical framework argued that the implementation of the diversification largely took place in the national system of innovation of the firm. This implied in particular that the national educational system could be adapted to the needs of the industry in terms of education of a competent workforce and university research. It also implied that national R&D organisations could support the venture (Chapter 2, Section 3.3).

Considering the aerospace industry as a whole, and not the specific products described in this empirical work, the three countries have provided the firms with both workforce and research.[12] The education policies of the countries during the building up of the firms was, and still is, oriented towards the support of the industry. The prospects for economic growth, employment, technological spillovers and prestige were all taken into account by the respective governments in shaping their education policies.

As the industry was already established in the countries it had a corresponding educational infrastructure. Hence, the need to develop a new one was not a necessity. Had the industry been radically new, with technological and product innovations – as was the case for the aerospace 20 to 50 years ago – an infrastructure would probably have been designed.[13] In the three cases studied, the established educational infrastructure was not used as a support for the development of the products. Technologies already existed and a workforce mastering these technologies was employed. Research and development was not carried out in universities.

In Section 2.6 of this chapter it was seen that national R&D organisations provided only limited support to the firms – with the exception of the Korean case. However, similar to the previous discussion about the educational system, some competences of the firms had been developed in joint research programmes with national R&D organisations. The national system was not directly used during the diversification, but the firms benefited from previous developments of technologies done within the national system of innovation.

Table 8.11: National Support for Diversification

	Dassault	Saab	Daewoo
Education	No	No	No
National R&D	Small	Small	High

Table 8.11 shows that diversification in the three firms did not benefit much from the support of national organisations whether in terms of education or of research and development. The Korean case is somewhat of an exception since the Agency for Defence Development initiated the programme of the KTX-1.

4.   SUCCESSES AND FAILURES IN DIVERSIFICATION

The three cases have now been analysed with regard to a number of dimensions. It was seen that the firms related to these dimensions to varying degrees. One might now ask if the firms succeeded in their new ventures. Was the Falcon a success? Did Saab survive with the Saab 340? Has Daewoo established itself as an aircraft manufacturer? This section will briefly discusses these questions.

The criteria of success of an operation are, however, problematic to assess. In this study, the focus has been both on the access to a new market and on technological developments. This indicates two dimensions of success and failure. A third dimension is the economic success of the operation, for example, whether or not the firm reached break-even with the new product.

The technological dimension can be assessed by evaluating whether or not the firm succeeded in developing and producing an aircraft. The fact that technologies in aircraft have to be certified by an external independent authority gives a clear answer to this dimension. However, this will not give an answer about how good the aircraft is compared to the competition. In terms of market, dimensions such as the number of aircraft produced and sold are not very interesting except if they can be compared among several firms for the same product and under the same conditions. The market share in volume of the firm in the new market can be a better indicator of its market success. This raises a problem especially in evaluating the case of Daewoo as its aerospace division is very young.

Assessing the economic success implies assessing if the firm really benefited from the diversification in economic terms. One way of doing this is to try to evaluate if the firm reached break-even, in other words if the sales of aircraft covered the costs involved in its development and production. Break-even in the aerospace industry is sometimes said to depend on the type of aircraft the firm produces. For example, a business jet manufacturer should sell between 200 and 300 aircraft, while this number is about 600 aircraft for a jetliner manufacturer (Carlier and Berger, 1996a, p. 179; McGuire, 1997, p. 117).

Break-even can be calculated at the very start of a programme or at its end. Calculating break-even at the start of a programme is always done on the basis of speculation as to the number and price of aircraft that will be sold during the coming two or three decades following the beginning of the venture. Hence, an *ex-ante* break-even calculation is just a rough estimation used by the firm to impress competitors and attract investors.

Calculating break-even at the end of a programme is also very problematic. As time goes on, the price of the aircraft changes as well as the cost of production. Besides the problem of development and production costs, it is always unclear whether the sales of spare parts and the maintenance of the aircraft should be included in the accounting of the firm. These manipulations make the estimation of *ex-post* break-even even more complicated. Therefore, break-even is almost never used in the aerospace industry as a performance measurement (Edlund, p.c., 2000).

Instead of break-even, a better way to evaluate the economic success of the venture is to follow the development of the new division of the firm and to try to assess its economic importance for the firm as a whole over time. These criteria of success will now be discussed for each firm.

4.1.   Dassault – a Great Success

The technological and market successes of the venture of Dassault are by no means problematic issues. The development of the Mystère-Falcon 20 led to an aircraft which precisely followed the requirements of Pan Am, and Dassault was able to deliver the first aircraft on time. The first contract with Pan Am, involving the purchase of 40 aircraft and 120 options, also represents the success of the firm to reach a new market. After the sale to Pan Am, the Mystère-Falcon 20 was sold to the French government and to a number of other firms.

With a total of 476 Falcon 20s produced in five different versions it can be stated that the programme was highly successful. An additional batch of 38 aircraft was also produced with upgraded avionics; the Falcon 200. In 1982 the production of the Falcon stopped (Berger, p.c., 1999).

At the end of the 1960s, the demand for smaller business jets led Dassault to develop the Falcon 10, with a capacity of six to eight passengers. During the 1970s, after a failed attempt to sell a jetliner, the Mercure, the firm focused on the business jet market and developed the Falcon 50.[14] In 1978, the Falcon 50 made its maiden flight. This aircraft had three jet engines, allowing for transatlantic flights. In 1984, the firm produced the Falcon 900, and in 1993, the Falcon 2000 was flying.

The success of the Falcons is now such that Dassault has established itself as a major business jet manufacturer, with a share in terms of aircraft delivered of 10% of the global business jet market and a share of 35% of the high-end business jet market. In 1998, the civil aircraft operations of Dassault accounted for 35% of the turnover of the firm (Berger, p.c., 2000).

4.2.   Saab – a Success Turning into a Failure

In the joint venture with Fairchild, Saab succeeded in developing and producing a regional aircraft, which rapidly became popular among regional airlines. In 1998, the Saab 340 was the regional aircraft most widely used in the United States, accounting for 16.2% of the total fleet's seating capacity – this despite growing competition (Aviation Week and Space Technology, 1998). The Saab 340 was produced in 456 units, in two different versions. In these terms, the Saab 340 was both a technological and market success.

Regional airlines operating the Saab 340 started to express their needs of a stretched version during the late 1980s. On the basis of these requirements, Saab launched the Saab 2000 in 1991. Powered by two brand new turboprops, the aircraft would carry up to 50 passengers. While the propeller blades were entirely redesigned, their combination with a new engine was to allow performances very close to the one of emerging regional jets. On shorter commuter flights, the time saved flying a regional jet would be almost insignificant as compared to flying the Saab 2000. Moreover the direct operating cost as well as the emission of toxic gases by the Saab 2000 would be much lower than the one of a regional jet. The choice of technologies was supported by the requirements of the market and the experience of Saab at the time. However, delays in the development of the aircraft limited dramatically the share of the Saab 2000 on the market for regional aircraft with 50 seats. Moreover, new and more efficient jet engines appeared during the 1990s.

During the 1990s, a succession of accidents with turboprop regional aircraft, though not manufactured by Saab, made bad publicity for the Swedish firm and the industry worldwide. It was then said that the age of propeller driven aircraft had ended and that travellers wanted the safety and comfort of modern regional jets.[15] The market for turboprop regional aircraft started to shrink in the United States and at the same time the market for regional jets increased. Saab was then in a situation where its technology was seen as out-of-date by the public, and there was no possibility of developing a new regional jet. It should also be stressed that in Sweden, the state did not financially support the production of civil aircraft, as was, and still is, the case in France, Canada or Brazil. As a result, the price tags of the Saab 340 and the Saab 2000 were too high as compared to the competition.

When combined, these three factors, i.e., delays in the Saab 2000 programme, choice of technology and lack of state subsidies, drove the decline of Saab's position on the market. In May 1999, the production of civil aircraft was stopped.[16] Since the Swedish Government was a risk-sharing partner in the venture, the loans supporting the development of the Saab 340 and Saab 2000 were never paid back by Saab.

The story of the Saab 340 is a story of both success and failure for the firm. The aircraft found a market and was very successful. The firm, however, did not manage the success properly and underestimated one important aspect of the aerospace industry – the financial support of the state for the production of civil aircraft.

4.3.   Daewoo – a Technological Success, but Will Markets Follow?

Daewoo succeeded in developing and producing a new aircraft. The way to success was long, but the firm managed to develop the technologies necessary for the aircraft. A market has also been identified and the firm has succeeded in selling the KTX-1 to the Korean Air Force. However, in order to be an economic success, the firm needs to sell its product to other air forces if it wants the venture to be economically successful.

It is still too early to assess the economic success or failure of the KTX-1 as its production only started in 1999. The Korean government ordered 80 aircraft for the Korean Air Force in 1998. This order will allow the firm to increase its competences both in development and in production, but what the firm needs now is an opportunity to sell the aircraft outside Korea. The problem is that the competition is very hard in a niche in which firms are already well established and are able to provide cheaper and better equipment.

During the 20 years of its existence, the Korean aerospace industry has overcome a number of challenges. It was reorganised in October 1999 with a merger of three of the main manufacturers, Samsung Aerospace, Hyundai Space and Aircraft and Daewoo's aerospace division, into the firm Korean Aerospace Industry LTD (KAI). Korean Air decided not to participate. The firms have pooled their facilities, personal resources and existing projects. The new Korea Aerospace Industry will be a sole aerospace system company in Korea, and the three original companies, still maintaining their identities, will function as subsystems or component suppliers. The merger will produce a consolidation of resources within Korea and eliminate the excessive competition among chaebols which proved to be mutually destructive (Chang, p.c., 2000).

NOTES

1.   This sum, of FRF48 million, was divided in two between the state-owned firm Sud Aviation and Dassault.
2.   Boeing provided both Dassault and Saab with various kinds of consulting. Engineers were exchanged between Dassault and Boeing. It should be noted that neither Dassault nor Saab were competing with Boeing on their new markets. Boeing was never involved in the business jet or regional aircraft markets.
3.   These financial difficulties were not related to the programme of the Saab 340.
4.   The Swedish Civil Aviation Administration is called Luftfartsverket.

5. As a matter of fact this happened in 1998 when the KTX-1 was finally bought by the Korean Air Force. There was never a competition between different alternatives.
6. Daewoo only had some production facilities which were of no use for the development of the aircraft.
7. Crossair had been the launch customer of the Saab 340 and of the Saab 2000.
8. Obviously, combinations of these actions occur and are certainly recurring. In order to understand each action, they need to be studied separately, recognizing that they may overlap.
9. Acquisitions are also frequent in other industries to support the rapid development of firms. For example, the development of the mobile telecommunication industry was largely based on the acquisition of small firms by large established ones (McKelvey et al., 1997).
10. This ideology changed in 1997 when Samsung studied the possibility of buying the Dutch aerospace firm Fokker.
11. The technological diffusion which took place earlier in the aerospace industry between the United States and Korea has been almost exclusively in the field of manufacturing. Korean engineers have been trained in American production facilities but never in development programmes.
12. Note that although Daewoo's engineers were trained in the United States, the Korean government had already started a number of university programmes supporting the aerospace industry during the 1970s.
13. See, for example, the building up of the mobile telecommunication industry in Sweden in McKelvey et al. (1997).
14. The Mercure was produced during the 1970s. It was a jetliner with a capacity of 150 passengers. Only eleven aircraft were sold to the French domestic airline Air Inter.
15. The irony of this is that although the Saab 340 has propellers, its engines are in fact turbojet engines (as opposed to piston engines) based on the same technologies as jet engines (Edlund, 1997, p. 111).
16. Note that despite all rumours about the death of the regional turboprop market, in 1999 the Canadian firm Bombardier started to sell a brand-new twin-turboprop, the Q-400 quiet regional jet.

9. Conclusions

It is my belief that flight is possible, and while I am taking up the investigation for pleasure rather than profit, I think there is a slight possibility of achieving fame and fortune from it.

Wilbur Wright [1]

The purpose of this study was to understand firm-level diversification within an institutional environment and to delineate the nature of the specific institutions affecting the process. To this end, five research questions were asked:

- Why do firms diversify?
- What is the role of national institutions and organisations in the firm's choice of a diversification strategy?
- How is diversification implemented within firms?
- What kind of learning mechanisms are used by firms for the generation and exploitation of the knowledge needed for their diversification?
- How do firms and supporting organisations interact in the process of diversification?

The theoretical taxonomy developed in Chapter 2 argued that the traditional diversification literature had reduced the process of diversification to a strategy internal to the firm. Moreover, this literature considered that the institutional environment of the firm was limited to a market in which firms interacted with buyers or sellers. Therefore, Chapter 2 was an attempt to integrate the diversification literature with another perspective, adding a broader concept of institutional environment – the systems of innovation approach. The firm was then described as operating within a system of innovation, although the nature of the system and its institutions were not clearly specified. National as well as sectoral organisations and institutions could be taken into account, and the possibility of overlap between national and sectoral systems was acknowledged.

The three case-studies, that have now been described and analysed in relation to the theoretical taxonomy, provide new insights into the process of diversification in large firms. These cases show that to comprehend the complexity of the process of diversification, it is simply not enough to consider the institutional environment in which the firm diversifies as being limited to the market. Neither is it enough, however, simply to consider that the firm diversifies in a broad institutional environment without clarifying what kinds of institutions are significant. Hence, these cases prove that it is the very nature of the specific institutions affecting the diversification that needs to be delineated.

Institutions matter during the whole process of diversification, from the initial decision making to the final steps of implementation. The embeddedness of the firm in its national system of innovation implies that transformations of the system can prompt the diversification, while the success of the implementation of the strategy is rooted in the degree of embeddedness of the firm in both the national and the sectoral systems of innovation.

Section 1 of this concluding chapter describes why and how firms diversify in both national and sectoral systems of innovation. The overlap between the systems is also discussed. This section underlines the important and multiple roles of institutions during the diversification process. While the concept of institution is broadly used in this description to explain how the strategy takes place in a firm, Section 2 details the nature of the specific institutions affecting the firm's strategy. Section 3 discusses the interactions between organisations and how these interactions influence the learning processes occurring in the diversifying firm. The concluding section outlines policy and management recommendations based upon the findings of this study.

1. DIVERSIFICATION IN NATIONAL AND SECTORAL SYSTEMS OF INNOVATION

The previous analysis in Chapter 7 and Chapter 8 has shown that diversification of firms should be analysed in both national and sectoral systems of innovation frameworks, since specific institutions and organisations from both systems were found to have a significance at different stages of the process. In the coming sections the whole process of diversification is described, following the shift of importance from national to sectoral systems of innovation. Before the diversification, institutions and organisations from the national system of innovation are seen as being more important to the firm than sectoral ones.

1.1. Triggering Diversification

In this sub-section, the reasons for diversification are presented in relation to the degree of embeddedness of the firm in the national system of innovation in which it operates and in relation to the existence of institutional lock-outs constraining the firm in its strategic choices. Afterwards, the emergence of opportunities is described as triggering diversification in firms.

To some extent, the firm is embedded in a national system of innovation. This embeddedness implies some interdependencies between the diversifying firm and other organisations in the system. This means that on the one hand, transformations of the system can induce transformations within the firm, triggering the diversification, and on the other hand, the firm can be constrained in its activities by its national institutional environment.

The main transformations of the system observed in the study were of a national institutional character. In Sweden, for example, changes in the perception of national security problems during the 1970s affected the way the government and the parliament regarded the defence industry. It resulted in the transformation of the Swedish national system of innovation by the reduction of military expenditures, thereby inducing Saab to diversify into civil activities. The Swedish case also exemplifies the fact that institutional changes do not necessarily concern the national system of innovation in which the firm operates. These changes can belong to the political sphere of the country. Since the political system and the national system of innovation are interconnected, transformations of one affect the other.

Existing institutions, such as laws regulating industry, can also impede the firm from entering a new sector and thereby act as barriers, locking the firm out of the industry. These institutional lock-outs are not necessarily designed consciously by organisations and by the state. They can have emerged in the national system of innovation in the course of the development of the system but are not identified as lock-outs before the firm decides to diversify. In France, for example, the aircraft industry was divided between private firms for the development and production of military airplanes and state-owned firms for civil airplanes. This structure had not been promoted by a law but had emerged after the Second World War as a follow-up of diverse political decisions. The result was the *de facto* exclusion of Dassault from the civil aircraft industry because of informal national institutions regulating the French aircraft industry.

Under these conditions of institutional lock-outs, diversification is triggered by the emergence of opportunities. When opportunities emerge in an industrial sector in which the firm is not already directly involved, the firm must understand their nature and evaluate how benefits can be reaped from them. Sectoral agencies, such as standards or certification organisations, can participate in the evaluation process of the opportunities since they are usually in a good position to understand the needs of the industry and the capacity of firms to fulfil these needs.

In Korea, Daewoo had been involved in the production of parts for the aerospace industry worldwide. However, Daewoo had not succeeded in being assigned the large programmes launched by the government. The fact that the Agency for Defence Development was looking for a partner to develop a trainer was the opportunity awaited by Daewoo. For both Saab and Dassault, the triggering opportunity was the emergence of a new market in which the firms could rapidly position themselves, taking advantage of their existing competences. In the particular case of Dassault, the French civil aviation authority had an important role in convincing both Dassault and the government about the benefits of Dassault's diversification for the country.

However, even if opportunities have emerged, firms still need to overcome the existing institutional lock-outs. This is done by convincing the state about the advantages of the venture for the national economy. These advantages took the form of employment and trade balance in the Swedish and French cases, and of technological spillovers and prestige in the Korean case. At this stage, the firm is finally ready to enter the diversification and start its implementation.

1.2. Implementing Diversification

While the national system of innovation of the firm is significant during the decision-making process, the sectoral system appears to be more important during the implementation of the diversification, or more precisely, the overlap between the two systems is crucial for the success of the diversification. The firm implements the diversification mainly in relation to organisations and under the influence of institutions from the sectoral system of innovation, particularly with regard to learning that is taking place within the firm, in interaction with other organisations. However, some elements of the knowledge necessary for diversification are also found in the national system, such as, at universities or technical institutes.

National and sectoral systems of innovation overlap because firms have to follow rules created by both the industry and the nation in which they operate. Moreover, some organisations fulfil innovation support in both national and sectoral systems. Institutions in the sectoral system can be created at national level, for example, through national industrial policies. They can also be created by organisations from various countries within the sector, as is often the case for certification regulations. The development of a business jet by Dassault during the 1960s and of a regional aircraft by Saab during the 1980s were both constrained by certification regulations. These regulations were mainly created by organisations within the aerospace sector. However, certification regulations can also easily be used as trade-barriers, as has often been the case between the United States and Europe. Hence, sectoral institutions can also have national characteristics. The diversifying firm must take stock of both national and sectoral institutions, assessing how they can be used to facilitate the diversification process.

Although created by national industrial policies, research organisations also overlap between national and sectoral systems. The ultimate aim of an industrial policy is not the industry *per se* but the development of the country's welfare; the industrial development being only an intermediate tool to reach this goal. In France, for example, the National Office for Aeronautic Studies and Research, ONERA, was created by the French state to help the aircraft industry reach national science and technology targets. Consequently, this organisation was intended to promote an industry and its possible spill-overs as well as to promote other benefits for the country as a whole.

The overlap between national and sectoral systems includes institutions and organisations supporting the diversification. Hence, learning processes occurring during the implementation of the diversification take place to a large extent in this overlap. Five main learning dimensions were identified in this study:

1. learning about the technologies involved in the new product and production process;
2. learning about the market and its characteristics;

3. learning how the financing of the venture can be carried out and how much should be invested;
4. learning how to manage a new venture and integrate it into the existing activity of the firm; and
5. learning how to assess and make use of the institutions regulating new sectors of activities.

While technology and market dimensions are obviously learned primarily with the support of organisations from the sectoral system of innovation, the other dimensions, i.e., financing, management and institutions, are learned at the overlap between national and sectoral systems.

This study has identified three types of organisation in the sectoral system of innovation, which interacted with the diversifying firm during the implementation of the strategy. These are independent research organisations, sectoral agencies and other firms.

National institutions also regulate these organisations, but not necessarily in the country where the diversification takes place. Swiss institutions influenced the firm Pilatus, but these did not affect the diversification process of Daewoo in Korea. They could have done so, however, if Pilatus had not been allowed to export its technologies to Korea. The interactions between these organisations will be described in more detail in Section 3.

With regard to the role of elements of the national system of innovation, some parts of the government, such as the Ministry of Industry and the Ministry of Defence, are predominantly important during the implementation of the strategy, particularly in terms of financing. The allocation of resources is done in accordance with existing science and technology policies or with other industrial policies. For example, since the diversification of Saab and Dassault would support the aircraft industry in France and Sweden, the respective governments were ready to grant the firms loans, thereby, sharing the risks of the development of a new aircraft with the firms.

The aforesaid description of the diversification process widens the understanding of the diversification of firms by using a systems of innovation approach. This description gives great importance to the role of institutions in the process as a whole. However, the nature of the institutions encountered varies considerably. Therefore, it is important to analyse the role of the specific institutions affecting the strategy.

2. INSTITUTIONS AFFECTING FIRMS' DIVERSIFICATION

Institutions were defined in this study as 'the rules of the game' (North, 1990, p. 3). However, such a concept is difficult to use since its definition is 'all-encompassing'. As a result, the concept of institutions is rather difficult to use as an analytical tool. How then does this study relate to the concept of institutions and what does it show concerning the role of specific institutions in the diversification of firms?

As Section 1.1 has shown, during the phase preceding the diversification, several kinds of institutions affect the choices made by the firm. Formal institutions, such as laws established by the state, can provide incentives and disincentives for firms. When formal institutions are established at the state level they can be transformed and adapted likewise, thus allowing diversification. Secondly, institutions can be informal and take the form of ideologies and traditions. These are more difficult to suppress because they build upon years of historical developments, both national and international. New laws formally established by the state can, however, restrain and transform these institutions and thereby facilitate the diversification process.

Still, such a dichotomy between formal and informal institutions is not precise enough. This study has shown that during the implementation of the diversification, several institutions were encountered that influenced the firm and its choices.

Four main subsets of institutions affecting the firm during the diversification process have been identified in this study. Furthermore, the study has proven that these institutions could have both national and sectoral characteristics. These institutions were as follows:

1. laws and policies regulating industry;
2. rules of behaviour regulating the relations between organisations;
3. standards and certification requirements; and
4. routines inside firms.

Although these institutions will now be discussed separately, they can, and often do, overlap, influencing each other in their effect on firms.[2]

2.1. Institutions as Laws and Policies Regulating Industry

The legal environment of the firm has implications at two different levels, i.e., on the strategy the firm chooses and on the outcomes of the strategy.

Firstly, laws resulting from, for example, science and technology policies or industrial policies of national states, constrain or induce the firms in their choices of strategies. Such an institution particularly affected Korean Airlines and Samsung in their decision to enter the defence industry during the mid-1970s, under the constraints of the Korean government.

Secondly, the legal environment of the firm has some impact on how the firm interacts with other organisations in the system of innovation, hence shaping the way the strategy is being carried out. Dassault had to find a way to integrate the state-owned manufacturer Sud Aviation in the civil venture, so that, on the one hand, funding would be granted by the state and on the other hand, Sud Aviation could reduce the production workload of Dassault by manufacturing the fuselage of the aircraft.

The definition of policies by the government does not, however, necessarily imply the creation of new laws but may provide an institutional framework in which the firm can decide upon its strategy. For example, by formulating science and technology policies the government indicates to firms which industrial sectors might be supported. Policies *per se* are not institutions but create new institutions or transform existing ones, thereby affecting the institutional environment. Changes in the Swedish national defence policy during the 1970s did not result in the creation of new laws but instead resulted in a situation where Saab had to diversify to accommodate its activities to its new institutional environment.

However, the interconnection between policies and institutions remains unclear. Policies can result in formal laws, or formal institutions, as well as in informal guidelines, the latter providing the firm with a supporting institutional environment for its operations. Understanding these interconnections could be the object of further investigation.

2.2. Institutions as Rules of Behaviour Regulating the Relations Between Organisations

Institutions regulate the relations between the various organisations of the system of innovation, whether national or sectoral. These institutions can be created by the legal system or be routines established between firms and other organisations. Rules of behaviour can, therefore, be a subset of the previously described institutions. For example, contractual relationships between firms follow established legal institutions that allow the fulfilment of contracts, legally protecting the firm in litigious cases. In the case of Saab, the firm was bound by contract with Fairchild to complete the development, the production and the certification of the aircraft. The contract was specific enough to detail the areas of responsibilities of both firms and contained clauses regarding delays and withdrawal of the venture by either firm.

However, rules of behaviour are not necessarily formal. The relationship between firms is based on a mutual understanding of each other's activity as well as on trust. During the process of diversification, the diversifying firm needs to understand how firms in the new industry behave. Understanding these rules is necessary for the diversifying firm to successfully interact with these firms. The development of trust relations between firms is a process that takes time, and it is, therefore, difficult to evaluate how such relations can be developed.

Daewoo had to develop its relationship with firms in the aerospace industry worldwide and show its capacity to fulfil the requirements of the industry, especially in terms of quality. Developing these relations was a process that took time and involved trial and error while getting contracts with established manufacturers. Trust is mainly an informal institution to be taken into account while diversifying. The fact that the firm was already established in other sectors and had proven itself to be trustworthy facilitated the process of being accepted in the aerospace sector.

There are, however, some elements of formal institutions in the development of trust between firms. A particular element, as identified in this study, is the certification of the product or of the production, following specific rules designed by independent organisations, as will be described in the next section.

2.3. Institutions as Standards and Certification Requirements

Some industrial sectors have to follow strict regulations when it comes to their products and production processes. Independent authorities assess whether firms comply or not with the regulations. In the aerospace sector, a very strong set of institutions are the certification regulations. These have two major impacts on firms. On the one hand, since certification is carried out by independent authorities, it allows firms to have an official basis for establishing their trust relations with other firms. On the other hand, certification regulations affect the development of new products by the firms, constraining the nature of the technologies used as well as the production process.

Certification is the official recognition by an independent organisation of the firm's capability to carry out its activities in the industry properly. This implies that certification allows for the development of trust relations between the diversifying firm and firms established in the industry. By showing their compliance with official certification regulations concerning the production of parts for the aerospace industry, Korean chaebols were able to slowly win the trust of other established aerospace firms worldwide, and thereby became accepted in the industry as a reliable partner.

The second, and more important, aspect of certification regulations is concerned with the creation of rules to which the firm must comply. If the industry and the state require the certification of a product and the production process, the firm must then follow these rules precisely, otherwise it will not be able to sell the product at all. Certification requirements, especially for safety, are usually established by single national organisations or by groups of national organisations coming from different countries. In the case of Saab, the firm had to follow the sets of regulations created by the American Federal Aviation Administration and by the European Joint Aviation Requirements. Although very similar in their content, these two sets of regulations presented some discrepancies that had to be taken into account by the firm and the certification authorities so that the aircraft would comply to both American and European certification requirements.

Certification regulations do not define any functionality of the product but define a number of requirements to which the product and the production process must comply in order to be certified. Technologies *per se* are not specified by certification rules, but their implementation in a product needs to be certified, showing their compliance with the regulations, whether in terms of safety, quality or other related issues. In France, Dassault used technologies developed for its military aircraft while developing the Mystère 20. It was not the technologies themselves that worried the certification authorities but their compliance with safety requirements. The firm carried out new tests to control the technologies, and certification officials often had to use their own judgement to accept or refuse the results of these tests, thereby allowing or rejecting technology transfers and technological innovations.

Although not identified in this study as an institution that affected the diversification process, standardisation must be mentioned here because of its similarities to certification. Standardisation strongly influences the choice of technologies and can be a hurdle for diversifying firms to overcome if they choose not to follow this institution. Standardisation precisely specifies the functionalities or the dimensions of a product, for example, the end signal of a radio base-station in a mobile telecommunication network or the diameter of a CD-ROM. As a result, the product can be used freely with technologies designed by other firms following the same standards. The technologies used to reach the functionalities of the product might differ between firms, but the outcome must be identical if the firm wants to have access to specific markets (Tassey, 1995, p. 162).

However, standardisation does not force the firm to comply with its rules as do certification regulations.[3] The firm may decide to develop a product outside the standard and attempt to create its own market. This is a risky strategy, but the possibility exists. Standards wars have long prevailed in industries such as the VCR industry or the mobile telecommunication industry and several standards can co-exist.

2.4. Institutions as Routines Inside Firms

Routines govern the way firms carry out their daily operations. Some of these routines are formally established by the management of the firm in order to organise its various activities, while others emerge informally within the organisation. The success of the strategy decided by the management of the firm will largely depend on how employees within the firm adapt to the new organisation. During the diversification, new routines are created to facilitate the process. However, existing routines within the firm might slow down the diversification. These must, therefore, be suppressed or at least ignored. The process by which routines are created and suppressed is both formally organised by the management of the firm and evolves informally as the strategy develops.

At Dassault, engineers followed the so-called 'small-steps policy' while designing a new aircraft. This strategy within the firm established routines as to how engineers were supposed to conceive an aircraft, taking into account knowledge previously developed within the firm and reducing the amount of risk. The 'small-steps policy' was not a formal routine in the firm, but it very strongly influenced choices of technologies and development of new aircraft within the firm.

To operationalise the strategy, some rigidities created by routines in the firm should be reduced. Since most of the routines are not established formally, it can be difficult to identify them, impeding the proper development of the diversification. Some new rigidities can also be created during the implementation of the strategy. For Saab's engineers, the joint venture with Fairchild implied new routines as to how the programme was to be managed. Engineers had to assimilate and follow these routines in coordination with American engineers despite the conflicts caused by these routines.

3.   INTERACTIVE LEARNING BETWEEN ORGANISATIONS

This study has shown that the success of the diversification depends on the interactions between the diversifying firm and other organisations as well as on the ability of the diversifying firm to take advantage of these other organisations. Section 1.2 and Section 2.4 of this chapter have demonstrated the existence of institutions regulating the interactions between organisations. The generation of knowledge necessary for the fulfilment of the strategy is based on the interactions between these various organisations and the firm as well as on the resulting interactive learning. The interactive learning that occurs allows the diversifying firm to gain access to the competences and the knowledge it needs for the venture.

Three sorts of organisations, now to be discussed, were observed in this study, i.e., supporting firms, research organisations and sectoral agencies. These are all the recipients of specific knowledge that can be used by the firm in the course of the implementation of the diversification. Section 1.2 of this chapter pointed out the fact that differences exist as to the nature of the learning dimensions these organisations could provide to the diversifying firm. Five learning dimensions of relevance for the diversification were analysed, i.e., technology, market, financing, management and institutions. These learning dimensions will now be discussed in relation to the organisations supporting diversification.

3.1.   Supporting Firms

In the sectoral system of innovation, supporting firms provide the diversifying firm with knowledge related to the five learning dimensions. It is, therefore, important for the diversifying firm to assess clearly which firms can be partners of the venture and what kind of partnership it should be. Firms established in the sector are already aware of where and how they can find the necessary knowledge for their existing activities. Hence, their support is crucial for diversifying firms. In the case of Saab, the support from Fairchild was essential in order to gain access to the regional aircraft market in the United States, to develop technologies and learn how to certify a civil aircraft. Moreover, Saab had to learn how to manage the diversification in cooperation with Fairchild. Finally, by reducing the financial burden of the development cost of the Saab 340 and by improving the confidence that the programme would be a success, Fairchild facilitated the financing of the programme both by the firms and by the Swedish state.

The interactions between the diversifying firm and the supporting firms gradually increase the stock of knowledge of both firms and allow the implementation of the diversification. The success of the venture is very much based on the organisation of the interactive learning that takes place between the firms. Daewoo lacked almost all necessary knowledge to develop an aircraft. The first partnership with Pilatus did not work out properly because of the conflicts of interest that emerged between the firms. Daewoo was, however, able to take a first step in understanding the technologies. The interactions with GECI, a consulting firm, provided Daewoo with the specific technological knowledge that was needed to develop the KTX-1.

Supporting firms can either be foreign or of the same nationality as the diversifying firm. In both cases, the institutional environment of the sector is important for the relations between the partners. However, if the firms belong to the same national system of innovation, national institutions might constrain the relations, as was the case, for example, between private and state-owned firms in France. In this particular case, the involvement of the state was needed in order to transform elements of the national institutional environment. This involvement allowed the venture to be carried out without obstruction.

3.2. Independent Research Organisations

Independent research organisations are private or public research organisations involved in the development of science and technologies for use in the industrial sector in which the firm diversifies. They support the diversifying firm by providing it with technological competences to be used in the diversification. National research organisations are not, however, completely independent, as most of their financing comes from the state. As a result, the main orientation of the research that is carried out follows national science and technology targets.

In this study, the role of research organisations was seen as being minor in the whole process of diversification. However, the Korean case showed how the interactions between the Agency for Defence Development and Daewoo spurred the development of technologies for the KTX-1. Since both organisations were new to the development of aircraft, they had to interact very closely with each other, constantly monitoring their progress.

3.3. Sectoral Agencies

Sectoral agencies certify that technologies are used according to specific rules, for example, rules of safety or quality. Although not studied in this work, organisations setting the standards of the industry may also be important in the process. The interaction between the firm and these organisations is important for the firm, in order to understand the specific institutions of the new industry and to learn how technologies can be used.

Certification authorities, as a form of sectoral agency, were seen to be extremely important for the diversifying firms, particularly in the French and the Swedish cases. The Swedish civil aviation administration followed the development of the Saab 340 very carefully and made the first truly European civil aircraft certification possible. The foresight of this organisation in finding solutions to simplify the certification of the Saab 340 was a great support for Saab. It accelerated the process of certifying the aircraft at a reasonable cost.

The interactive learning taking place between the firm and the certifying organisation implies that the firm learns about the institutions and also that the organisation develops its own competences. Certifying new technologies often implies that the certification authority must use its own judgement, hence learning how the institutions it created can gradually be transformed.

4.   CONCLUDING REMARKS

This study has shown the combined influence of national and sectoral systems of innovation on the diversifying firm. The relations between organisations in the systems follow a number of institutions. Moreover, the previous section has shown that learning occurs in interaction between these organisations. What then are the conclusions of this study in terms of public policy and of firms' strategic management?

4.1. Public Policy Implications

The role of the state in the diversification was proven to be more important during the decision phase than during the implementation of the strategy. A shift of importance was identified as moving from the national system of innovation in which the firm operates to the sectoral system into which the firm diversifies. This has some direct consequences for an industrial policy supporting diversification in firms.

Institutional lock-outs can block the diversification of firms in specific industries. Hence, one main conclusion in terms of policy implication rests on the identification and elimination of these institutional lock-outs. Such a policy should be concerned, firstly, by the identification of the nature of institutional lock-outs, as well as by the understanding of how they have emerged. Secondly, such a policy must focus on suppressing these lock-outs.

Identification of institutional lock-outs is done at the level of the national system of innovation. The interactions between the firm, sectoral agencies and the state provide information as to diversification opportunities available to the firm. Through the precise evaluation of these interactions, it is possible to identify why the firm is not able to engage in the strategy. Note that history matters; the present institutional environment of the firm is the result of events in the past. This was clearly demonstrated in the three cases. The institutional lock-outs were the result of long processes of industrial developments involving the relations between firms and the state. For example, the difficulties Dassault had in diversifying dated back to the mid-1940s, and the very tight customer–supplier relations between Saab and the Swedish state did not give Saab the opportunity to diversify at all since the Swedish state was not interested in civil aircraft until the late 1970s.

When institutional lock-outs are identified and analysed they must be suppressed or at least their effects on the firm must be relaxed. This work must also be done in close collaboration with the industry, in a symbiosis which allows both the firm and the government to identify the advantages of facilitating the diversification. Moreover, this symbiosis will allow the identification of the nature of the institutional environment needed by the firm in order to take advantage of new opportunities. This means that some national institutions will have to be suppressed or adapted to the new industry, but it also means that new ones will have to be created.

By reducing its military expenditures, the Swedish state created a break in the traditional relations it had with Saab. The whole procedure of financing military aircraft was redesigned, requiring the development of military programmes at fixed costs. The new institutions that were promoted and the termination of old ones fostered the diversification of Saab. Thus, supporting the diversification of firms in new industries is not only a question of financially assisting firms.

Although financing should not be the only role of the state in supporting diversification, it is a very important part of a supportive innovation policy. When coming to the question of financing, the government must evaluate the potential benefits of the diversification for the country as well as the cost of not taking advantage of these benefits. For the country, these benefits can be employment, technological development, industrial growth or other related advantages. The three cases have shown that the state had an interest in the diversification of the firms. In the French and the Swedish cases, the state was interested in supporting the industry in order to avoid problems with unemployment. In the Korean case, the state wanted the development of the aircraft industry for reasons of prestige as well as for the expected technological spillovers. The coordination of the efforts between the firms and the state towards a new sector is necessary for successful diversification in the long term.

Finally, a diversification policy should be oriented towards supporting the development of the firms in the new sector. This should be done through an efficient educational structure, providing a competent workforce, as well as through research and development. The fact that the French and the Swedish aerospace industries had developed over many decades, with the support of the state, facilitated the diversification. In Korea, such infrastructures hardly existed and were still under development during the diversification of Daewoo, making the process of knowledge accumulation long and difficult for the firm.

4.2.   Firms' Strategy Implications

Whether in a growth phase or exposed to risks in its existing market, the firm evaluating possibilities of diversification can follow a number of recommendations, allowing for a successful implementation of the strategy. Before evaluating possibilities of diversification, the management of the firm needs to understand the constraints of its national institutional environment and how these constraints will affect the strategy. When institutions block the process of diversification, the firm needs to find ways to overturn these barriers with the support of the government and of sectoral agencies. In particular, this implies that before starting the diversification, the firm must be well aware of the government's industrial as well as science and technology policies in order to be able to relate the strategy to government industrial targets.

This conclusion links back to the policy implications of this study. The interactions between the state, the firm and sectoral organisations provide information as to the needs of the state and the capacity of the firm. By frequenting the Ministry of Industry and the Ministry of Defence, Marcel Dassault was able to understand the needs of the state with regard to its industrial policy for the aircraft industry and to forthcoming military programmes. This understanding, combined with the support of the French civil aviation authorities, helped Dassault to launch the business jet programme. The then CEO of Saab, Sten Gustafsson, was also involved in several discussions with the Swedish Minister of Industry, arguing for the future of the Swedish aerospace industry and identifying issues of importance for the state, such as employment and prestige of the industry.

Thus, the choice of a sector into which the firm can diversify is largely influenced by national institutions. This shows that the management of the firm must not only look at its technological competences, including production and development of new products stemming from its existing facilities and R&D activity, but must also look at other competences, such as its understanding of the market, its capacity to organise new ventures and to which extent it can assess the institutional environment of the firm.

Although the choice of a sector is not necessarily based solely on technology relatedness, this aspect greatly facilitates a successful diversification. Building on the existing competences of the firm in terms of technology must not lure the firm as to the assessment of other competences needed for the diversification, however. Market and institutional relatedness are also to be taken into account. The firm must evaluate the risks of the diversification and reduce the uncertainties related to the strategy through the identification of other organisations that can support the firm efficiently.

For both Dassault and Saab, the diversification was related in terms of technologies and not in terms of institutions or market. This fact helped the firms to develop the aircraft and gain the confidence from the state that the project would succeed. This latter aspect facilitated the financial support of the ventures by the state. In the case of Dassault, the fact that the firm early on found a strong customer reduced the amount of risks of the venture even more.

While the diversification is being implemented, the firm needs to know how it can take advantage of all its competences. It must also be well aware of the difficulties implied by the institutional environment of the new sector. In other words, the firm should focus on the five learning dimensions, i.e., the technologies, the market, the financing, the management and the institutions in relation to the new sector. Besides these learning dimensions, the firm needs to evaluate clearly which organisations in both its national and sectoral systems of innovation will be able to provide new competences through interactive learning. The clear assessment of the competences of the firm and of the industrial needs of the government are keys to success in a diversification venture.

NOTES

1. Wilbur Wright performed the first complete circular flight in a motor-driven airplane on 20 September 1904. Along with his brother Orville, he is one of the pioneers of aeroplane development.
2. This does not mean that these are the only institutional forms existing in an institutional environment. Other institutions exist but were not found relevant in relation to the diversification process.
3. However, some standards cannot be ignored by the firm. For example, the bandwidth of radio frequencies which can be used by firms in the mobile telecommunication business is fixed by national organizations.

References

Published Material:

Amit, R. and Livnat, J. (1988), 'Diversification Strategies, Business Cycles and Economic Performance', *Strategic Management Journal*, 9, 99–110.

Amsden, Alice (1989), *Asia's Next Giant*, New York, Oxford: Oxford University Press.

Andersson, Hans (1989), *Saab Aircraft since 1937*, Washington, D.C.: Smithsonian Institution Press..

Ann, Young-Su (1997), 'Korea's Aircraft Industry: Using Strategic Alliances to Reach a New Level of Sophistication', *KIET Economic Review*, 2 (9), 13–17.

Ann, Young-Su (1998), 'Low Localisation Level of Korea's Aircraft Part Industry', *KIET Economic Review*, 3 (2), 22–24.

Annual Report Saab-Scania (1968).

Annual Report Saab-Scania (1969).

Annual Report Saab-Scania (1970).

Annual Report Saab-Scania (1971).

Annual Report Saab-Scania (1972).

Annual Report Saab-Scania (1973).

Annual Report Saab-Scania (1974).

Annual Report Saab-Scania (1975).

Annual Report Saab-Scania (1976).

Annual Report Saab-Scania (1977).

Annual Report Saab-Scania (1978).

Annual Report Saab-Scania (1979).

Annual Report Saab-Scania (1980).

Annual Report Saab-Scania (1981).

Ansoff, Igor (1957), 'Strategies for Diversification', *Harvard Business Review*, 35 (5), 113–124.

Ashford, Douglas E. (ed.) (1992), *History and Context in Comparative Public Policy*, Pittsburgh: University of Pittsburgh Press.

Aviation Week and Space Technology (1998), Strong Passenger Demand Propels U.S. Regionals, 18 May 1998.

Barnard, R.H. and Philpott, D.R. (1989), *Aircraft Flight – A Description of the Physical Principles of Aircraft Flight*, Longman Scientific and Technical.

Cantwell, John (1995), 'The Globalisation of Technology: What Remains of the Product Cycle Model', *Cambridge Journal of Economics*, 19 (1), 155–174.

Carlier, Claude (1983), *L'Histoire de l'Aéronautique Française 1945–1975*, Lavauzelle.

Carlier, Claude (1992), *Marcel Dassault – La Légende d'un Siècle*, Paris, Librairie Académique Perrin.

Carlier, Claude (1997), *Chronologie Aérospatiale Politique et Militaire 1945–1995*, Paris: Economica.

Carlier, Claude and Berger, Luc (1996a), *L'entreprise – Dassault, 50 Ans d'Aventure Aéronautique*, Edition du Chêne – Hachette Livre.

Carlier, Claude and Berger, Luc (1996b), *Les Programmes – Dassault, 50 Ans d'Aventure Aéronautique*, Edition du Chêne – Hachette Livre.

Carlsson, Bo (ed.) (1992), *Technological Systems and Economic Performance: the Case of Factory Automation*, Boston, Massachusetts and London: Kluwer Academic Publishers.

Carlsson, Bo and Stankiewicz, Richard (1992), 'On the Nature, Function and Composition of Technological Systems', in Bo Carlsson (ed.), *Technological Systems and Economic Performance: the Case of Factory Automation*, Boston, Massachusetts and London: Kluwer Academic Publishers, pp. 21–57.

Carroll, Sidney L. (1975), 'The Market for Commercial Airliners', in Caves R.E. and Roberts M.J. (eds), *Regulating the Market*, Cambridge: Ballinger, pp. 145–169.

Chandler, Alfred (1977), *The Visible Hand – The Managerial Revolution in American Business*, Cambridge, Massachusetts and London: The Belknap Press of Harvard University Press.

Chandler, Alfred (1990), *Scale and Scope – The Dynamics of Industrial Capitalism*, Cambridge, Massachusetts and London: The Belknap Press of Harvard University Press.

Chung, Kae-H, and Lee, Hak-Chong (eds) (1989), *Korean Managerial Dynamics*, New York: Praeger.

Cohen, W.M. and Levinthal, D.A. (1990), 'Absorptive Capacity: a New Perspective on Learning and Innovation', *Administrative Science Quarterly*, 35, 128–152.

Dassault, Marcel (1970), *Le Talisman*, Edition J'ai Lu.

David, Paul (1990), 'Clio and the Economics of QWERTY', in Christopher Freeman (ed.), *The Economics of Innovation*, Aldershot, UK and Brookfield, US: Edward Elgar, pp. 390–395.

Detrie, Jean-Pierre and Ramanantsoa, Bernard (1986), 'Diversification – the Key Factors for Success', *Long Range Planning*, **19** (1), 31–37.

Dörfer, Ingemar (1973), *System 37, Viggen – Arms, Technology and the Domestication of Glory*, Universitetsförlaget.

Dosi, Giovani, Freeman, Christopher; Nelson, Richard; Silverberg, Gerald and Soete, Luc (eds) (1988), *Technical Change and Economic Theory*, London: Pinter.

Dyer, W. Gibb and Wilkins, Alan L. (1991), 'Better Stories, Not Better Constructs, to Generate Better Theory: a Rejoinder to Eisenhardt', *Academy of Management Review*, **16** (3), 613–619.

Edlund, Ulf (1997), Jet, Tubine, Turbojet, Turboprop, Turbofan – Differences and Similarities, in *Mekanisten*, No. 1997:4, p. 110–113.

Edquist, Charles (ed.) (1997a), *Systems of Innovation, Technologies, Institutions and Organisations*, London: Pinter.

Edquist, Charles (1997b), 'Introduction', in Charles Edquist (ed.), *Systems of Innovation, Technologies, Institutions and Organisations*, London: Pinter, pp. 1–35.

Edquist, Charles (2000), 'Innovation Policy – A Systemic Approach', in Daniele Archibugi and Bengt-Åke Lundvall (eds), *The Globalising Learning Economy: Major Socio-Economic Trends andd European Innovation Policy*, Oxford: Oxford University Press.

Edquist, Charles and Hommen, Leif (1999), 'Public Technology Procurement and Innovation Theory', in Charles Edquist, Leif Hommen and Lena Tsipouri (eds), *Technology Procurement and Innovation*, Boston/Dordrecht/London: Kluwer Academic, pp. 1–70.

Edquist, Charles and Johnson, Björn (1997), 'Institution and Innovation: a Conceptual Discussion', in Charles Edquist (ed.), *Systems of Innovation, Technologies, Institutions and Organisations*, London: Pinter, pp. 36–63.

Edquist, Charles and Lundvall, Bengt-Åke (1993), 'Comparing the Danish and the Swedish Systems of Innovation', in Richard Nelson (ed.), *National Systems of Innovation: a Comparative Analysis*, New York: Oxford University Press, pp. 265–298.

Edquist, Charles and McKelvey, Maureen (1998), 'High R&D Intensity Without High Tech Products: a Swedish Paradox?', in Klaus Nielsen and Björn Johnson (eds), *Institutions and Economic Change – New Perspectives on Markets, Firms and Technology*, Cheltenham, UK and Northampton, MA, USA: Edward Elgar, pp. 131–149.

Edquist, Charles and Texier, François (1996), 'The Growth Pattern of Swedish Industry' in *Innovation Systems and Competitiveness*, Osmo Kuusi (ed.), Helsinki : Taloustieto Oy, pp. 103–122.

Edquist, Charles; McKelvey, Maureen and Hommen, Leif (1998), 'Product Versus Process Innovation: Implications for employment', in Jonathan Michie and Angelo Reati (eds), *Employment, Technology and Economic Needs – Theory, Evidence, and Public Policy*, Cheltenham, UK and Northampton, MA, USA: Edward Elgar, pp. 128–152.

Edquist, Charles; McKelvey, Maureen and Hommen, Leif (2000), *Innovations and Employment: A Systems of Innovation Perspective on Process Versus Product Innovation*, Cheltenham, UK and Northampton, MA, USA: Edward Elgar.

Eisenhardt, Kathleen M. (1989), 'Building Theories from Case Study Research', *Academy of Management Review*, **14** (4), 532–550.

Eliasson, Gunnar (1995), *Teknologigenerator eller Nationellt Prestigeprojekt?*, Stockholm: City University Press.

English, Dave (1999), *Slipping the Surly Bonds – Great Quotations on Flight*, McGraw-Hill.

Enright, Michael J. (1994), 'Regional Clusters and Firm Strategy', working paper, Harvard Business School.

Feldman, Elliot J. (1985), *Concorde and Dissent – Explaining High Technology Project Failures in Britain and France*, Cambridge: Cambridge University Press.

Feldman, Jonathan (1997), 'Diversification after the Cold War: Results of the National Defence Economy Survey, Working Paper No. 112, Center for Urban Policy Research, Rutgers, the State University of New Jersey.

Feldman, Jonathan (1998), 'The Conversion of Defence Engineer's Skills: Explaining Success and Failure Through Customer-Based Learning, Teaming, and Managerial Integration at Boeing-Vertol', paper presented at the Second Klein Symposium on the Management of Technology, Smeal College of Business Administration, Pennsylvania State University, University Park, Pennsylvania, 15 September 1997.

Feldman, Jonathan (1999a), 'Can Saab Diversify?: Lessons From Civil Spin-offs in the 1970s and 1980s', Tema T Working Paper No 206, University of Linköping, Sweden.

Feldman, Jonathan (1999b), 'Civil Diversification, Learning, and Institutional Change: Growth Through Knowledge and Power', *Environment and Planning*, 31, 1805–1824.

Flight International (1973), 'Europlane Details Revealed', 24 May 1973, 765–766.

Flight International (1980a), 'Swedish Study Recommends Civil Emphasis', 2 February 1980, 290.

Flight International (1980b), 'Volvo and Garrett to Co-operate', 9 February 1980, 365.

Flight International (1998a), 'Daewoo Starts Work on Modified KT-1', 4–10 October 1998, 9.

Flight International (1998b), 'Good Flying?', 21–27 October 1998, 45–49.

Flight International (1998c), 'Compromise and Change', 21–27 October 1998, 42–44.

FLIK 1978, Flygindustriskomitténs Betänkande, Del 1, Ds Fö 1978:8.

FLIK 1980, Flygindustriskomitténs Betänkande, Del 2, Ds I 1980:2.

Flygbladet Number 2521, 28 April 1977.

Flygbladet Number 2529, 16 June 1977.

Flygbladet Number 2532, 30 June 1977.

Flygbladet Number 2532 extrablad, 30 June 1977 .

Flygbladet Number 2541, 22 September 1977.

Flygbladet Number 2551, 14 November 1977.

Flygbladet Number 2564, 2 February 1978.

Flygbladet Number 2567, 23 February 1978.

Flygbladet Number 2575, 1–2, 8 April 1978.

Flygbladet Number 2576, 13 April 1978.

Flygbladet Number 2588, 25 May 1978.

Flygbladet Number 2605, 19 October 1978.

Flygbladet Number 2618 special bilaga, 5 January 1979.

Flygbladet Number 2622, 1 February 1979.

Flygbladet Number 2629 specialbilaga, 1 March 1979.

Flygbladet Number 2645, 10 May 1979.

Flygbladet Number 2654, 26 June 1979.

Flygbladet Number 2689 extra bilaga, 22 February 1980.

Flygbladet Number 2690, 28 February 1980.

Flygbladet Number 2696, 11 April 1980.

Flygbladet Number 2698, 24 April 1980.

Flygbladet Number 2701, 17 May 1980.

Flygbladet Number 2703, 11 June 1980.

Flygbladet Number 2706, 19 June 1980.

Flygbladet Number 2707, 26 June 1980.

Flygbladet Number 2716, 11 September 1980.

Flygbladet Number 2721, 16 October 1980.

Flygbladet Number 2722, 23 October 1980.

Flygbladet Number 2728, 4 December 1980.

Flygbladet Number 2731, 15 January 1981.

Flygbladet Number 2760, 6 August 1981.
Flygbladet Number 2766, 17 September 1981.
Flygbladet Number 2770, 8 October 1981.
Flygbladet Number 2850, 26 January 1983.
Flygbladet Number 2866, 28 April 1983.
Fölster, Stephan (1993), 'De Teknologiska Spridningseffekterna av JAS: en Ny Empirisk Metod', (stencil), Stockholm : IUI.
Freeman, Christopher (1987), *Technology Policy and Economic Performance – Lessons from Japan*, London: Pinter.
Freeman, Christopher (1995), 'The "National Systems of Innovation" in Historical Perspective', *Cambridge Journal of Economics*, 19, 5–24.
Freeman, Christopher and Perez, Carlota (1988), 'Structural Crises of Adjustment, Business Cycles and Investment Behaviour', in Giovani Dosi, Christopher Freeman, Richard Nelson, Gerald Silverberg and Luc Soete (eds), *Technical Change and Economic Theory*, London: Pinter, pp. 38–66.
Gambardella, Alfonso and Torrisi, Salvatore (1998), 'Does Technological Convergence Imply Convergence in Markets? Evidence From the Electronic Industry', in *Research Policy*, 27, 445–463.
Gandt, Robert, (1995), *Skygods – The Rise and Fall of Pan Am*, New York : William Morrow and Company Inc.
Gates, Brian (1978), *Falcon Mystère 20 Production History*, Midland Counties.
George, Alexander L. (1979), 'Case studies and Theory Development: the Method of Structured, Focused Comparison', in Paul G. Lauren (ed.), *Diplomacy: New Approaches in History, Theory and Policy*, New York: The Free Press, pp. 43–68.
Granstrand, Ove (1984), 'Technology Procurement as a Special Form of Buyer-Seller Interaction in Industrial Marketing', *CIM–Report* No: 84:06, Department of Industrial Management, Chalmers University of Technology, Sweden.
Granstrand, Ove (1998), 'Towards a Theory of the Technology-Based Firm', *Research Policy*, 27, 465–489.
Granstrand, Ove and Alänge, Sverker (1995), 'The Evolution of Corporate Entrepreneurship in Swedish Industry – Was Schumpeter Wrong?', *Journal of Evolutionary Economics*, 5, 133–156.
Granstrand, Ove and Sjölander, Sören (1990), 'The Acquisition of Technology and Small Firms by Large Firms', *Journal of Economic Behaviour and Organisation*, 13, 367–387.
Granstrand, Ove; Patel, Pari and Pavitt, Keith (1997), 'Multi-Technology Corporations: Why They Have "Distributed" Rather Than "Distinctive Core" Competences', *California Management Review*, **39** (4), 8–25.
Håkansson, Håkan (1989), *Corporate Technological Behaviour: Co-operation and Networks*, London: Routledge.
Håkansson, Håkan (1990), 'Technological Collaboration in Industrial Networks', *European Management Journal*, **8** (3), 371–379.
Hawkins, Richard; Mansell, Robin, and Skea, Jim, (eds) (1995), *Standards, Innovation and Competitiveness – The Politics and Economics of Standards in Natural and Technical Environment*, Aldershot, UK and Brookfield, US: Edward Elgar.

Hobday, Michael (1995), *Innovation in East Asia – the Challenge to Japan*, Aldershot, UK and Brookfield, US: Edward Elgar.

Hodgson, Geoffrey (1988), *Economics and Institutions – A Manifesto for a Modern Institutional Economics*, Polity Press.

ITC (1998), *The Changing Structure of the Global Large Civil Aircraft Industry and Market – Implications for the Competitiveness of the US Industry*, Investigation No 332–384, publication 3143, US International Trade Commission, pp. 15–20.

Jacobs, Norman (1985), *The Korean Road to Modernization and Development*, Urbana, Illinois: University of Illinois Press.

Jacobsson, Staffan and Ehrnberg, Ellinor (1997), 'Technological Discontinuities and Incumbent's Performance: an Analytical Framework', in Charles Edquist (ed.), *Systems of Innovation, Technologies, Institutions and Organisations*, London: Pinter, pp. 318–341.

Johnson, Björn (1992), 'Institutional Learning', in Bengt-Åke Lundvall (ed.), *National Systems of Innovation – Toward a Theory of Innovation and Interactive Learning*, London: Pinter, pp. 23–44.

Jones, Leroy and Sakong, Il (1980), *Governmnet, Business, and Entrepreneurship in Economic Development: The Korean Case*, Cambridge, Massachusetts and London, England: Harvard University Press.

Kaiserfeld, Thomas (1999), 'A Case Study of the Swedish Public Technology Procurement Project "The Computer in the School" (COMPIS), 1981–1988', in Charles Edquist, Leif Hommen and Lena Tsipouri (eds), *Technology Procurement and Innovation*, Boston/Dordrecht/London: Kluwer Academic, pp. 121–141.

Kelley, M. and Watkins, T. (1995), 'The Myth of Specialised Military Contractors', *Technology Review*, **98** (3), 52–58.

Kennedy, A.P. (1979), 'Joint Airworthiness Requirements – Their History and Progress', *Aircraft Engineering*, May 1979.

Keon, Michael (1977), *Korean Phoenix – A Nation From the Ashes*, London: Prentice-Hall International.

Kim, Chan; Hwang, Peter and Burgers, William (1989), 'Global Diversification Strategy And Corporate Profit Performance', *Strategic Management Journal*, 10, 45–57.

Kim, Jun-Mo (1998), 'Targeting the Future: Asian Aerospace, Its Current Status and Challenges', *Journal of Korea Technology Innovation and Society,* 12, 338–350.

Kim, Ki-Dong, and Kim, Chong (1989), 'Korean Value Systems and Managerial Practices', in Kae-H Chung and Hak-Chong Lee (eds), *Korean Managerial Dynamics*, New York: Praeger, pp. 207–216 .

Kim, Linsu (1997) *Imitation to Innovation – The Dynamics of Korea's Technological Learning*, Boston: Harvard Business Press.

Klofsten, Magnus and Pettersson Thomas (1984), *Regionalflygbolagens Flygplansköp – En Studie av Bakomliggande Faktorer*, Master Study at the Department of Economics of Linköpings University, Sweden.

Köhler, Karl-Gustav (1984), 'JAS-Spelet', *Insyn,* 2–76.

Kuter, Laurence (1973), *The Great Gamble – the Boeing 747: the Boeing – Pan Am Project to Develop, Produce, and Introduce the 747*, Birmingham: Ala.

Lall, Sanjaya (1996), *Learning from the Asian Tigers, Studies in Technology and Industrial Policy*, MacMillan Press.

Lawrence, Philip and Braddon, Derek (eds) (1999), *Strategic Issues in European Aerospace Industry*, Aldershot, UK and Brookfield, USA: Ashgate.

Leary, William M. (ed.) (1995), *From Airbus to Airship – The History of Civil and Commercial Aviation; Infrastructure and Environment*, Washington and London: Smithsonian Institution Press.

Lee, Sang-M (1989), 'Management Styles of Korean Chaebols', in Kae-H Chung and Hak-Chong Lee (eds) *Korean Managerial Dynamics*, New York: Praeger, 181–194.

Lemaire, René (1992), 'L'Industrie Aéronautique de la Région Bordelaise', *in Cahiers de la Mémoire de Bordeaux*, William Blake and co., pp. 83–107.

Lindén, Johan (1991), *JAS 39 Gripen, Den Havererade Stormaktsdrömmen*, Broderskaps Förlag / Säkerhet and Nedrustning.

Llerena, Patrick and Cohendet, Patrick (1997), 'Learning, Technical Change, and Public Policy: How to Create and Exploit Diversity', in Charles Edquist (ed.), *Systems of Innovation, Technologies, Institutions and Organisations*, London: Pinter, pp. 223–241.

Lorne, Jean-Michel (1996a), *L'Industrie Aéronautique et Spatiale Coréenne : Qui Fait Quoi?*, Les Notes des Postes d'Expansion Economiques, French Trade Commission in Seoul.

Lorne, Jean-Michel (1996b), *Mythes et Réalités de l'Industrie Aéronautique Coréenne*, document from the French Trade Commission in Seoul.

Lundvall, Bengt-Åke (ed.) (1992a), *National Systems of Innovation – Toward a Theory of Innovation and Interactive Learning*, London: Pinter.

Lundvall, Bengt-Åke (1992b), 'Introduction', in Bengt-Åke Lundvall (ed.), *National Systems of Innovation – Toward a Theory of Innovation and Interactive Learning*, London: Pinter, pp. 1–19.

MacDonald, James (1985), 'R and D and the Directions of Diversification', *Review of Economics and Statistics*, **67** (4), 583–590.

Malerba, Franco and Breschi, Stefano (1997), 'Sectoral Innovation Systems: Technological Regimes, Schumpetarian Dynamics and Spatial Boundaries', in Charles Edquist (ed.), *Systems of Innovation, Technologies, Institutions and Organisations*, London: Pinter, pp. 130–156.

Malerba, Franco; Breschi, Stefano and Lissoni, Francesco (1998), 'Knowledge Proximity and Technological Diversification: An Analysis of the Determinants of Technological Diversification in Europe, United States and Japan', in François Texier and Charles Edquist (eds), *Innovation Systems and European Integration on CD-ROM*, University of Linköping, Sweden.

McGuire, Steven (1997), *Airbus Industry – Conflict and Co-operation in US-EC Trade Relations*, MacMillan Press.

McKelvey, Maureen (1996a), 'Discontinuities in Genetic Engineering for Pharmaceuticals? Firm Jumps and Lock-in in Systems of Innovation', *Technology Analysis and Strategic Management*, **8** (2), 107–116.

McKelvey, Maureen (1996b), *Evolutionary Innovations, the Case of Biotechnology*, Oxford: Oxford University Press.

McKelvey, Maureen (1997), 'Using Evolutionary Theory to define Systems of Innovation', in Charles Edquist (ed.), *Systems of Innovation, Technologies, Institutions and Organisations*, London: Pinter, pp. 200–222.

McKelvey, Maureen and Texier, François (2000), 'Surviving Technological Discontinuities Through Evolutionary Systems of Innovation: Ericsson and Mobile Telecommunication', in Bart Norteboom and Paulo Saviotti (eds), *Technology and Knowledge: from the Firm to Innovation Systems*, Cheltenham, UK and Northampton, MA, USA: Edward Elgar, pp. 227–248.

McKelvey, Maureen; Texier, François and Alm, Håkan (1997), 'The Dynamics of High-Tech Industry: Swedish Firms Developing Mobile Telecommunication Systems', in François Texier and Charles Edquist (eds), *Innovation Systems and European Integration on CD-ROM*, Linköping University, Sweden.

Meurling, John and Jeans, Richard (1994), *The Mobile Phone Book, the Invention of the Mobile Telephone Industry*, Communications Week International.

Montgomery, Cynthia (1994), 'Corporate Diversification', *Journal of Economic Perspectives*, **8** (3), 163–178.

Montgomery, Cynthia and Hariharan, S. (1991), 'Diversified Expansion by Large Established Firms', *Journal of Economic Behaviour and Organisation*, **15** (1), 71–89.

Mowery, David (1987), *Alliance Politics and Economics – Multinational Joint Ventures in Commercial Aircraft*, Cambridge, MA: Ballinger Pub. Co.

Mowery, David (1999), 'The Computer Software Industry', in David Mowery and Richard Nelson (eds) (1999), *Sources of Industrial Leadership – Studies of Seven Countries*, Cambridge: Cambridge University Press, pp. 133–168.

Mowery, David and Nelson, Richard (1999), 'Sources of Industrial Leadership', in David Mowery and Richard Nelson (eds), *Sources of Industrial Leadership – Studies of Seven Countries*, Cambridge: Cambridge University Press, pp. 359–382.

Mowery, David and Nelson, Richard (eds) (1999), *Sources of Industrial Leadership – Studies of Seven Countries*, Cambridge: Cambridge University Press.

Mowery, David and Rosenberg, Nathan (1989), *Technology and the Pursuit of Economic Growth,* Cambridge: Cambridge University Press.

Mueller, D.C. (1969), 'A Theory of Conglomerate Mergers', *Quarterly Journal of Economics*, 643–695.

Nadler, David and Tushman, Michael (1997), 'A Congruence Model for Organisation Problem Solving', in Michael L. Tushman and Philip Anderson (eds), *Managing Strategic Innovation and Change*, New York and Oxford: Oxford University Press, pp. 159–171.

Nelson, Richard (ed.) (1993), *National Systems of Innovation: a Comparative Analysis*, Oxford: Oxford University Press.

Nelson, Richard and Winter, Sidney (1982), *An Evolutionary Theory of Economic Change*, Cambridge, Massachusetts and London: The Belknap Press of Harvard University Press.

Nilsson, Göran B. (1973), 'Om det Fortfarande Behovet av Källkritik: Jämte Några Reflexioner över Midsommaren 1941', *Historisk Tidskrift*, 1, 173–211.

North, Douglas (1990), *Institutions, Institutional Change and Economic Performance*, Cambridge: Cambridge University Press.

Orlebar, Christopher (1986), *The Concorde Story – 21 Years in Service*, London: Reed Books Limited.

Oskarsson, Christer (1993), *Technology Diversification – The Phenomenon, its Causes and Effect*, Ph.D. Study, Department of Industrial Management and Economics, Chalmers University, Sweden.

Owen, Kenneth (1997), *Concorde and the Americans, International Politics of the Supersonic Transport*, Smithsonian History of Aviation Series, Washington and London: Smithsonian Institution Press.

Penrose, Edith (1959), *The Theory of the Growth of the Firm*, Oxford: Oxford University Press.

Phillips, Almarin; Phillips, Paul and Phillips, Thomas (1994), *Biz Jets – Technology and Market Structure in the Corporate Jet Aircraft Industry*, Dordrecht: Kluwer Academic.

Pilat, Dirk (1994), *The Economics of Rapid Growth : Experience of Japan and Korea*, Aldershot, UK and Brookfield, US: Edward Elgar.

Porter, Donald J. (1985), *The Cessna Citations*, McGraw-Hill.

Ramanujam, Vasudevan and Varadarajan, P. (1989), 'Research on Corporate Diversification: a Synthesis', *Strategic Management Journal*, 10, 523–551.

Richardson, George B. (1972), 'The Organisation of Industry', *Economic Journal*, 82, 883–896.

Rondi, Laura; Sembenelli, Alessandro and Ragazzi, Elena (1996), 'Determinants of Diversification Patterns', in Stephen Davies and Bruce Lyons (eds), *Industrial Organisation in the European Union*, Oxford: Clarendon, pp. 168–183.

Rumelt, Richard (1974), *Strategy, Structure and Economic Performance*, Cambridge, Massachusetts: Harvard University Press.

Sabbach Karl (1996), *Twenty-First-Century Jet – The Making and Marketing of the Boing 777*, New York: Scribner.

Samuels, Richard and Whipple, Benjamin (1989), 'Defence Production and Industrial Development, The Case of Japanese Aircraft', in Chalmers Johnson, Laura D'Andrea Tyson, John Zysman (eds), *Politics and Productivity, The Real Story of Why Japan Works*, Cambridge, Mass.: Ballinger.

Saxenian, Anna-Lee (1994), *Regional Advantage : Culture and Competition in Silicon Valley and Route 128*, Cambridge, Massachussetts: Harvard University Press.

Scherer, Fredrich M. and Ravenscraft, D. (1984), 'Growth by Diversification: Entrepreneurial Behaviour in Large-Scale United States Enterprises', *Journal of Economics*, **4** (4),199–218.

Scherer, Fredrich M. and Ross, David (1990), *Industrial Market Structure and Economic Performance*, Third Edition, Boston: Houghton Mifflin Company.

Schild, Ingrid (1996), *The Politics of International Collaboration in Polar Research*, Ph.D. Study, University of Sussex, Science Policy Research Unit, England.

Segelod, Esbjörn (1995), *Renewal Through Internal Development*, Aldershot, UK and Brookfield, US: Avebury.

Sehlberg, Bo (1988), *340 – The Story*, Förlagshuset Norden AB.

Tassey, Gregory (1995), 'The Roles of Standards as Technology Infrastructure', in Richard Hawkins, Robin Mansell, and Jim Skea (eds), *Standards, Innovation and Competitiveness – The Politics and Economics of Standards in Natural and Technical Environment*, Aldershot, UK and Brookfield, US: Edward Elgar, pp. 161–191.

Teece, David (1980), 'Economies of Scope and the Scope of the Enterprise', *Journal of Economic Behaviour and Organisation*, 1, 223–247.

Teece, David (1982), 'Towards an Economic Theory of the Multiproduct Firm', *Journal of Economic Behaviour and Organisation*, 3, 39–63.

Teece, David (1988), 'Technological Change And The Nature of The Firm', in Giovani Dosi, Christopher Freeman, Richard Nelson, Gerald Silverberg, and Luc Soete (eds), *Technical Change and Economic Theory*, London: Pinter, pp. 256–281.

Teece, David (1992), 'Strategies for Capturing the Financial Benefits from Technological Innovation, in Rosenberg', in Richard Landau and David Mowery (eds), *Technology and the Wealth of Nations*, Stanford, California: Stanford University Press, pp. 175–205.

Teece, David; Rumelt, Richard; Dosi, Giovani and Winter, Sidney (1994), 'Understanding Corporate Coherence, Theory and Evidence', *Journal of Economic Behaviour and Organisation*, 23, 1–30.

Texier, François (1998), 'Diversification in Systems of Innovation – an Institutional Approach', paper presented at the European Association for Evolutionary Political Economy (EAEPE) conference in Lisbon, 6–9 November 1998.

Texier, François and Charles Edquist (eds) (1998), *Innovation Systems and European Integration on CD-ROM*, University of Linköping, Sweden.

Thornton, David (1995), *The Politics of an International Industrial Collaboration*, St. Martin's Press.

Trimble, William F. (ed.) (1995), *From Airbus to Airship – The History of Civil and Commercial Aviation; Pioneers and Operations*, Washington and London: Smithsonian Institution Press.

Tushman, Michael; Anderson, Philip and O'Reilly Charles (1997), 'Technology Cycles, Innovation Streams, and Ambidextrous Organisations: Organisation Renewal Through Innovation Streams and Strategic Change', in Michael L. Tushman and Philip Anderson (eds), *Managing Strategic Innovation and Change*, New York and Oxford: Oxford University Press, pp. 3–23.

Tyson, Laura D'Andrea (1992), *Who's Bashing Whom – Trade Conflicts in High-Technology Industries*, Washington: Institute for International Economics.

Utterback, James (1994), *Mastering the Dynamics of Innovation*, Boston, Massachusetts: Harvard University Press.

Very, Pierre (1993), 'Success in Diversification: Building on Core Competences', *Long Range Planning*, **26** (5), 80–92.

Vincenti, Walter G. (1990), *What Engineers Know and How They Know It – Analytical Studies from Aeronautical History*, Baltimore and London: The Johns Hopkins University Press.

Weidenbaum, M. (1973), 'Industrial Adjustments to Military Expenditure: Shifts and Cutbacks', in Bernard Udis (ed.), *The Economic Consequences of Reduced Military Spending*, Lexington, MA: Lexington Books, pp. 253–287.

Whitley, Richard (1992), *Business Systems in East Asia*, London: Sage.

Yin, Robert K. (1994), *Case Study Research: Design and Methods*, second edition, Thousand Oaks, CA: Sage.

Zander, Ivo (1997), 'Technological Diversification in the Multinational Corporation – Historical Evolution and Future Prospects', *Research Policy*, 26, 209–227.

Unpublished Material:
ASF (1980), Agreement between Saab and Fairchild, 25 January 1980.
ASS (1980), Agreement between the Swedish state and Saab, 26 February 1980.
Déplante, Paul, (1961), logbook December 1961 to November 1962.
Déplante, Paul, (1962), logbook December 1962 to December 1963.
Déplante, Paul, (1963), logbook December 1963 to December 1964.
Déplante, Paul, (1964), logbook December 1964 to March 1965.
Déplante, Paul, (1965), logbook March 1965 to July 1965.
Europlane Limited (1972), Marketing Group Report on Feasibility, Study Phase 1.
Hedblom, Ingmar, 'The Certification of the Saab 340'.
Hwang, Chin-Young (1998), 'Diversification Path in the Korean Aerospace Industry'.
Hwang, Chin-Young (1999), 'Aggressive-Incremental Strategy: Daewoo Heavy Industries Ltd.', Research chapter, Science Policy Research Unit.
ITA (1962), *Le Mystère 20*, Document Confidentiel de l'Institut des Transports Aériens.
Lemaire, René and Parvaud Pierre (1995), *Du Mystère 20 au Falcon 2000*.
Malerba, Franco (1999), Sectoral Systems of Innovation and Production, ESSY Project, Milan, June 1999.
MMB (1980a), Minutes of the Management Board, 19 February 1980, Farmingdale, New York.
MMB (1980b), Minutes of the Management Board, 28–29 April 1980, Farmingdale, New York.
MMB (1980c), Minutes of the Management Board, 20 March 1980, Farmingdale, New York.
MMB (1980d), Minutes of the Management Board, 22 May 1980, Farmingdale, New York.
MMB (1980e), Minutes of the Management Board, 18 June 1980, Linköping.
MMB (1980f), Minutes of the Management Board, 15–16 July 1980, Farmingdale, New York.
MMB (1980g), Minutes of the Management Board, 13–14 August 1980, Farmingdale, New York.
MMB (1980h), Minutes of the Management Board, 15–16 September 1980, Linköping.
MMB (1980i), Minutes of the Management Board, 12–13 November 1980, Linköping.
MMB (1980j), Minutes of the Management Board, 18–19 November 1980, Farmingdale, New York.
MMB (1980h), Minutes of the Management Board, 16–17 December 1980, Farmingdale, New York.
MMB (1981a), Minutes of the Management Board, 24 February 1981, Linköping.
MMB (1981b), Minutes of the Management Board, 24 March 1981, Farmingdale, New York.
MMB (1981c), Minutes of the Management Board, 28 May 1981, London.
MMB (1981d), Minutes of the Management Board, 29 June 1981, New York.
MMB (1981e), Minutes of the Extraordinary Management Board, August 11, 1981, Farmingdale, New York.

MMB (1981f), Minutes of the Management Board, 11 August 1981, Farmingdale, New York.

MMB (1981g), Minutes of the Management Board, 26 August 1981, San Antonio.

MMB (1981h), Minutes of the Management Board, 22 September 1981, Linköping.

MMB (1981i), Minutes of the Management Board, 19 October 1981, Farmingdale, New York.

MMB (1981j), Minutes of the Management Board, 19 November 1981, Linköping.

MMB (1982a), Minutes of the Management Board, 10 February 1982, Linköping.

MMB (1982b), Minutes of the Management Board, 11 March 1982, Farmingdale, New York.

MMB (1982c), Minutes of the Management Board, 14 April 1982, Linköping.

MMB (1982d), Minutes of the Management Board, 18 May 1982.

MMB (1982c), Minutes of the Management Board, 17 June 1982, Linköping.

MMB (1982d), Minutes of the Management Board, 10 August 1982, San Antonio.

MMB (1982e), Minutes of the Management Board, 15 September 1982, Farmingdale, New York.

MMB (1983a), Minutes of the Management Board, 26 January 1983, Farmingdale, New York.

QSF (1971), Quiet Short Field Aircraft Project, Intern Document from MBB, BAC and Saab.

Personal communication to the author (letters, fax and email):

Ann, Young-Su, June 1999.

Åsling, Nils G., 10 August 1999.

Berger, Luc, 21 October 1999.

Carlier, Claude, 7 February 2000.

Chang, Keun-Ho, 5 January 2000.

Chassagne, Paul, 25 October 1999.

Edlund, Ulf, January 2000.

Etesse, André, 10 January 2000.

Faherty, John, 29 November 1999.

Hedblom, Ingmar, 10 October 1999.

Hwang, Chin-Young, 15 April 1999.

Lee, Jong-Won, 22 December 1999.

Lemaire, René, 29 January 2000

Leroudier, Bernard, 7 January 2000.

Nordström, Lars-Erik, 30 November 1999.

Ra, Duck Joo, 17 March 2000

Rodling, Sture, 12 October 1999.

Sebold, Robert, 20 October 1999.

Interviews for the chapter on the Dassault Mystère 20:

Claude Carlier, Ph.D. in Aeronautics History, Professor at the Sorbonne, Director of the Centre of Aeronautic and Space History. Interview at the Ministry of Defence in Paris, 27 August 1997.

Jacques Estèbe, former Vice President of Dassault Aviation, Director of the Project Mystère 20 at Dassault in 1963 (retired). Interview in St Médard en Jalles (France), 1 September 1997.

Paul Chassagne, Technical Director of the project Mystère 20 (retired). Interview in Bordeaux (France), 2 September 1997.

René Lemaire, in charge of the development of the first prototype of the Mystère 20 (retired). Interview in Bordeaux (France), 2 September 1997; 12 May 1999; as well as several informal discussions.

Bernard Leroudier, former certification engineer at Dassault, responsible for the certification of the Falcon 20 (retired), 28 May 1999.

Jean Delacroix, former general director of the SGAC during the certification of the Falcon 20 (retired), 13 May 1999.

Poisson-Quinton, telephone interview, ONERA Organisation Nationale des Etudes et Recherches Aéronautiques (retired), 12 May 1999.

Jean Cabrière, telephone interview, former Chief Technical Director of Dassault (retired), St Cloud, 31 May 1999.

André Etesse, vice CEO of Dassault, St Cloud (retired), 5 June 1999.

Interviews for the chapter on the Saab 340:

Nils G. Åsling, Minister of Industry October 1976 – October 1978 (retired), 21 October 1998.

Erik Bratt, telephone interview, Chief Design Engineer at Saab (retired), 9 September 1998.

Ulf Edlund, Strategic Manager at Saab, Project Manager of the 340, 1979 – 1981, 3 May 1996 and 11 September 1996.

Olof Esping, Project Manager of the 340 from 1981 to 1984 (retired), 10 September 1998.

Jack Faherty, telephone interview, Business Manager Fairchild (retired), 6 April 1999.

Sten Gustafsson, Former CEO of Saab between 1978 and 1983 (retired), 14 Septembre 1998. Informal telephone conversation 28 November 1999.

Ingmar Hedblom, Luftfartsverkets Certification Manager of the 340, 15 October 1998.

Erik Krönmark, Defence Minister of Sweden October 1976 – October 1978 (retired), 23 October 1998.

Milton Mobärg, Security Officer of the 340, 10 September 1998.

Lars-Erik Nordström, Director of Luftfartsverkets Flight Safety Department and Chairman of the Saab 340 JAR Joint Validation Committee (retired), 9 October 1998.

Sture Rodling, Chief Test Engineer of the 340, 4 September 1998.

Robert Sebold, telephone interview, Business Manager of the 340, Fairchild (retired), 4 December 1998.

Erik Sjöberg, First Test Pilot of the 340 (retired), 2 September 1998.

Interviews for the chapter on the Daewoo KTX-1:

Firms:

Daewoo Heavy Industries Ltd, 28 January 1999.

GECI International, email to the author, 15 March 1999.

Hyundai Space and Aircraft Co. Ltd, 22 January 1999.

Korean Air, 12 February 1999.
Pilatus, telephone interview, 9 March 1999.
Samsung Aerospace, 26 January 1999.

Research organisations
Agency for Defence Development (ADD), 27 January 1999.
Korea Aerospace Research Institute (KARI), 27 January 1999.
Korea Institute for Industrial Economics and Trade (KIET), 29 January 1999.

Ministry and other organisations
Ministry of Commerce, Industry and Energy (MOCIE), 25 January 1999.
Korea Aerospace Industry Association (KAIA), 25 January 1999.

Appendix A: Interview Protocols

Protocol 1: civil servants and certification authorities

Relations industry – government
- Why did the government want an aircraft industry, both military and civilian?
- What did the government think about the aircraft industry?
- Were there some controversies or disagreements within the government about the issue of the aircraft industry?
- Why was the aircraft industry considered important by the government?
- What were the expectations of the government?
- What was the general opinion (public opinion) about the aircraft industry?
- How was the government ready to support the industry?
- How were the activities of the firm discussed at the government level?
- How did the government negotiate the diversification of the firm?
- What kind of incentives were given to the firm to diversify?

Education and national/regional research and development
- Were specific university programmes or universities created to support the diversification?
- How were these universities financed?
- Were specific national research centres used to support the diversification?
- How could they relate to the activities of the firms?
- What were the conditions of the relations?
- How were they financed?

National infrastructure support
- Was there a national industrial programme from which the diversification could benefit?
- Were science parks created, aiming at creating new knowledge for the aerospace industry?
- Did the firm interact with other organisations not mentioned earlier?
- Did the firm profit from tax reductions because of the diversification?
- How did standards or certification procedures affect the diversification?

Certification
- How was the problem of certification considered?
- Were there needs of new specialised personnel for the certification?
- How were the relations between the firm and the certifying organisation?
- How did the two organisations work together?
- What were the major problems with the certification?
- How were they tackled?

Protocol 2: managers and engineers of the firm

External factors
- What were the external factors influencing the decision about diversification in the firm?
- How did the firm react to these external factors?
- Was the firm positive to diversifying?
- How did the firm negotiate the diversification with the state?
- Was it an open negotiation or was it forced by the state?
- What kind of guarantees were given by the state in the event of the programme failing?

Internal factors
Growth of the firm
- What was the general economic situation of the firm during the period preceding the diversification?
- What were the general policy lines concerning the future of the firm?
- Was the firm in a growth trend or did it intend to grow and expand its activities?
- What was the opinion of the management about the eventual growth of the firm?
- What was important for the growth of the firm according to the management?
- In what terms did the management want to see the firm grow? Profits, employment, market shares?

Use of resources
- What were the major resources of the firm, in terms of competences, technologies and physical assets?
- Did the firm have some special competences?
- Could these competences be considered as an advantage against competitors?
- Did the management of the firm consider that some of the resources of the firm could be used better?
- Were there some discussions about the use of these unused resources?
- Was the management trying to find ways to reduce costs in the firm by using internal synergies?
- How was the firm positioned in its previous markets, before diversification?

Opportunities
- Was the management of the firm willing to enter new ventures?
- Was the management conservative concerning the activity of the firm?
- What kind of opportunities did the management of the firm consider as viable for the firm?
- How did the management plan to take advantage of these opportunities?
- What were the actions taken by the management of the firm to implement the diversification?

Acquisition of other firms
- Did the firm acquire other firms?
- Under what conditions were these firms acquired?

- How were these firms integrated to the main firm?
- What were the difficulties encountered?
- Were there some clear separations between the firms after the acquisition?
- How did the 'old' firm look at the 'new' firm?
- Did it raise some problems?

Contractual relationships with other firms
- Did the firm seek the help of other firms through contracting during the diversification process?
- What did the firm get out of this collaboration?
- Did the firm outsource some of the development of the new product?
- What were the terms of the contract?
- What were the difficulties encountered during the joint work?
- How were these difficulties coped with?
- What kinds of relations were developed with the contracted firm?
- Had the firm already been involved with the contracted firm?
- If not, why was the firm selected?

Internal research and development
- Why did the firm choose this option?
- What kinds of technologies were needed that did not exist inside the firm?
- How did the firm organise the internal development?
- How many people were working with research and development?
- How did the project relate to the previous activity of the firm?
- What kind of competences could be used directly on the new project?
- Was there a need to transfer some technologies from the previous activity?
- What were the difficulties?
- How were the teams created?
- How did they react to their new assignments?
- What was the size of the R&D effort (in money and in number of people) compared to the global activity of the firm?
- Was it considered as large as compared to the rest of the firm?

Education and national/regional research and development
- Did the firm interact with universities?
- Was the firm involved in the design of specific educational profiles?
- Did the firm finance university research?
- How did the firm interact with other private or national research centres?
- What kinds of research centres were involved?
- What were the conditions of the relations?

National infrastructure support
- Was there a national industrial programme from which the diversification could benefit?
- Did the diversification answer an expressed desire of the government?
- Was the firm involved in a science park or other kind of infrastructure?
- Did the firm interact with other organisations not mentioned earlier?

Specific institutions
- Did the firm profit from tax reductions because of the diversification?
- How did standards or certification procedures affect the diversification?

Managing New Knowledge and Uncertainties
Management
- How was the project managed?
- Was the new activity separated from the old activity of the firm?
- What were the relationships between the new and the old activity?
- Was the management of the new activity free to do what they wanted?

Investment
- What was the size of the investment in the new venture in terms of personnel and money?
- Was it considered as important?
- Did the new management have difficulties in funding the activity?
- From where did the funding come?
- Was the investment enough or was it too small?

Technology and product
- How did the management cope with the new technology?
- How did the engineers cope with the new technology?
- How did the new technology relate to the old technology?
- What kind of existing technologies could be used in the new product?
- What were the problems with this adaptation?
- What new competences had to be developed?
- What were the relationships between the new product and the old product?
- How much time did the development take?

Market
- How did the management cope with the new market?
- What kind of new competences were needed for marketing?
- Where were these new competences found?
- How did the management consider the new market?
- What kinds of difficulties were experienced which were not related to either the product or the market?
- What kinds of decisions were taken by the management to tackle these difficulties? Personnel, investments, education?

Institutions
- How was the problem of certification considered?
- Were there needs of new specialized personnel for the certification?
- What were the relationships between the firm and the certifying organization?
- How did the two organizations work together?
- What was the major problem with the certification?
- How much time did the certification take?

Index